Civil Society Knowledge Networks

CRITICAL FRONTIERS OF THEORY, RESEARCH, AND POLICY IN INTERNATIONAL DEVELOPMENT STUDIES

Series Editors

Naomi Hossain, Briony Jones, Alfredo Saad Filho,
Benjamin Selwyn, and Fiona Tregenna

The contemporary world is characterized by massive wealth alongside widespread poverty, inequality, and environmental destruction—all bound up through class, race, and gender dynamics of inequality and oppression.

Critical Frontiers of Theory, Research, and Policy in International Development Studies, the official book series of the Development Studies Association of the UK, was established to contribute to critical thinking about local, national, and global processes of structural transformation. The series publishes cutting-edge monographs that promote critical development studies as an interdisciplinary and applied field and shape the theory, practice, and teaching of international development for a new generation of scholars, students, and practitioners. As the series evolves, we wish to publish a diverse and inclusive range of authors whose work engages in critical, multidisciplinary, decolonial, and methodologically plural development studies.

Recently published in the series

The Invisible Hand(out)
Aid, Trade, and Unequal Globalization
Samuel Brazys

The Rise and Fall of Neoliberal Rentier Capitalism
The Political Economy of the 20th and 21st Centuries
Luiz Carlos Bresser-Pereira

The Spectre of State Capitalism
Ilias Alami and Adam D. Dixon

Business of the State
Why State Ownership Matters for Resource Governance
Jewellord T. Nem Singh

Disrupted Development in the Congo
The Fragile Foundations of the African Mining Consensus
Ben Radley

Politics and the Urban Frontier
Transformation and Divergence in Late Urbanizing East Africa
Tom Goodfellow

Equity, Evaluation, and International Cooperation
In Pursuit of Proximate Peers in an African City
Gabriella Y. Carolini

They Eat Our Sweat
Transport Labor, Corruption, and Everyday Survival in Urban Nigeria
Daniel E. Agbiboa

Civil Society Knowledge Networks

International Development and the Globalization of Ideas

E. Fouksman

OXFORD
UNIVERSITY PRESS

OXFORD
UNIVERSITY PRESS

Great Clarendon Street, Oxford, OX2 6DP,
United Kingdom

Oxford University Press is a department of the University of Oxford.
It furthers the University's objective of excellence in research, scholarship,
and education by publishing worldwide. Oxford is a registered trade mark of
Oxford University Press in the UK and in certain other countries.

Published in the United States of America by Oxford University Press
198 Madison Avenue, New York, NY 10016, United States of America

British Library Cataloguing in Publication Data

Data available

Library of Congress Control Number: 2025944761

ISBN 9780198943693

DOI: 10.1093/9780198943723.001.0001

Printed and bound by
CPI Group (UK) Ltd, Croydon, CR0 4YY

The manufacturer's authorized representative in the EU for product safety is
Oxford University Press España S.A. of Parque Empresarial San Fernando de Henares,
Avenida de Castilla, 2 - 28830 Madrid (www.oup.es/en or product.safety@oup.com).
OUP España S.A. also acts as importer into Spain of products made by the manufacturer.

MIX
Paper | Supporting
responsible forestry
FSC® C013604

To Andrew, who made it possible

And Levy, who began at its completion

Acknowledgements

This book would not have happened without the generosity, trust, and aid of people across four different continents and many different years. I cannot list them all here, but I am especially grateful to William Beinart, Nandini Gooptu, and Miles Tendi, all of whom gave their time, thought, and patience when this project was taking shape during my time at the University of Oxford, together with David Lewis and Jonny Steinberg, who propelled the project forward with generous feedback and encouragement. Also at Oxford was a community of friends and fellow-scholars without whom researching and writing would have been a far lonelier endeavour. I cannot list them all, but am especially grateful to Meghan Bailey, Alex Barker, Hannah Dawson, Chris Desvernine, Nina Hall, Eva Lam, Libby Longino, Josh Makepeace, Andrew McCall, Chris McConnachie, Rosanna Nichol, Willy Oppenheim, Ellie Ott, Caitlin Prentice, and Francis Vergunst. In more recent years this project was sustained by the input, encouragement, and sometimes prodding of Jacklyn Cock, Sharon Gerwirtz, and Billy Holzberg. I am also grateful to Andrew Fischer and the editorial board at Oxford University Press for supporting the book, and the anonymous reviewers who gave thoughtful and constructive feedback on the manuscript.

The book also would not exist without the generosity of all the people in Kenya, Ethiopia, and Kyrgyzstan who gifted me hours and hours of their time and energy. In Kenya, I am particularly grateful to Wolde, Dr Hussein, Hassan, Liban, and all the people in Beliqo who spoke with me during the dry and hot days of an August Ramadan. In Kyrgyzstan, all of the staff members of AKF Kg, MSRI, and MSDSP were gracious and welcoming, but I must particularly thank Chad for taking a leap of faith and initially inviting me to do research with AKF Kg, Laurie and Pirjan for their enthusiastic support of my work with the climate change adaptation project, and the residents of Saro-Kamush for the warmth of their welcome (and an unforgettable birthday celebration).

Besides time, I have many to thank in both Kenya and Kyrgyzstan for their gift of hospitality. Hassan and Habiba in Kenya, and Nicolle, Pirjan, and Eliza and Nurmat in Kyrgyzstan, all welcomed me as a complete stranger into their homes for indefinite lengths of time, and their families graciously and kindly did the same. I am taught and humbled by their trust and open generosity. I must also thank my translators, Salad Choki and Maksat Kazubekova, for their patience, perseverance, and dedication to this work.

The person most difficult to thank, because his unbounded love and support has pervaded every aspect of this work, is Andrew. How could I ever enumerate the encouragement, conversations, nourishment, and necessary distractions, not to mention the hours upon hours of editing that you have gifted me? It is impossible. Thank you.

Portions of this book draw on material published in three earlier works:

- E. Fouksman, Civil Society Knowledge Networks: How International Development Institutions Reshape the Geography of Knowledge. *Third World Quarterly*, 38(8) (2017), pp. 1847–1872.
- E. Fouksman, Global Authenticity, Local Authority: Epistemic Power, Discursive Geographies, and the Creation of Civil Society Knowledge Networks. In J. Glückler, H.-D. Meyer, and L. Suarsana, eds. *Knowledge and Civil Society*, Knowledge and Space Series vol. 17. New York: Springer, 2022, published under a Creative Commons Attribution 4.0 License (CC BY 4.0), pp. 209-232.
- E. Fouksman, Inside the Anti-Politics Machine: Civil Society Mediation of Everyday Encounters with the State. In W. Adebanwi, ed. *Everyday State and Democracy in Africa: Ethnographic Encounters*. Athens, OH: Ohio University Press, 2022, pp. 118-138.

Material from these publications has been adapted, expanded, and integrated into this book. All reused content is used in accordance with the relevant publication agreements or publisher permission.

Contents

1
Introducing Civil Society Knowledge Networks

Picture a small village in a narrow valley nestled in the lower reaches of the Tian Shan Mountains, in the southwest corner of Kyrgyzstan, the 'Switzerland of Central Asia'. It perches on the edge of a cliff overlooking a wide riverbed with a shallow brown river running down its middle and snowy mountain peaks visible at each end of the valley. Once the village had been on the river's banks, but flooding and widening caused the village to move ever further. Indeed, the village is named Saro-Kamush, Kyrgyz for the yellow reeds that grow in the river. On the green-brown hillsides around Saro-Kamush graze herds of horses and sheep, pointing to the semi-nomadic pastoralist livelihoods of the residents of the village. Every summer many in the village leave with all of the herds to pitch their yurts on summer pastures high in the mountains.

Or picture instead a vast unfolding flatland, scrubby bush and acacia trees failing to mask the bare parched earth, swept by hot, dry winds. The flatness is broken by a series of hills on one horizon and the shock of the rising bulk of a plateau in the north, blocking any hope of a mobile phone signal. A river winds through the landscape, sometimes vast and swollen, sometimes down to a trickle or disappearing entirely, the only flash of verdant green a strip of forest on either side. An occasional village is sprinkled in here and there, close to the rocky dirt road that cuts through the bush. No electricity lines break the vista. This is a small corner of northern Kenya, a part of the country that used to be the Northern Frontier District. People in Kenya's metropolises speak of it as 'upcountry', a word synonymous with remoteness. The people here, the majority of whom belong to the Borana ethnic group, are largely pastoralist, many still walking with their herds. They once lived in small movable villages of woven huts that followed the animals, but more and more stay in permanent villages of mud-walled houses. One such village is Beliqo, tucked around a curve of the Ewaso Niro, a three-kilometre walk from the river. Many of its residents are gone for long stretches of time with their herds, but many stay, preferring to have access to the village's primary

Civil Society Knowledge Networks. E. Fouksman, Oxford University Press. © Elizaveta Fouksman (2026).
DOI: 10.1093/9780198943723.003.0001

school, small dispensary, and, most importantly, food aid, which is crucial to surviving the increasingly lengthy and frequent droughts that wrack this already arid land.

Now picture two gleaming high-rises. One is in Geneva, Switzerland, just a block or two from Lake Geneva. Much of the building is dedicated to the various ventures, charitable and commercial, of His Highness the Aga Khan, spiritual leader of the Ismaili community,[1] billionaire, business magnate, and philanthropist. No trace of the spiritual role of the Aga Khan is visible in the building, one floor of which is dedicated to the Aga Khan Foundation, the charitable branch of the Aga Khan Development Network. It is filled with largely European and North American nationals that administer or guide the many branches of the foundation, which run development projects in education, health, livelihood creation, and natural resource management around the globe.

The other high-rise is in San Francisco, California. One of its floors houses the open-plan offices of another charitable foundation—The Christensen Fund. People sit at their desks, looking into computer screens, tapping on keyboards. Floor-to-ceiling windows offer views of the city and the bay beyond, but even more eye-catching is the art on the walls: tapestries and paintings that are indigenous or aboriginal, their origins ranging from Central Asia to East Africa to the Pacific Islands to the US Southwest. This art is the first clue to the interests of the foundation, interests that not only focused on indigenous culture but also combined this with ecology and the environment—in other words, biocultural diversity, the view that cultural diversity is crucial to maintaining biological diversity and the ecological wellbeing of the planet (Loh & Harmon 2005).

What connects these villages and offices? What connects a pastoralist people in the remote north of Kenya, struggling in the face of increasing drought, violent resource-based ethnic conflict, food insecurity, and aid dependence, to the people sitting in the bright offices of a foundation on the other side of the globe? Although the people in Beliqo village might have shrugged at such a question, those in the foundation were quick to answer—Beliqo residents showed an interest in conserving their riverine forest and reviving the traditional knowledge and customs that surround forest and river use, an interest expressed in grant applications to the foundation, and one that aligned with its broad aims. Thus resources—in the form of thousands of dollars—flowed annually from the foundation to the village. The same processes seemingly

[1] The Aga Khan is the current imam of Nizari Ismailism, a denomination within Shia Islam with between 12 million and 15 million followers. Ismaili Muslims are spread through South Asia, the Middle East, East Africa, and Central Asia, as well as Europe and North America.

connected Saro-Kamush and the Geneva offices of the Aga Khan Foundation. These offices administered and oversaw a climate change adaptation project as part of their natural resource management work, and pointed to increasing climate instability and natural disasters experienced by the residents of Saro-Kamush as good reasons for them to be enthusiastic about taking part in the climate change adaptation project.

But this is too simple a story. It ignores the technological, geographical, social, and linguistic barriers around Beliqo and Saro-Kamush that could not have been overcome without intermediaries—in this case, non-governmental organizations (NGOs). How would each village have even heard of these foundations? How could it have composed and sent in grant applications with limited access to information technology, not to mention knowledge of the language and rhetoric needed to write a grant application successfully? And why would a people often in dire straits, struggling with food and human security or natural disasters, care about conserving a forest, or be interested in learning about climate change?

I. Civil Society Knowledge Networks and the Globalization of Ideas

This book traces geographies of knowledge within current practices of development, aiming to understand the ways in which such epistemic geographies form and change. It is concerned with the way ideas travel—and the way they mutate, interact, and impact individuals and communities along the way. I construct this geography of ideas by examining the way flows of knowledge straddle what Pieterse (1995, p. 49) terms the 'tandem operation of local/global dynamics'. As such, this work draws on the scholarship around socio-cultural globalization, which explores the shifting scale and depth of interconnections between cultures and peoples around the globe. This literature focuses largely on mechanisms of interconnection such as information technology (i.e., the internet, mobile phones, and social media), the media (such as television), and global consumer culture (i.e., global brands like MacDonald's).[2] In contrast, this book looks at a very different route for the flow of ideas: development institutions such as NGOs, the charities and foundations that fund them, and the grassroots movements or local activists they support. My research conceptualizes networks of such organizations, the

[2] For foundational work in this area, see for instance Bordo, Taylor, and Williamson (2003); Dicken (2003); Held and McGrew (2003); Lechener and Boli (2004).

communities they work in, and the foundations that fund them as *civil society knowledge networks*. These networks are uniquely positioned to create connections and shift the content and application of knowledge, not only in the global South but also within broader international epistemic communities. In particular, this book uses the lens of environmentally focused development interventions to focus on the ways rhetoric, ideas, and practices are created and negotiated between and within a variety of participants and actors in the development project.

This work uses the model of civil society knowledge networks to explore the formation of development-focused epistemic communities that span the global North and global South (or the minority and majority world), linking the local and the global, the traditional and the expert, through the flow of ideas. In doing so, I build on the work of Castells (2005), who posits the existence of a 'network society' in which the globe is increasingly integrated through the sharing of ideas via information technology. Castells argues that the network is a key form of spatial organization that links to both agency and structure (Fernández-Ardèvol & Ribera-Fumaz 2023). However, Castells himself acknowledges that much of the world continues to be left out of the network society. As Castells has written recently, 'the logic of networks means that they include and exclude at the same time . . . not everything and everybody is included in the core of the network society but all human experience in our time is affected by the dynamics generated in this core' (Castells 2023: 941). This is particularly true for pockets of the global South, parts of which still lack electricity, much less information technology. These dynamics of inclusion and exclusion mirror the spatial concentration of wealth and power, poverty and marginality (Castells 2023). Yet I argue that networks of development institutions cross through these concentrations, and in so doing play a key role in weaving together a 'network society', often creating points of epistemic exchange in places where accessing information technology remains challenging. Indeed, this book demonstrates that even in communities that are becoming connected to the technological 'network society', development actors play a key role in transforming local ideas and worldviews through their engagement—while being themselves transformed in turn. This makes development institutions vital to understanding the way ideas move and interact through local/global 'knowledge networks'.

This work asks a number of questions about the knowledge relationships between the development-focused organizations in civil society knowledge networks, as well as between these organizations and the communities they work with in the global South. How are ideas around development and the environment spread and used, or contested and adapted, through civil society networks and in local communities? How do local communities themselves create, influence, implement, or ignore ecological and developmental values, knowledge, and rhetoric? How are the knowledge and practices of local communities shaped by ideas propagated by such networks, and what role do communities have in shaping and creating this content themselves?

II. Grounding the Inquiry: Historical Roots of Knowledge and Development

The development project has been shaped and formed by knowledge production and spread, from colonialism to the modernization approaches of the 1950s and 1960s through the present. This book has its analytical roots in this history, and builds on a long tradition of critical scholarship on development theory and discourse (such as Cowen & Shenton 1996; Leys 1996; Ziai 2015). The roots of this lie in colonial knowledge production and its legacy. The colonized 'other' was studied and categorized in the 'scientific' and empirical tradition of the Enlightenment, both for the sake of administration and control through classification and for scholarship (Said 1994 [1978]). This knowledge could be gained via a system of classification, categorization, and 'scientific' understanding—in the words of Michael Adas, a Western impulse to 'measure and catalogue the worlds they were "discovering"' (1989: 2). This was achieved via both the curiosity of Western scholar-adventurers and scholar-administrators, as well as more formal state mechanisms such as the census and land surveys (Cohn 1990; Cohn 1996). Much of this knowledge was constructed or imagined, in particular due to the colonizer's view of colonized societies as static, unchanging, and primordial (Ranger 1992).

By imagining and constructing social categories, colonial knowledge and the Enlightenment approach towards classification and categorization drew many of the still-existing lines of social division in the global South, be they ethnic, caste, or religious. The colonized themselves also played an active role in this process, both filling the social categories created by the colonialists and providing information and details to flesh out colonial knowledge (Lonsdale 1989). But although the process was far from unidirectional, it was the colonizers that played the key role in creating and solidifying social categories and divisions, both through colonial knowledge creation and through putting that knowledge to use via administrative policies. The creation of knowledge—knowledge bound within the framework of Western Enlightenment thinking—directly influenced the creation and implementation of colonial rule.

Yet as Washbrook (1999) points out, it was not only the Enlightenment tradition that influenced the way the West sought to know the colonized Other. European Romanticism also drove this interest. The Romantics sought not only to know the culture and traditions of the colonized but also to privilege their uniqueness and value. They prized this knowledge as a source of Western renewal and transformation. This privileging of local and indigenous knowledge (as constructed and understood by the West) is a theme that will continue to echo through Western engagement with the global South, including via the development project. It is also a theme that will recur repeatedly throughout this book.

The creation and spread of knowledge and discourse that shaped colonial rule continued to shape the post-colonial development project. Indeed, many theorists and historians of development (particularly within the post-development tradition) have drawn a direct line from the aims of the colonial project (framed as a form of trusteeship or guidance over colonies' immanent development (Cowen & Shenton 1996)) to contemporary development interventions (Sachs 1992a). The post-war Keynesian consensus and the modernization approach of the 1950s and 1960s were explicitly framed in terms of expertise and the spread of technical knowledge rather than social justice or redistribution (Abrahamsen 2000). This expertise was meant to help post-colonial states travel along the same path as wealthy nations to achieve industrialization. Such expertise was built on colonial knowledge and the colonial understanding of social reality, be it ethnicity, religion, or even the interaction between humans and their environment (Ziai 2015). It also depended on the continuing use of experts, many from the West, to explain how states and societies are best run (Ingham 1993; Evans & Stephens 1988; Mitchell 2002). In this manner, knowledge continued to travel largely from the West to the rest, with Western actors interpreting and shaping both development discourse and practice.

Modernization approaches were critiqued via dependency theory, which pointed out the way 'periphery economies' were shaped by unequal economic, technological, and cultural power relations with the global North (Leys 1996; Munck & O'Herean 1999). Yet despite its critiques and influence on development theory and discourse in the 1970s, the 1980s and 1990s saw the rise of the Washington consensus around neoliberalism and structural adjustment programmes, which imposed a neoliberal and free-market ideology on the states and economies of the global South, led by technocratic expertise of global institutions such as the International Monetary Fund and the World Bank. On the heels of the Washington consensus came the good governance agenda, with Western institutions emphasizing (and often tying aid funding to) the importance of what they termed democratic practices and government transparency and accountability—a set of ideas that will emerge repeatedly throughout this book (Abrahamsen 2000).

The spectacular failure of structural adjustment programmes and the Washington consensus has led to pushback against technocratic, Western-imposed development approaches. Much of this pushback has taken the form of what Munck has called the '"Holy Trinity" of engendered, sustainable and bottom-up development' (1999: 202). Although such participatory approaches began from a critical or even radical standpoint towards development, often linked to postdevelopment critiques, by the early 2000s they had become embedded, at least discursively, in mainstream development practice, personified, for instance, by the World Bank's 'Voices of the Poor' study (Narayan et al. 2000). These more contextualized, decentralized approaches to development coincided with the spread of post-colonial and postmodern perspectives, which privilege the specificity and context-dependence of any group of actors and promote 'the validity and salience of local knowledge' (Beinart 2000: 280)—for example, emphasizing the value of indigenous conservation systems (Berkes 1999; Berkes et al. 2000) or culturally specific ways of interpreting gender relations, such as Islamic feminism (Mahmood 2005). In development practice, this post-colonial turn puts a premium on the role of participatory decision-making and knowledge, on local self-governance and locally led civil society organizations (Chambers 1983; Chambers 1986; Hickey & Mohan 2004), and on multiple pathways to development. In short, the Western-based and expert-led modernization approach has—in theory—been challenged by a locally bound, participatory, and context-specific approach.

But how deep has this challenge been? Alongside the rhetoric of context specificity, local knowledge, and community participation, development as both a universal aim and practice has continued to be 'the central organizing concept of our time' (Cowen & Shenton 1995b). For instance, while in the early 2000s participatory approaches became ever more prominent in development practice, so too did the widespread acceptance of the United Nations' Millennium Development Goals, followed by the Sustainable Development Goals, which set the overall, universal aims of development. The privileging and lauding of local ideas, itself a universalizing discourse rooted in Romantic Orientalism and continued in participatory approaches to development, coexists alongside a continued search for knowledge of universal development aims and solutions, rooted in the Enlightenment and then colonial views of progress and shared humanity. As this book will demonstrate, the development project has become the key place of negotiation and enactment of these two visions, often held simultaneously by the same development actors.

III. A Geography of Civil Society Knowledge Networks

These same tensions are echoed by a range of globalization scholarship which posits that the world is in the process of being increasingly knit together by a set of (more or less) shared values and cultural assumptions.[3] Indeed, the globalization debate explores the link between local specificity, global influence, and homogenizing universalist forces, be they economic or cultural, since 'the central problem of today's global interactions is the tension between cultural homogenization and cultural heterogenization' (Appadurai 1990: 295). The answers that emerge out of this interrogation reimagine the local and the global scales as not sealed off from each other but rather porous and interconnected. Thus understanding cultural and social change becomes a matter of 'rethinking difference *through* connection' while acknowledging the influence of transnational movements and public spheres (Gupta & Ferguson 1992: 8). That is precisely what this work sets out to do through the prism of development.

By looking at the ways in which development-focused organizations connect a variety of scales into civil society knowledge networks, this book examines the way development can act as a crucial agent that forges epistemic links between different geographies, cultures, and worldviews. Colonial knowledge production is thus an analytical springboard for this work, launching it towards an exploration of development's role in transnational flows of not only people and resources but also discourse and ideas. This work uses development and those involved in it to examine the world 'from the standpoint of participants located at the intersection of the most remote forces, connections and imaginations' (Burawoy 2001: 148). It looks at the way connections between a variety of scales are both produced and experienced by development-focused civil society organizations and the people they work with, connections that purposely set out to bridge the local and the global, but may end up doing so in surprising, unexpected, and even unnoticed ways.

[3] Pieterse (1995); Boli and Thomas (1999); Meyer (1999); Kaldor (2003); Castells (2005).

This book builds on and contributes to a scholarly lineage focused on the evolution and contestation of 'grand theories' of development (such as modernization, dependency, neoliberalism, participatory approaches, and bottom-up development). In particular, books from the 1990s like Leys' *The Rise and Fall of Development Theory* (1996), Cowen and Shenton's *Doctrines of Development* (1996), and Moore and Schmitz's *Debating Development Discourse* (1995) trace the evolution and contestation of 'development theory' by focusing on the rhetorical, discursive, and ideological foundations of how development practice is justified, ordered, and understood. This book builds on this tradition, but rather than focus exclusively on the analysis of discourse and ideology that emanates from global development institutions and the theoretical structures that underpin such ideology, it focuses on the way more pointed epistemic content sits within (and in the process shapes and reshapes) these ideologies. For instance, how do ideas around climate change interact with ideological commitments to participation?

In other words, while the book is grounded in the many critical overviews of the evolution and contestation of development discourse and theory, it focuses less exclusively on development *theory* (i.e., what Pieterse (2009, p. 1) terms 'organized reflections on development') and rather examines both paradigmatic and concrete knowledge and ideas that are used by the people and institutions involved in development (ranging from theoretical and ideological approaches such as 'bottom-up development' to concepts and practices such as 'climate change adaptation' or 'monitoring and evaluation', or even linguistic knowledge, such as the ability to speak and write in English).

In investigating the way networks of development institutions create and spread ideas across different scales of institutions and geographies, I do not mean to say that the flow of knowledge in such networks is unidirectional, moving simply from the West to the rest. The people that development organizations set out to work with and aid are not passive recipients. This work will demonstrate that local actors are very much agents, not subjects, in these networks. They pursue their own agendas and fuse the knowledge of development institutions with their own ideas into new hybrids. Civil society knowledge networks thus lead not to homogenization but to an increasing diversity in the way the global is adapted or 'indigenized' (Appadurai 1990) by the local. Indeed, while this work builds on some of the core ideas and conceptual categories of the literature around 'epistemic communities' (Adler & Haas 1992), I point to the limitations of the way this term has been used to focus on Western 'experts' and policymakers. Ideas within civil society knowledge networks also emerge from what is labelled 'traditional', 'indigenous', or 'local' knowledge (Briggs 2005). Yet, as this work will demonstrate, this process is complex and far from obvious. Local communities in the developing world not only adopt and implement the ideas that are spread through such networks but also repurpose them to promote and enact their own aims and ideologies. These ideas are often grounded in knowledge that comes from below—knowledge produced by what Gramsci (1970) calls 'organic intellectuals'. The categories of local and global are themselves contested, and are often porous and blend into each other (Ferguson 2006). In exploring the way development creates epistemic links, this work investigates the overlapping boundaries and interpenetration of spatial categories, pointing to the ways in which such distinctions have been privileged, reinforced, or romanticized by international environmental movements and development institutions.

IV. Exploring the Global–Local Connection: Two Case Studies

This project thus looks at the way development creates, reshapes, and spreads knowledge. It does so through the two multi-sited case studies described at the opening of this chapter. The first is a network whose global node is The Christensen Fund, an international foundation based in San Francisco but working all over the globe, and at the time of research actively creating and involved in one particular global approach towards environmental activism: that of biocultural diversity. One of the many organizations they funded is an NGO in Nairobi, the Kivulini Trust, which was itself an outgrowth of their work in the region. Amongst the many local NGOs that Kivulini connected to The Christensen Fund was the Waso Trustland Project, a small non-profit that for many years had been a land-rights advocacy organization for the peoples of Isiolo district in the north of the country. At the time of research, the organization was gradually shifting its focus to ecological and cultural concerns. Finally, the last node in this network is Beliqo, a village where Waso Trustland was running a project to conserve a local riverine forest from logging by setting up a community forest association. The project was funded by The Christensen Fund, fuelled by advice from Kivulini, and built on existing organizations in the village.

The second of the two case studies also includes an international foundation—the Aga Khan Foundation (AKF), with its headquarters in Geneva. I focus on the work AKF funded and assisted in the Kyrgyz Republic, through both its national branch in Kyrgyzstan (AKF Kg) and the Kyrgyz

NGO that implemented their projects (Mountain Society Development Support Programme Kyrgyzstan, or MSDSP Kg). Although the focus of both AKF and its Kyrgyz partners was primarily on livelihood, education, and health, at the time when this book was being researched the foundation was supporting one project that was outside its usual portfolio in Kyrgyzstan: a project focused on climate change adaptation. The project was structured to consist of an assessment of climate change impacts and then a series of trainings on climate change adaptation in selected villages. After the trainings, the villages created an adaptation plan and competed for a mini-grant of US$4,000 to do one of the projects on the plan. I zero in on this project, the staff in these organizations that support it, and one Kyrgyz mountain village where the project is run: Saro-Kamush. In this village I look closely at the ideas, perceptions, and worldviews around climate change, ecology, activism, civil society, and governance of both the participants of the climate change adaptation project and the village residents more broadly.

Each case study conceptualizes these organizations into a network, held together not only by flows of resources but also by shared (and sometimes contested or subverted) knowledge. While both of the networks are engaged in ecologically focused interventions (and thus knowledge of the environment), environmental ideas in and of themselves are *not* the focus of this work. It would be far beyond the scope of this book to delve into an analysis of the many varieties and strands of environmentalism or even biocultural diversity and climate change adaptation in any detail. The case-study networks share, dispute, and recreate understandings of not only ecological interventions but also participatory development, good governance, and expertise and authority. Thus environmental interventions, while themselves complex, varied, and contested, are used by this work as a *lens* through which to examine civil society knowledge networks. Both of the case studies look at the way development organizations create, spread, and utilize ideas around the relationship of humans with the natural world. Yet these organizations and the local communities they work in also develop and contest such ideas, in the process producing and utilizing knowledge themselves. One of the key findings of this work is that despite each case-study intervention having environmental aims, the ideas valued by most of the organizations and communities involved in the projects are *not* around the environment but rather around politics, rights, livelihood, governance, and civic involvement. For instance, we shall see that the residents in the village of Saro-Kamush learn few specific facts about the causal links between climate change and their own experiences of a changing climate, despite participating in a climate change adaptation project. However, they do acquire many ideas about accessing resources from the state and development organizations, or self-organizing around infrastructure projects.

It is worth noting that I am interested above all in the ways knowledge is created, spread, and contested across a range of scales via development. As such, the aim here is not normative: I do not set out to criticize or evaluate the efficacy of these organizations or their work, or to critique the project of development as a whole. There is plenty of work to this effect already.[4] At the same time, this work does not attempt to trace the relationship between development policy and development practice but rather the way development institutions (including their actions in the world) create and influence the spread of ideas and worldviews. Such ideas can surface as policy but they may also lie in the realm of more specific, individual concerns. Finally, while power dynamics within the networks is a subtheme in much of this work, it is not the sole focal point of the analysis. I move away from simple hierarchies of power (and their subversion) and broaden the discussion to include 'power that is productive rather than repressive, that comes from below as well as above, that is heterogeneous, diffuse, immanent and unstable' (Lewis & Mosse 2006: 3). I highlight and analyse such wide-ranging relationships of power to the extent that they affect the ways in which ideas are created, transmitted, and reshaped.

V. Book Structure

Chapter 2 lays the groundwork for the book's ethnography. It briefly summarizes the key theoretical traditions that this work draws on: in particular, it looks at the scholarship around both knowledge and civil society, with a focus on the way both are rooted in global/local dynamics and geography. The chapter also highlights the definitional pluralism of a number of terms—global, civil society, local, and environmentalism—and sets the broad definitions that will be used throughout the work. The chapter goes on to provide the background and structure of the case-study ethnographies using a geographically organized narrative of each location and organization. This is where the reader will find succinct descriptions of the main characters, as well as organizational and inter-personal dynamics in the case studies. The chapter concludes with a brief historical and political background of Kenya

[4] See, for instance, Escobar (1995); Fisher (1997); Cooley and Ron (2002); Reimann (2005, 2006); Bano (2008); Matanga (2010).

and Kyrgyzstan, with a focus on the particular details that are essential to understanding the two case studies.

The following three empirical chapters are organized both geographically and thematically. Rather than being divided by case study, the three empirical chapters correspond to organizational and geographic categories in both case-study networks—the two villages and the local organizations and global movements and foundations, national- and regional-level NGOs, and finally the two villages. Each chapter is organized thematically, and then each theme is subdivided into the two cases. The goal of the analysis is thus not to be explicitly comparative between the two cases but rather to *utilize* their differences and similarities to broaden and deepen the argument.

The first of the empirical chapters, Chapter 3, explores how knowledge within civil society networks affects and is affected by the local. It examines questions of connection and disconnection within the network society, pointing out the way civil society networks bring connections—particularly in the case of Kenya—to environmental ideas but also to the international aid system and state resources. The chapter also explores ideas and worldviews around the environment, civic involvement, development organizations, and government institutions in each village. It thus unpicks what is learned, what is ignored, and what is adapted from each development project by the local community, and in turn the ways local communities forge agency within the resource constraints imposed by international actors and foundations. The chapter also looks closely at the way development institutions interact with local communities. In particular, the chapter looks at the way programmes operate in practice, in contrast to institutional rhetoric around how programmes *should* be run (particularly when it comes to participation).

Chapter 4 goes on to examine networks of NGOs that act as intermediaries between the global and the local, unpicking how such intermediaries transfer and shape ideas from both below and above. I argue that while such networks can consist of organizations that have very different aims and goals, they are able to function as a network by adopting the rhetoric and ideas of one global movement. The chapter also charts how the intermediaries transform ideas from above into action—or at least plans for action. They do so in part by designating expertise, in particular by equating expertise with Westerners or at least those with Western education. Yet they also implement the global nodes' search for legitimacy and authenticity through local knowledge. The chapter outlines the way these intermediaries establish connection with or presume knowledge of the grassroots, particularly through adopting the framework of participatory development. It also looks at actors outside the network, in particular the state, and how such intermediary development institutions forge relationships with the state to access its resources, provide longevity to their programming, and in return supplement the (dis)functioning of the state.

Chapter 5 looks at global movements that promote key ideas in the networks—such as climate change adaptation or biocultural diversity—and the international foundations that create and propagate them. The focus is on the relationship between the two, using The Christensen Fund as an example of the way global civil society institutions can foster and create global movements around novel concepts (in this case, biocultural diversity) and The Aga Khan Foundation as an example of the way that such institutions can 'plug into' and adopt global movements (such as climate change adaptation). The chapter also demonstrates how such transnational institutions forge wider global networks. They do so not only through funding paths to and from other global institutions but also by cultivating relationships with academic and governmental institutions via conferences, workshops, and university networks. This chapter also investigates the way the two foundations attempt to build authenticity and legitimacy by trying to forge connections to locals or at least NGO intermediaries through field visits, workshops, and festivals.

The concluding Chapter 6 then ties together the key themes that emerge out of the empirical material. It focuses on the tension between agency and alignment within the networks, as well as the classification and privileging of certain types of ideas over others. Both are essential processes for the functioning of civil society knowledge networks and illustrate how these networks expand our understanding of the way development shapes contemporary geographies of knowledge.

2

Theories, Methods, and Background

I. Theorizing Knowledge, Local and Global

The impetus for this work came from the call for an ethnography of the global by scholars such as Burawoy (2001), Moore (2004), and Ferguson (2006). This call is for a deeper and richer exploration of the way in which the local is being woven into a tapestry of the global, as well as the processes and means by which the global is constituted, understood, and instrumentalized. Indeed, it is also a call to examine the extent to which the local–global dichotomy is a useful way of understanding how various points of the globe are interconnected, and the effects of such connections. This work is an exploration of one corner of this vast terrain, using development-focused civil society and environmentally focused development interventions as a lens to examine the complexities of these connections. The goal of this work is to use our two case studies to piece together a particular geography of knowledge: knowledge that is transferred and shared; knowledge that is utilized and ignored, challenged, and transformed; knowledge that shapes values and thus actions.

To do this, the book takes as its starting point the anthropological literature around knowledge and 'knowledge making' through social relations (Dilley 2010; Marchand 2010b). For Marchand (2010a), one of the central questions of anthropological inquiry is 'how do we come to know?', and this is one of the key questions of this work. In particular, this book is interested in the far-from-linear processes of knowledge transfer and exchange, paying particular attention to the messy and unequal processes through which knowledge is articulated and transformed (Marchand 2010a).

The book uses the metaphor of knowledge 'flows' to conceptualize these processes. This term has been contested, for instance, by James Ferguson, who suggests that 'hopping' rather than flowing is more appropriate terminology for the 'point to point connectivity and networking of enclaves' that ignores the terrain that lies between (Ferguson 2006: 47–48). While in accord with the spirit of this critique, I would argue that it is built on too narrow a definition of the word 'flow', which is widely used in mathematics

Civil Society Knowledge Networks. E. Fouksman, Oxford University Press. © Elizaveta Fouksman (2026).
DOI: 10.1093/9780198943723.003.0002

and engineering to refer to movement from node to node in a network, and explicitly does not require engagement with the space between nodes (Pieterse & Black 2004). Thus I conceptualize the flow of knowledge and ideas within these two case-study networks as *saltatory flows* (those that propagate by leaps and bounds). Using the concept of *saltatory flows* allows us to pay attention to the inequalities and disjunctures as well as the multi-directional nature of such flows. These flows have eddies, backwashes, and counter-currents, as the power dynamics as well as the different relationships and points of connection of the case-study networks facilitate diverse dynamics of exchange and contestation.

The unevenness within knowledge flows plays a key role in another essential distinction within this project—the differences within the scope, privilege, and power of knowledge at the global and the local levels, which are also referred to by actors in the networks as 'expert' and 'indigenous' knowledge. Although this work actively engages in the contestations, distinctions, and gaps between these categories, it is vital to acknowledge that the categories themselves are blurred, fluid, and flawed. Simply understanding the global as 'an enveloping level of coverage' (Ferguson 2006: 42) and the local as representative of 'grounded authenticity' is misleading. Often the local is well integrated into and savvy in its use of the global, so the assumption that the global somehow supersedes the local in power and reach can be problematic. And what emerges in this book is the importance of 'meso' geographies, neither quite local or global (Johnson et al. 2023)—for instance, national NGOs that are neither global in scope nor deeply connected to particular communities. The aim of this book is thus not to decide whether global/local is a justified dichotomy but rather to illuminate a more complex relationship than a dichotomy between any two terms could capture.

A categorical distinction that parallels the global/local division is that between 'expert' and 'indigenous' or 'local' knowledge. The latter category is one that will be referenced repeatedly throughout this work, as it was used frequently by the globally situated actors in the case studies. *Indigenous knowledge* 'evolve[s] by adaptive processes and [is] handed down through generations by cultural transmission . . . [that] is time, place and culture specific' (Ifejika Speranza et al. 2010 296; see also Fernando 2003). The concept is now common parlance within global institutions (Sillitoe 2010) and acts as an overarching global discourse that can connect indigenous groups or local communities to a global movement by positing the existence of a shared, distinctly indigenous worldview (Groenfeldt 2003). Such a 'global indigenous worldview' seems to qualify the idea of indigenous knowledge as locally situated. Indeed, Groenfeldt (2003) makes the case that such a globally unified indigenous movement has utilized Western techniques for its own aims, via academic journals, conferences, and legal norms. And, as will be analysed throughout this book, global movements have instrumentalized local or indigenous knowledge for global aims as well.

In short, categories like global/expert and local/indigenous are deeply interconnected, and one of the contributions of this work is a critique of the institutions and practices within development that presume them to be distinct and laud one as more 'authentic' than another. Indeed, a long scholarly tradition has documented the ways in which the opposition between 'scientific' or expert knowledge and indigenous knowledge is institutionally produced in the global North, with the two categories having methodological and epistemological similarities, along with a long historical interweave (see, for instance, Fernando 2003). Indeed, some of the critiques of the construction of local or indigenous knowledge within development practice echo critiques of participatory approaches to development, particularly in the ways in which such approaches can reproduce local inequities in power and voice (Cooke & Kothari 2001; Beinart & Brown 2013). And Agrawal (1995, 2002, 2005a) has pointed out the inherent contradiction behind the promotion of indigenous knowledge by the West: indigenous knowledge is valuable to the West because it can advance both scientific knowledge and development, yet these are the very forces that are destroying indigenous knowledge. This tension between privileging local and indigenous knowledge and pursuing universalizing development goals will emerge as a key theme in the chapters to come.

This work critically engages with a construction of not only 'local' but also 'global' geographies of knowledge and the complex relationship between the two. In particular, I make use of three conceptual approaches to the global or transnational geographies of knowledge: epistemic communities, knowledge commons, and the network society. An *epistemic community* is, in the words of Peter Haas (1992: 3), a 'network of professionals with recognized expertise and competence in a particular domain and an authoritative claim to policy-relevant knowledge'. Epistemic communities have a shared way of knowing, which includes shared values, causal beliefs, and, importantly, discursive practices. The epistemic community literature highlights the relationship between discourse and action, pointing out that communication and 'the negotiations of meanings, understandings and beliefs' are what allows for a shared set of values and 'moral vision' (Adler & Haas 1992: 389) that then allows for action within the policy arena.

This book expands the epistemic community concept from Haas' original definition. It challenges two aspects: the necessity for an epistemic community, first, to consist of 'experts' or 'professionals' and, second, to act as advisors to state actors in creating policy. Instead, the book broadens the definition to include literal 'communities of knowledge', peopled not only by recognized professionals (a culturally biased and elitist vision of epistemic authority) but also by any agents involved in generating a cohesive transnational discourse around a particular issue. Epistemic communities could include organic intellectuals—groups of people who might not define themselves as intellectuals by profession but emerge to voice the aspirations and identity of a group or class (Gramsci 1970). This could include communities that produce indigenous or local knowledge as well as the civil society actors discussed in the latter half of this chapter. Moreover, the role of epistemic communities does not have to be limited to advising the state. Non-state actors, including local movements and civil society organizations, take action based on the consensus of such transnational epistemic communities. I thus suggest an opening and flattening of the epistemic community concept against the original highly hierarchical framing of the term: a geographic and conceptual expansion that also involves looking at the role of the local and meso in such communities.

Another useful way of conceptualizing such a wide and open community of knowledge without the exclusivity of the original epistemic community concept is the idea of the *knowledge commons*. If the word 'commons' refers to a 'complex ecosystem' in which 'a resource is shared by a group of people that is subject to social dilemmas' (Hess & Ostrom 2007: 3), then conceptualizing knowledge as one such resource allows us to examine the way it is accessed, shared, or enclosed (putting it outside of the knowledge commons). Unlike the original idea of epistemic communities, the knowledge commons has been imagined across a variety of geographies—local, global, 'or somewhere in between' (Hess & Ostrom 2007: 9). The conceptual language associated with the knowledge commons is both more open and more egalitarian than that used for epistemic communities. Each individual within a knowledge commons is both a generator and contributor of ideas, regardless of rank within an epistemic hierarchy, rather than just a consumer of knowledge. As such, 'connection and sharing of ideas without exerting individual ownership of the ideas allows the knowledge to move freely and grow' (Joranson 2008: 68).

Yet while the commons is conceptually useful in imagining both global and local realms of knowledge as a shared resource, the idea of a commons lacks the descriptive tools to analyse the *ways* in which knowledge is unevenly created, contested, and shared within the process of its social construction. Indeed, even authors writing on the knowledge commons often use the visual of a network rather than a commons. As Boyle (2003: 74) writes, the commons can help 'reimagine creation, innovation, and speech on a global network', and Kranich (2007: 88, 94) refers to knowledge commons as 'resource-sharing networks' and 'networked environments'. This takes us to the final spatial metaphor used extensively in this book: the knowledge network.

An alternative way to conceptualize a geography of knowledge is to use the idea of networks of interconnected idea creators, contesters, and transmitters, particularly Manuel Castells' (2005, 2023) global '*network society*'. This is a social structure 'based on networks . . . that generate, process, and distribute information on the basis of the knowledge accumulated in the nodes of the networks' (2005: 7) that cross national boundaries and create global connections and flows of information and knowledge.

There is a strong focus on the transformative effect of information technology in Castells' work. The case studies to come will extend the network society beyond the impact of information technology, demonstrating that other social structures—namely, civil society organizations—can enable its functioning, even when, as will be argued later in this work, technological connectivity fails. Indeed, a danger of the knowledge network framework is ignoring all of the forces—social, cultural, economic, political—outside of the network in question that in fact affect both the actors and the knowledge created within the network. Mejias (2009: 12) calls this 'nodocentrism': 'the assertion that only nodes need to be mapped, explained or accounted for'. He makes a case for what he terms paranodality, or the space outside of the network:

> As far as the network is concerned, the paranodal . . . gives nodes their history and identity: shifts in the paranodal translate into changes in the location of nodes and the relationships between them, and consequently into changes in the network itself. In short, the instability of paranodal space is what animates the network, and to attempt to render paranodal space invisible is to arrive at less, not more, complete explanations of the network as a social reality. (2009: 12)

The problem with attempting to trace all such paranodal influences is that it becomes a totalizing research task. It is impossible to consider the possible influence of all outside forces on a specific knowledge network, and this book does not attempt this—but it does look at influences such as academia or the state as paranodal actors in our case-study networks.

II. Civil Society Geographies: From Global Civil Society to NGOization

This book thus traces both the *geography* and the *mechanisms* of knowledge creation and exchange, examining the ways in which macro, meso, and micro social scales interact and influence one another with an increasing density of interconnection. The actors that make these interconnections are an equally vital part of the argument: these are development-focused civil society organizations. Like the categories of global and local, civil society is a fraught term, evolving from the Enlightenment concept of a *civil* (that is, civilized) society, ruled by law with a state monopoly over violence, to Hegel and Marx's idea of a bourgeois society between the state and the family that is produced by the emergence of capitalism (Kaldor 2003). In the twentieth century, Gramsci used the term to denote a sphere separate from both market and state (though intimately linked to the functioning of the latter) that can either support or challenge the existing ruling order and its ideology and develop an alternative hegemony (Gramsci 1971; Buttigieg 1995; Lewis 2002). This view of the concept influenced an activist, social movement version of the term which emerged in the 1980s and 1990s in conjunction with the dissident movements in eastern Europe at the end of the Cold War. In this view, civil society can be a site of struggle and resistance. At the same time, the concept became linked to NGOs and charities that could shoulder some of the responsibilities of the state by providing service delivery (McIlwaine 2007). This neoliberal version of civil society is in tension with the Marxist and Gramscian activist one but has been utilized extensively by neoliberal visions of international development. This neoliberal version co-exists with a postmodern one (Keane 2003), which emphasizes diversity and plurality, in contrast to the shared cosmopolitanism of the activist model or the civic-mindedness of the neoliberal version. The contemporary concept of civil society could thus be referred to as civil societies, and some social theorists deplore the conceptual looseness of the term, arguing that its very popularity (particularly amongst development practitioners) leads to ambiguities, confusions, and contradictions (Kumar 2000). Yet in the words of Jean and John Comaroff (1999: 7–8), 'to bemoan the lack of coherence and specificity of the concept of civil society . . . seems rather to miss the point. So too does the effort to pin it down, to wrestle away its inherent ambiguities.'

The concept of civil society used within this work is based on the history of the term traced by Habermas (1989) and the way the term has been situated within the global by Kaldor (2003) and Keane (2003). It can be understood as *the space outside of (though often engaged with) the formal mechanisms of the state, the private realm of the family, and the economic realm of the market where individuals form movements, institutions, and groups to engage with social issues of collective concern.* The use of the term here emerges from common uses of the term by development practitioners, and thus is grounded in practice and utility. Of course, defining the term does not eliminate its controversies, in particular those related to what David Rieff (1999) has described as a 'prescriptive' idealization of the political utility of civil society. Civil society can reproduce 'dominations and segmentations, hegemonies and exclusions' (Burawoy 2004: 1616). While this work makes no claim that civil society is necessarily useful, egalitarian, or democratic, its aim is *not* to engage with such normative debates beyond acknowledging them and rather to construct an analytical model of some of the epistemic outcomes of civil society networks.

This book focuses on one particular type of civil society: international development organizations in their variety, including NGOs, the charitable foundations that fund them, and the grassroots movements and community-based organizations (CBOs) they encourage and support. Development, with its theoreticians, policymakers, and implementers, has its own long history and analytical literature, as outlined in Chapter 1. This work does not operate within the instrumental view of development practice, with its pragmatic managerial and policy concerns and its aspirational 'will to improve' the human condition (Li 2007). Rather, it builds on long-standing analytical scholarship that deconstructs the development project by critically demonstrating its inherent contradictions, hegemonies, and hierarchies (see, for instance, Ferguson 1994; Cowen & Shenton 1995a, 1995b; Escobar 1995; Scott 1998). In particular, it draws on this analytical tradition when it comes to the relationship between civil society and the state, and the development rhetoric and practice that calls itself participatory, bottom-up, or indigenous. Yet, as noted in Chapter 1, the book looks beyond the 'grand theories' of development (such as modernization, dependency, neoliberalism, participatory approaches, and bottom-up development) to also see the way in which these underpinning ideologies interact with more focused ideas around topics such as the environment, good governance, livelihood, and agricultural policy. The overall aim of the book is thus to look at development and the actors involved in it as a set of social processes, one amongst many, that knits together a diversity of ideas, perspectives, values, and aims across a variety of spaces and places into a tangled web of meaning. It is the structure and functioning of such a web that forms the crux of this inquiry.

The foundation of this argument emerges when the scholarship on international development and civil society meets that of the sociology of globalization. It is built on the assumption that actors are deeply embedded in a rich institutional environments (Boli & Thomas 1999; Meyer 1999, 2010). Indeed, the case studies will demonstrate that even places that seem initially lacking in formal or state-recognized institutions in fact have a complex institutional environment—more specifically, a bounty of development-focused civil society institutions. Such a rich institutional environment creates systems of meaning that penetrate beyond the boundaries of individual actors, 'constructing agency, identity and activity' (Meyer 2010: 4). This book examines the way civil society in the form of development institutions enables, empowers, and shapes the opportunities of many human actors by providing linkages to political, technological, financial, and information resources.

Such networks of civil society institutions can operate globally and transnationally. Particularly useful for conceptualizing this is the concept of *global civil society*, or 'the groups, networks and movements which comprise the mechanisms through which individuals negotiate and renegotiate social contracts or political bargains on a global level' (Kaldor 2003: 78). Development institutions are one of these mechanisms, connected by transnational civic networks, allowing local campaigns to receive global attention and support and global campaigns to trickle down to the local level. Keck and Sikkink (1999) reframe these as *transnational advocacy networks* whose formation is motivated by core similarities in ideas, values, and norms. Information exchange is the key function of such networks, and they both constitute and rely on connections and flows of information, funds, and services. At the same time, transnational advocacy networks can be arenas of struggle as well as diffusion, shaping and challenging shared norms. As Hall (2022) has argued, scholarship on transnational advocacy can conflate or flatten distinct elements of such campaigns by focusing largely on what happens at large global summits, and ignoring the particular needs (both national and more local) of the members of such networks. This book contests and nuances both of these terms by focusing not only on the global or transnational aspects of civil society and advocacy but also on their national, regional, and grassroots counterparts.

Whether conceptualized as global civil society or transnational networks, NGOs and other development institutions are able to operate because they are embedded within a global public sphere built on a set of shared 'civic religions' such as human rights and environmentalism (Kaldor 2003). As Anderson and Rieff (2005) point out, development-focused civil society attempts to represent the 'universal' needs and rights of the world's peoples.

Indeed, this is a key critique of '*NGOization*'—that in the process of playing the role of 'new citizen saviours' and contributors to human progress, NGOs decide on what this progress *is*, becoming the gatekeepers for a 'global market of worthy and just causes' (Reimann 2005: 38, 46). As such, transnational networks of development institutions operate based on a widely accepted (but not uncontested) assumption of the moral universality of their values (Anderson and Rieff 2005). The reliance of NGOs on universalist discourses to shape their agenda is tied into their relationship to donors, another key part of the NGOization critique, which points out that NGO agendas are often driven by the need to continue receiving funding and thus are a reflection of funders' interests rather than local needs. Yet, as the case studies that follow show, the way ideas and agendas spread and are adapted is more convoluted than the simple question of "who has the money." By sharing a set of universalist values or goals, NGOs are able to move resources from a wide variety of funders, while donors in turn use the information and discourse generated by NGOs to legitimize their own existence (Ebrahim 2003). At the same time, this work will show that this depiction of universal values and global civic religions is too flat: it ignores the agency of actors within and around development institutions to redefine the agenda. Such actors both appeal to these values and subvert them; they both take up such 'universal' ideas and adapt them to local needs and approaches.

The NGOization critique has more broadly pointed out the ways in which civil society can be depoliticizing, undemocratic, and unaccountable (Choudry & Kapoor 2013). Participatory approaches to development are one response to this critique. *Participatory development* promises to build on the local and indigenous knowledge discussed earlier in the chapter to challenge power hierarchies in development projects and provide responsive development interventions (Chambers 1983, 1986, 2004; Gaventa 2004; Hickey & Mohan 2004). The assumptions and incoherencies of these approaches have now been thoroughly critiqued and deconstructed, particularly for their rarefaction of 'community' and 'local knowledge'; their neglect of local hierarchies, power dynamics, and motivations; and their tendency to find the ideas and needs that they set out to see (Cleaver 2001; Cooke & Kothari 2001; Kothari 2001; Mosse 2001, 2003, 2005). Many of these critiques emerge in the case studies that follow. Yet ideas of participation, alongside concepts such as 'local', 'community', 'bottom-up', and 'grassroots' development, still hold immense power and appeal within development institutions. One of the subthemes of this work is to understand why this is and how both participation and the local are used and understood within the case-study networks.

III. The Lens of Environmentalism(s)

A useful lens for narrowing an exploration of the way that geographies of knowledge and civil society networks come together is environmentalism. Environmentalism is a dynamic example of a transnational movement operating on multiple tiers of a complex global network, ranging from local projects to national policies to transnational advocacy organizations. Of course, environmentalism is far from *one* movement—there are many strands, rhetorics, aims, and geographies of environmentalism. However, there are certain common factors tying these disparate strands together. Environmental movements are built not only on the assumption of a shared humanity but also on a shared experience of the physical world. Yet environmentalism includes many different priorities and discourses: some focus on indigenous knowledge and resource rights, others on scientific priorities and state-led fortress conservation, and yet others on the private sector as a vehicle for environmental improvement (Guha & Martínez-Alier 2000). Its substrands within development work can go by many names, including sustainable development and natural resource management, and have been critiqued for treating the environment as something to be managed, exploited and controlled for the sake of ongoing, 'sustainable' growth within a competitive productivist paradigm (rather than challenging such a paradigm) (Sachs 2009b). This book is less concerned with the content of environmental movement(s) themselves than environmentalism as epistemic communities tied together through international linkages (Jeon & Yoon 2006). This ties into the substantial literature on the relative value and privilege of global versus local environmental knowledge, such as that highlighted by Beinart (2000).

The multi-sited case studies in this book are themselves part of contrasting strands of environmentalism. In *The Environmentalism of the Poor* (2002), Martínez-Alier divides environmental movements and their history into three broad 'clusters', though the boundaries between these clusters are blurred and blended. One of these clusters is what Martínez-Alier terms the 'Gospel of Eco-Efficiency', which could equally well be called sustainable development. Here, the rhetoric is not of nature but rather of natural resources, with a focus on 'scientific management' (2002: 7). This cluster of ideas and movements advocates two types of solutions to ecological problems: economic (for instance, through carbon taxes or REDD (Reducing Emissions from Deforestation and Forest Degradation) programmes) and scientific (through green technology such as solar power and more efficient agricultural technologies).

The Swiss–Kyrgyz case-study network fits precisely into this environmental vision. The development intervention that lies at the heart of this case study is a climate change adaptation project, itself housed within the natural resource management programme within the Aga Khan Foundation Kyrgyzstan (AKF Kg) and their partner NGO, Mountain Society Development and Support Programme (MSDSP) Kg. Adaptation has grown on the development agenda since the early 2000s, increasing in popularity both with donors and implementing organizations. Its aim is to adjust 'natural or human systems in response to actual or expected climatic stimuli or their effects, which moderates harm or exploits beneficial opportunities' (Klein et al. 2007: 750), or, in the words of Thornton and Manasfi (2010: 132), to 'climate-proof development'. The focus on adaptation is a move away from mitigating climate change and represents a more politically and economically neutral agenda of preparing communities and countries for its effects, often in ways that neatly 'mainstream' into current development programmes around natural resource management. Indeed, AKF's climate change adaptation project never mentioned the words 'environmentalism' or even 'nature'; instead, its rhetoric was of infrastructural and economic ways to address a changing climate.

Besides being an increasingly powerful global call to action within the development sphere, climate change adaptation also makes for a useful epistemic lens for this work in its concerns with multi-scale dynamics—at least in the academic literature, if not in practice (Agrawal et al. 2009). Climate change is a global phenomenon, linked to global systems of economics, governance, consumption patterns, and activism. At the same time, much of the focus of adaptation programmes, including that of AKF, has been on the local. While adaptation programmes have searched for technologically based, reproducible solutions, they have also adopted some of the rhetoric and methods of participatory development. As such, they have attempted to integrate community-generated ideas and grassroots involvement. These approaches have their own critics based on the multi-scale nature of climate change noted above: local communities cannot easily engage with national or global priorities for adaptation (Thornton & Manasfi 2010). Thus even within the strand of climate change adaptation, global/local dynamics and the geography of knowledge (as well as resources and power) play a key role in determining the way adaptation is understood and put into practice.

Besides 'geo-efficiency', another broad strand of environmentalism is what Martínez-Alier calls the Cult of Wilderness. This cluster values and idealizes wilderness for its intrinsic aesthetic and moral merits. The applications of this strand within international development can range from fortress conservation to co-management with local communities, though co-management is often seen as a failure or last resort. In contrast, the third cluster in Martínez-Alier's delineation is what he calls Environmentalism of the Poor but can also be termed Environmental Justice or Popular Environmentalism. This refers to South-based resistance to the environmental impacts of economic development—an archetypal example is indigenous communities protesting dam-building projects. This resistance could emerge out of livelihood concerns, territorial rights, or cultural or traditional beliefs around the sacredness of nature—in short, either material or sacred interests.

While The Christensen Fund's (TCF's) focus on biocultural diversity in the 2010s had clear affiliations with the Cult of Wilderness in its love for landscapes and biodiversity, its mandate of promoting biocultural diversity also fit into the Environmentalism of the Poor. Supporters of biocultural diversity argue that cultural diversity is essential to preserve biodiversity and stop ecological degradation. Although the term was brought into use by Posey (1996), the arguments around biodiversity were first formalized in the Declaration of Belém in 1988, when a gathering of indigenous and 'traditional' peoples met with scientists and environmentalists at the First International Congress of Ethnobiology in Belém, Brazil. The Declaration argues that 'there is an inextricable link between cultural and biological diversity'. It recognizes that social, cultural, and economic systems hold both the problems and solutions to biological problems (Cocks 2006). Biocultural diversity advocates underscore the link between the knowledge and cultural traditions of 'indigenous' and 'traditional' peoples and the protection of diverse landscapes, flora, and fauna.

Biocultural diversity is a global idea and movement, yet it privileges local and indigenous knowledge—not simply as an inherent good but as a way to resolve global problems of biodiversity loss and resultant ecological degradation. Thus the global movements to support and preserve indigenous knowledge and biocultural diversity epitomize the complex relationship between the global and local dynamics of knowledge production. TCF's approach contrasts with AKF's climate change adaptation project, yet both have simultaneous engagement both with the rhetoric of the local and particular and the global scope of ecological problems.

IV. Introducing the Case Studies

a. Constructing Multi-Sited Case Studies

This book is based on two multi-sited case studies to tease out the detailed dynamics and particularities within the process of creating, spreading, and contesting knowledge within networks of development organizations and communities. The fieldwork for these case studies was spread across three years, with immersive periods at each of the four countries and eight organizations that comprise the two case studies. The fieldwork drew on ethnographic methods, involving extended homestays with my interlocutors, and many semi-structured interviews as well as observations, participation in organizational and village life, and informal conversations. Research participants were free to decide if they preferred me to use their real first or full names or a pseudonym. As many chose to use their given names, for consistency's sake I use only first/given names throughout this work. Some participants chose to be anonymized, in which case a pseudonym is used for their given name.

If, in the words of David Mosse (2005: 4), 'the project cycle . . . insures the separation of planners and implementers', this work brings the two together, along with the communities where the implementers work. The case studies were designed to examine how all three are nodes in an epistemic network, integrated to some degree but also with discrete individual levels where knowledge is generated and transmitted. In this way, they are a means to examine forces of cultural and social globalization 'from the standpoint of participants located at the intersection of the most remote forces, connections and imaginations' (Burawoy 2001: 148). Thus connections and flows (along with disconnections and tensions) are as much a part of the case study as the individual nodes themselves. As Marcus (1995: 105) has argued, a research 'site' need not be geographically defined, with 'multi-sited research . . . designed around chains, paths, threads, conjunctions or juxtapositions of locations . . . with an explicit, posited logic of association or connection among sites that in fact defines the argument [of the project]' (see also Urry 2000). Such multi-sited research design is the foundation of this research project; the chains and threads connecting different tiers of the cases are as central to the empirical data as each individual location.

One of the difficulties of selecting and designing case studies is deciding where each case begins and ends. This is particularly true of the multi-sited network model—besides all of the nodes that comprise each knowledge network, there are many other social, political, and contextual forces that influence the way each of the case-study networks functions. As with any empirical research project, it is impossible to examine every possible variable that ties into each case study. However, as mentioned in the previous chapter, this work does go out of its way to engage with this limitation by exploring Mejias' (2009) concept of 'paranodality', or what lies outside the network but still influences it. Each case study does include one of the most influential and primary of such paranodal forces: the state. The state is the one agent outside the network that emerged again and again in conversations throughout my fieldwork. As a result, each case includes an exploration of the relationship between the civil society organizations in question and local and national government institutions. Other external forces will also play a role in the chapters that follow, particularly universities and academia.

Another key difficulty of approaching research questions via a case study lies in the issue of theory-making, of generalizing from the particular to the universal. As Molyneux (2001: 273) points out, 'since any ethnographic account of development and globalization is necessarily partial and selective, at best it can provide a focused illumination of a part of a complex whole'. As such, this study does not attempt to use the cases deductively to produce universalizing theory but rather to explore the usefulness of the framework laid out in this chapter in making sense of the particularity and complexity of the two cases in question (Yin 2009).

The two case-study networks have been chosen precisely on this basis of similarity and contrast. Both include a geographically remote, semi-nomadic pastoralist people who were concerned with the livelihood implications of sustainable resource use, disillusioned with the state, and were being encouraged to engage in ecologically focused initiatives by regional NGOs tied to international private foundations. Both of these foundations were interested in funding environmentally related programmes, and thus were connected to global environmental movements—though to different flavours of environmentalism in each case. However, conducting a comparative case study in two different parts of the world enabled me to examine the role of cultural, political, and historical specificities in the ways these networks interacted with the local. At the same time, looking at two different foundations with two different visions of development let me examine the ways in which different organizational cultures and epistemic commitments influenced the way such a network functions. Thus the end goal of using the two case studies is not simply to compare and contrast them to clarify their distinctiveness and particularity, but also to tease out the dynamics of similarly

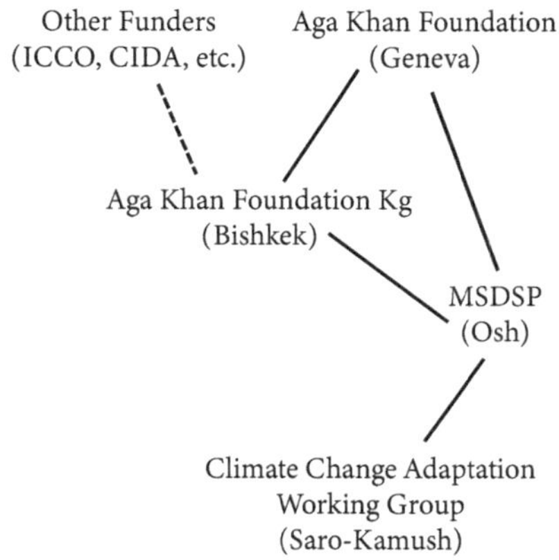

Figure 2.1 Swiss-Kyrgyz network

structured civil society knowledge networks within two different geographic and institutional contexts.

It is not easy to keep track of all of the actors, individuals, organizations, and agendas in this book (see Figures 2.1 and 2.3 for a schematic overview of the networks). Two multi-sited case studies, each with four or five different sites, make for a complicated web of interests, contexts, and personalities. This section gives a brief introduction to each of the organizations, locations, and major personalities within this project (with names highlighted in bold for quick reference), and briefly describes their relationships to each other.

b. Case Study One: From Saro-Kamush to Geneva via Kara-Kulja, Osh, and Bishkek

i. Saro-Kamush and Zalgat Alma/The Climate Change Adaptation Working Group

The village of Saro-Kamush (Сары-Камыш, alternatively transliterated as Sary-Kamysh) is the local node of the Swiss–Kyrgyz case-study network (see Figure 2.2 for a map). At the time of research in the mid-2010s, this was a village of about 900 people, a 20-minute drive outside of Kara-Kulja (Кара-Кулжа, also transliterated as Kara Kuldja), situated next to a river-canyon and surrounded by mountain foothills, with a great snowy range closing off the ends of the long valley in which the village nestles. The village was run by the (elected) village elder, with a council of elders to advise him or her, though local political power actually lay with subdistrict and district councils

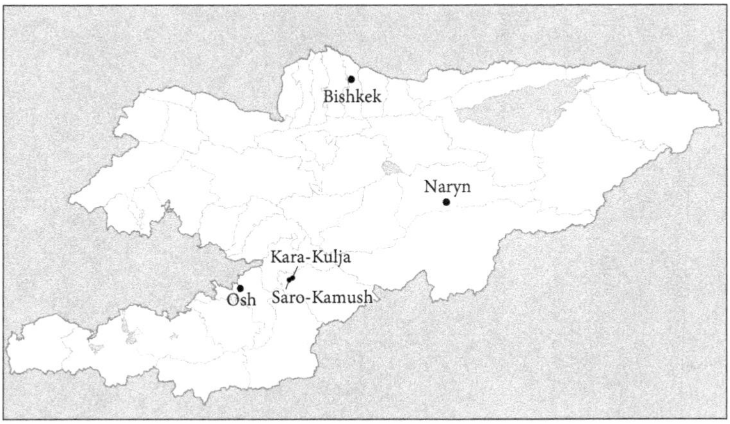

Figure 2.2 Map of the Kyrgyz Republic

(for which the village members can stand in elections). Although at a lower altitude than many of the other villages in the district, it is still a mountain village, where the main occupation is herding. The residents are semi-nomadic pastoralists, many leaving the village in the summer to move up to summer pastures with their cows, sheep, and horses, living in yurts and (for a fee) looking after not only their own livestock but also those of their neighbours that choose to stay in the village for the summer. Both in winter and summer, the animals graze on communal pastures that are under the use of the village (which is technically 'renting' them from the government in a long-term lease); animal-owners pay a different level of pasture tax depending on the numbers of animals they put out to pasture.

Yet while every family in the village owned at least a few sheep, a major source of income while I was there was remittances from family members in Bishkek or abroad, largely in Kazakhstan or Russia. This echoed the economy of the country as a whole, where the largest source of income is remittances. Every single house where I conducted interviews had at least one member of the younger generation (20–40-year-olds) working away, and it was income from such remittances that funded the rather high standard of living in the village—every family had at least one TV and many had a car. Everyone had a mobile phone, and I saw one woman with an iPad, bought for her by a brother working in Moscow.

Those working abroad were typically working in menial labour such as cleaning or cashiering or selling goods at the market—frequently with university degrees in hand. Migrants willingly submitted to substandard living conditions such as terrible crowding in order to be able to send remittances home. And not everyone was successful—**Eliza** and **Nurmat**, the couple I lived with in the village, who were in their early 30s, spent most of their 20s trying to make it abroad, first in Kazakhstan reselling goods, then in Bishkek reselling scrap metal, and finally in Moscow (just Eliza) working as a cashier. In Eliza's words, they were never successful at any of this—they always just barely managed to break even. Although many young people were sending money home in this way, and though their families did express gratitude and even dependence, they also deplored the lack of employment opportunities in the village and in the Kyrgyz Republic as a whole. When I asked why more young people did not choose to be herders, I was told that herding simply did not make enough money for discretionary spending—it was just enough for food, but that is about it. This migration was nearly always temporary, even when successful, and many young people returned to herding or other local pursuits afterwards.

The associational life of the village largely revolved around the village mosque and the village clinic, and consisted in informal associations based around religious life or fundraising for village necessities such as a new clinic or new kindergarten. Besides these two focal points, much of the organizational life in the village—particularly that with external links or funding—centred on the village school. The school had about a dozen staff members and a hundred or so children, and was both a primary and secondary school. Both the husband and wife in the family that hosted me are teachers in the school, and **Maksat**, my translator, was one of the Russian teachers there (her sister is the principal of the school).

During my time in the village in 2013, Saro-Kamush was about two-thirds of the way through MSDSP Kg's Climate Change Adaptation project (described in more detail below)—they had completed an assessment, the information session, and the plan-creating session, and had formed a working group, applied for a mini-grant, and won the grant. Their mini-grant proposal to the project was to clean out the main canal in the village, which was blocked up with sedimentary run-off, and place a concrete pipe with a bridge/road over it in one spot so that vehicles could get from the village road to the fields where fodder is being grown. (Before the project, people would use horses to get across the canal when it was full.) At the time I was in the village the mini-grant paperwork was signed, materials were being bought, and work was just starting.

The main point person for the mini-grant project was **Nurmat**, the 33-year-old physical education teacher in the school and my host in the village. In his 20s, Nurmat had founded and led a registered local CBO (or 'jamat' (fund), as they were known in the village) called **Zhalgiz Alma**

(Single Apple). This was initially an active micro-credit/micro-savings organization but had been inactive for several years because Nurmat had left the village to work abroad, and the person who took over mismanaged the funds, though the CBO was still registered with the state. Both the working group and MSDSP saw that working with an existing registered agency—even one that had been inactive for years—was to their advantage, as it had a bank account and recognition from the state in the form of a licence. The registered members of the group overlapped largely (though not exclusively) with the members of the adaptation plan working group.

ii. MSDSP Kg and the Climate Change Adaptation Programme

The MSDSP Kyrgyz Republic (**MSDSP Kg** or **MSDSP Kyrgyzstan** at the time of the research) 2012 annual report introduces the organization as an 'initiative' of the Aga Khan Foundation. This rather ambivalent statement about the relationship between the two agencies, despite the implied hierarchy, means that MSDSP can present an independent front to the world when necessary—it is registered as a stand-alone NGO in Kyrgyzstan, is often referred to as a 'local' partner organization on grant applications, and operates in a different city. Besides the large head office (with more staff members than AKF Kg) in Osh, the Kyrgyz Republic's second-biggest city and its major metropolis in the south, MSDSP also had offices in Naryn in the centre of the country and Alai, Chong-Alai, and Kara-Kulja in the southern provinces. The head office, which was located in a gated compound in a central part of Osh, had its own drivers, car, engineer, agricultural specialist, and even a cook who sold lunch to the staff in the lunch room. Its staff was entirely Kyrgyz,[1] and in 2012 it had a budget of over US$2 million to spend on programming. However, MSDSP is closely interwoven with AKF Kg, with some staff members based in AKF Kg's Bishkek office. While AKF Kg focuses on fundraising, grant-writing (and thus programme creation), collaborations, and trainings, MSDSP Kg largely focuses on making programming happen. This means that it can have a degree of autonomy in interpreting programming and designing and tweaking implementations—a process which often points to MSDSP's organizational values and interests.

The director of MSDSP Kg, **Talant**, holds large sway over the way programmes are run and executed. In particular, Talant took quite a lot of credit and agency when it came to the **climate change adaptation project**, the focal point of this case study. Although the programme was largely designed and

[1] With the exception of only one staff member, Laila, the reporting manager for MSDSP whose role was to write up the programme reports and who was born in Mongolian and educated in Europe.

initially researched and tested by **Laurie**, an American consultant, Talant told me that the idea was originally his. The programme itself had gone through three iterations: the first was a year long, finished in 2012, and was funded by the Interchurch Organization for Development Cooperation (ICCO); the second was two years long, ran from 2012 to 2014, and was funded by the **Prince Sadruddin Aga Khan Fund for the Environment** (PSAKFE); the third was three years long, started in spring 2013, and was funded by the Canadian International Development Agency (CIDA). It is the second iteration that I use as a lens in this case study; however, I do refer to the materials and staff members of all three in the book. The second iteration of the programme was run by **Pirjan**, the project manager based in the Osh office of MSDSP, with the help of **Aizada**, the project specialist based in Naryn district and tasked with overseeing the projects there. Besides Pirjan, Aizada, and Laurie, I also spent time with **Alibek**, the MSDSP staff member then carrying out an evaluation of the programme, as well as **Erkin**, the former project manager of the first version of the project.

The programme ran in MSDSP's operating areas: Naryn district in the centre of the country and Osh district in the south. The stated goal of the climate change adaptation project was to spread information about climate change and enable local communities to develop pragmatic climate change adaptation plans that would be integrated into local governance structures as part of the broader regional development plan (AKF Kg 2010). Although the second iteration of the programme was housed within MSDSP's natural resource management programme, a major aspect of the programme was building local civil society—indeed, the first iteration of the project was under the civil society programme at MSDSP, and the title of both the first and third rounds of the programme is 'building local civil society through climate change adaptation and resilience in Kyrgyzstan'.

The programme conducted participatory assessments of the possible consequences of climate change on selected mountain villages—for instance, glacial lakes rising and flooding the village, or more avalanches or mudslides as more melting snow comes down in the spring, or droughts and extreme weather. The programme then returned to conduct an information session that teaches community members about climate change. It then returned again for a session about creating an adaptation plan for climate change impacts—for instance, the plan could suggest planting more trees to hold slopes in place or reinforcing riverbanks and moving houses to higher ground. At this point, participants selected a small working group whose role was to solidify the plan and integrate it into local government institutions. The last part of the programme allowed the group to select one part of the plan to turn into a project proposal, which they submitted to MSDSP as a mini-grant proposal. Not all villages won the grant, but the two-thirds or so that did received US$4,000 to carry out the adaptation, which was supposed to be run by the working group. The aim was to have the villages learn not only about climate change and adaptation but also about how to develop proposals and get such projects off the ground.

The climate change adaptation project emphasized the importance of creating a relationship with local and national government structures. This meant not only adding the climate change adaptation plans produced by participating villages to the local development plan but also integrating the programme with the national-level Ministry of Emergency Situations—and the choice of this Ministry, rather than one devoted to agriculture or pastoralism or the environment, is significant in demonstrating the disaster risk reduction lean of the programme. The programme was also a way for MSDSP to become a part of a coalition of Kyrgyz NGOs working on climate change who lobbied for and commented on a national-level climate change adaptation plan.

Both the Naryn and Kara-Kulja regional offices of MSDSP played a role in this research, as the climate change adaptation project was conducted in both regions. Because the project was at different stages in the two districts, I was able to observe Pirjan and Aizada conducting training in the earlier stages of the programme in Naryn district and then immerse myself in the working group and mini-project during the later phase of the programme in Kara-Kulja district. I also draw on time spent at both offices to discuss the relationship between the MSDSP head office and the regional branches. Of the two, the Naryn office was far more prominent, with more staff and a larger building in the small town of Naryn, the closest the mountainous centre of the country has to a metropolis. The Kara-Kulja office was far smaller: it had fewer than half a dozen staff members and took up two small rooms in a government administration building. Kara-Kulja itself is a large village, though it is the administrative and market hub for the subdistrict.

iii. Aga Khan Foundation Kyrgyzstan

The offices of the **Aga Khan Foundation Kyrgyz Republic** (AKF Kg; commonly referred to as the Aga Khan Foundation Kyrgyzstan at the time of the research) were in Bishkek, the capital of the Kyrgyz Republic, in a gleaming new high-rise devoted to a cross-section of Aga Khan Development Network agencies. AKF Kg had a floor to itself, though this could hardly hold the desks of the nearly two dozen people that worked there. The organization received visits from the programme staff in AKF Geneva every three to six months; AKF Kg (as well as their NGO partner MSDSP Kg) staff members visited the Geneva office for training and workshops a few times a year; and AKF Geneva, AKF Kg, and AKF MSDSP held an annual strategy planning retreat together. However, AKF Kg had a large degree of autonomy to design its own programming and find its own funding. In 2013, AKF Kg and MSDSP combined had a budget of US$3.6 million, and of this $1.4 million came from the Aga Khan, referred to by staff as His Highness or HH funding. The rest came from a cross-section of external funders, including the European Union (EU), the United States Agency for International Development (USAID), the Norwegian, German, and Canadian governments, the World Bank, and small foundations such as The Christensen Fund. The resulting autonomy is reflected in AKF's climate change adaptation project. The initial idea and imperative for the project was widely attributed to Laurie, the American hired as a consultant by AKF Kg to advise on environmental and natural resource management programming. In the view of both staff at AKF's Geneva office and at AKF Kg, Laurie developed the programme together with the then-head of fundraising at AKF Kg, as well as Talant, head of MSDSP Kg.

A handful of MSDSP staff members were also based at the AKF Kg Bishkek office. These included Mavluda, the communications coordinator (the equivalent of a press secretary or publicist) of MSDSP Kg, and Rahat, the project manager for the third iteration of the climate change adaptation project. Indeed, though the staff of both organizations drew a line between AKF Kg, which had a primarily fundraising and reporting role, and MSDSP Kg, which was AKF's implementing partner and legally an independent organization, in practice the two organizations were highly integrated and interdependent. Despite being in different cities, AKF largely supervised and directed the activities of MSDSP. In turn, Talant, MSDSP's director, seemed to have a strong voice in AKF.

AKF Kg was externally orientated, not only towards international donors but also towards Kyrgyz NGOs and government agencies. For instance, during my time at AKF Kg's office, I attended several meetings of the Mountain Partnership, a collection of natural resource management NGOs focused on mountain societies. These meetings were hosted by the Aga Khan Development Network (AKDN) in their own meeting rooms. Even programme-related meetings at AKF Kg sometimes included outside organizations working on similar interventions, such as an agricultural greenhouse project meeting I attended where several other Kyrgyz and international NGOs shared their work. Likewise, AKF Kg collaborates with other AKDN agencies, most of whose Kyrgyz branches were located in the same high-rise in Bishkek. The most important of these for this project is the University of Central Asia (UCA)—indeed, the role of universities and academia as an additional 'node' in civil society knowledge networks will come up repeatedly throughout the case studies. UCA was the Aga Khan's ambitious project to run a world-class university in Central Asia, with campuses planned accross three countries—the Kyrgyz Republic, Kazakhstan, and Tajikistan—each based not in a major city but rather in a small town in a remote, often mountainous region of each country. The research for this book was initially facilitated by UCA's Mountain Society Research Institute (at the time it was the Mountain Society Research Centre), which was focused on conducting applied research linked to Central Asia, livelihoods, and natural resources that involves both foreign and local academics, and which played into AKF Kg's programming decisions.

iv. The Aga Khan Foundation, Geneva

The **Aga Khan Foundation** is an international charity, headquartered in Geneva, with fundraising branches in the US, Canada, and the UK. It was started in 1967 by Aga Khan IV, the socialite, businessman, philanthropist, and European-based head of the Ismaili Muslim community at the time of the research. (Aga Khan IV died in 2025, with the title passing to his son, Rahim al-Hussaini, who became Aga Khan V.) While AKF is a personal foundation in that it draws on the funds of the Aga Khan, it is also an operating foundation in that it runs and manages its own projects. In fact, it also fundraises from other international development agencies, including the United Nations (UN), the World Bank, and other intergovernmental organizations.

In the 2010s, AKF had five thematic areas of focus: rural development (which includes natural resource management), health, education, civil society, and the environment (which includes disaster risk management). At the time, its programmes were largely in Central Asia, the Middle East, East Africa, and South Asia. While AKF was avowedly secular and emphasizes that it is not a religious organization, the Ismaili connection did play a role in its work. Not only did AKF work in parts of the world with significant Ismaili minorities but it also draws on the Ismaili community, particularly the expatriate community in North America and Europe, for funds, know-how, volunteers, and staffing. This relationship with the Ismaili community is not formalized but was mentioned to me repeatedly in informal contexts. The office gossip among expats in AKF's Kyrgyzstan head office often referred to the fact that the then-CEO of AKF Kg was the first non-Ismaili to head that branch of AKF.

Because of the Aga Khan's status as the equivalent of a head of state, his agencies had formalized relationships with the governments of the states where they were located. The Aga Khan had a diplomatic office and staff in all such countries to formally liaise with the state and build relationships with members of government. As will be discussed more in the empirical chapters that follow, this has a specific impact on the way organizations and projects in this network connect with the state.

AKF was linked to the larger AKDN, which is a collection of for-profit and non-profit enterprises ranging from a hotel chain to a fund for traditional culture. Although the different agencies sometimes cooperated, they were largely independent. The only other agency of AKDN that played an active role in this research is the UCA, described in more detail below. AKF itself was divided into the head office in Geneva, fundraising offices in Europe and North America, and country offices in the countries where AKF runs its programmes. Although staff at the head office at times described the country offices as merely branches of AKF, at other times they insisted that the country offices have a large degree of autonomy. **Mark**, the head of the natural resource management programme in the head office in Geneva, stressed the freedom of each country office, while Geneva simply 'raises [their] profiles' by bringing country office ideas to the board while providing some basic oversight.

The head office of AKF was also the site of PSAKFE (in 2017, PSAKFE was folded into the Aga Khan Agency for Habitat (AKAH)). In the words of **David**, the head of PSAKFE at the time of the research, PSAKFE was a small internal fund (he was the only staff member) with the aim of integrating environmental perspectives across all of AKF's programmes. PSAKFE gave US$20,000 as initial seed money to the climate change adaptation project run by AKF Kg that forms the heart of this case study, though iterations of the programme have also been funded by ICCO and CIDA.

c. Case Study Two: From Beliqo to San Francisco via Isiolo and Nairobi

i. Beliqo Village and the Community Forest Association

Beliqo village (also sometimes spelled Biliqo) is a collection of low mud houses and woven huts in Merti District, Isiolo County, Eastern Province, northern Kenya (mapped in Figure 2.4). This is an arid and semi-arid region, where the main source of livelihood is pastoralism and which struggles under the pressure of worsening annual droughts. Animals are herded over communally held 'trust lands'. The rights to the land are vested in the communities that reside on them and are held in trust by the elected county council. Community members spoke of the councillors with a mixture of respect (most are community elders) and exasperation at the corruption that seems to plague the council, which has been accused of controlling access and ownership of the land for personal gain.

Beliqo is located 3 kilometres from the banks of the Waso Nyiro River. The river is one verdant strip in this arid region, and the ecosystem around Beliqo village, referred to as Charri, is home to a riverine forest. In the 2010s, this forest was under threat from loggers, both from within the local community and from neighbouring non-pastoralist ethnic groups. It was also threatened by charcoal-burners, who burned the tree trunks down into charcoal. The forest is key for grazing goats and sheep, as well as a source of firewood and building material for the village.

According to the 2009 Kenya census, Beliqo had a population of around 1,000 while I was there, though according to the sub-area chief, the number was closer to 2,000 (most likely because it included herders away from the village during the census). Village life is a relatively new phenomenon for the Borana (Dahl 1979), who have begun adopting a more sedentary lifestyle in order to give children a primary education and to have access to medicine and, crucially, to food aid during times of drought. Indeed, about two-thirds of the families in Beliqo subsisted for half of each year on food aid provided by the World Food Programme. Both primary schools and food aid encouraged families to stay in the village, either sending one family member out to the grasslands with the family's livestock or hiring poorer members of the village as herders. Although a minority of adults in the village had completed

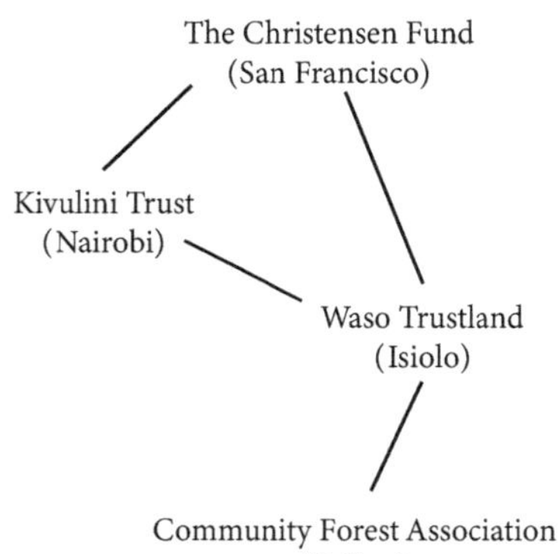

Figure 2.3 Kenya network

primary school, a majority (though far from all) of the village children attend by the 2010s.

The political administration of the village was divided between the area chief, Chief Golo at the time of the research, and the sub-area chief, **Chief Dima**, both of whom were appointed by the government. The area votes for a councillor to sit on the county council and represent the area's interests. The ethnic group dominant in the village, and in Isiolo County as a whole, is the Borana, a Muslim pastoralist people (Isack 1986). The village was six hours by bus over an unpaved road from Isiolo, the nearest metropolitan centre, and did not have electricity or a mobile-phone network while I was there. It did have a primary school, a mosque, and a dispensary, but to consult with a doctor or nurse, use a mobile-phone, or attend secondary school, one had to travel at least an hour and a half further north to the small town of Merti. As no one in the village owned a vehicle, to do so they had to either catch the bus that came by every other day or ride on the top of a passing lorry, an unreliable and uncomfortable option that was considered inappropriate for women or youths. In other words, Beliqo was infrastructurally isolated, with limited communication and transportation links to the rest of the country.

However, despite this, Beliqo hosted a kaleidoscope of formally registered and community-based organizations concerned with a variety of social causes. According to Chief Dima and several other village members, civil society groups began appearing in Beliqo in the late 1990s. The civil society landscape was fluid, with groups appearing and disbanding and others continuing in name while inactive. At a rough estimate, there were close to 20 groups in the village while I was there, most with between 10 and 20 members, varying in scope, membership, and levels of activities, ranging from youth and women's groups to herders' organizations, savings groups, and natural resource-use groups. Fourteen of these civil society groups became members of the **Beliqo Community Forest Association** (CFA), which was structured as an umbrella group, with a handful of decision-making posts and a representative of each of these groups on the CFA committee. Waso Trustland brought knowledge of the **2005 Kenya Forests Act**, which shifted management of Kenya's forests away from the government to the communities, legally enabling communities to both make use of and be responsible for the forests. When Waso Trustland suggested that the village form a CFA of their own with a biocultural diversity bent and TCF funding, there had already been an active grassroots resource-use and conservation group called REAR-Charri in the village. The CFA grew out of REAR-Charri with the organizational and legislative knowledge—as well as the continued involvement—of Waso Trustland. The CFA's mandate was to protect the riverine forest around the village from logging and burning, which they are able to do by hiring a few local guards to patrol the forest under the Forests Act's authority. They also started a tree nursery, built a community meeting hall, and helped Waso Trustland collect stories about the river—all tie-ins to TCF's then-emphasis on biocultural diversity.

ii. Waso Trustland

Waso Trustland Project (WTL) was an organization rooted in the suspicion of the state, both nationally and more crucially locally. It was also rooted in the centrality of land and land issues to the region. Tensions between land rights, ethnic divides, and political privileging have been and are felt throughout Kenya, but land rights are a particularly sensitive topic in the north of Kenya, where most of the land is 'trustland' formalized by the Trustland Act—communal land open to use and grazing by the pastoralist communities that survive off it, and held in trust by the elected county council. WTL began in 1996 as an organization concerned with the abuse of the Trustland Act, both by the government more broadly and the Isiolo county council in particular. WTL's founder and head, the charismatic and respected Borana elder and activist **Hassan**, as well as its long-time administrator and jack-of-all-trades **Liban**, were committed to investigating any possibility of 'land-grabbing' or land-related corruption. They were particularly concerned with past council attempts to sell off trustland to 'foreigners' (that is, those not native to Isiolo County) without the knowledge, participation, or benefit of local communities. WTL was also deeply concerned with council-led conservation efforts in the district. For example, Hassan was worried about the founding of game reserves that could curtail pastoralist land, that were not set up with community knowledge or consent, and that were not structured in such a way that financial gains from tourism would go to locals.

Waso Trustland demonstrated, agitated, drew media attention, and litigated against perceived corruption or misuse of power. Hassan had been jailed twice during such protests on charges of 'incitement'. However, WTL's stated mission was broad, encompassing peace work (in northern Kenya the connection is obvious, as much ethnic conflict is centred around land-use disputes), as well as AIDS, cultural heritage, and environmentalism, particularly as it is linked to natural resource use. In Hassan's view, much of the conflict in the region came from tensions over land access and resource use. Indeed, WTL's involvement with conservation around Beliqo village arose from a concern with water rights and the use and misuse of the Waso (or Ewaso) Niro River. The Waso Niro is the main lifeline for a region that is arid and semi-arid and prone to severe droughts. WTL became involved in the emerging conflict between the farmers of central Kenya, who were diverting the water upriver for agricultural use (often, according to Hassan, to water large flower farms that sold flowers for export), and the pastoralists downstream in northern Kenya, who rely on the river to water their livestock and were facing a severely curtailed water flow. From this concern with the misuse of water, WTL shifted its attention to similar concerns surrounding the use of the riverine forest in the vicinity of Beliqo village.

Over its history, WTL moved from focusing on litigation and agitation to working more directly with village communities in Isiolo County. This often took the shape of workshops and meetings in villages, which Hassan and Liban used as a way to spread information on land and resource rights and to get a feel for the challenges facing pastoralist communities around these rights. Two concerns emerged repeatedly in Beliqo village: outside communities logging the forest and farmers in central Kenya diverting water from the river. This happened at the same time that TCF, WTL's main funder, encouraged the organization to expand beyond advocacy and engage with more ecological and cultural issues in the region. These two factors together led to the broadening of WTL's activities and to the formation of the CFA in Beliqo under its guidance.

iii. Kivulini Heritage Trust

One of Wast Trustland's key partner organisations (and its link to international foundations) was the Nairobi-based NGO **Kivulini Heritage Trust**. Kivulini was housed in a modest three-room office in a wealthy part of Nairobi, whose occupants included its founder and then-head **Hussein** (commonly referred to as Dr Hussien by colleagues and fellow activists), as

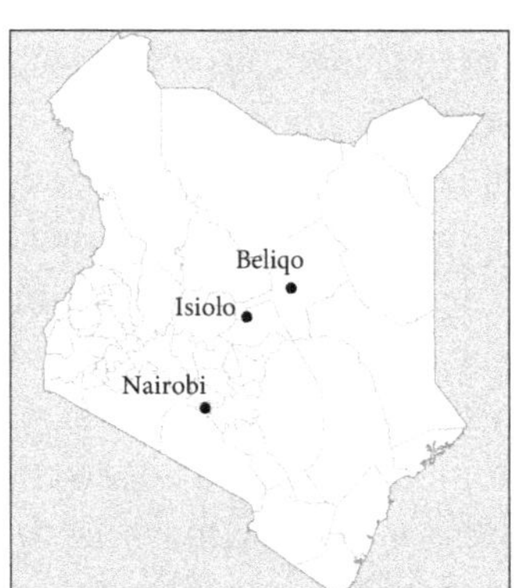

Figure 2.4 Map of Kenya

well as **Fatuma**, the organization's administrator, along with a pro bono consultant. Hussein was an ethno-biologist with a DPhil from Oxford who at the time worked as the director of Kenya's National Museum (Kivulini was his side project). His doctoral work focused on the honeybird, a bird that lives in a symbiotic relationship with some of the peoples of northern Kenya, leading them to honey and relying on them to break open the hive. This perhaps is the perfect analogy for Hussein's and Kivulini's focus: on the connection between peoples and landscapes, culture and nature, and the way the two interact to the mutual benefit of both. Kivulini was a strong partner of The Christensen Fund. After Hussein worked for TCF for two years as a consultant and field officer in East Africa, Kivulini was founded at the urging of TCF's executive director. Indeed, Kivulini's mission statement was in many ways an echo of TCF's: to support 'communities' endeavors to sustain environmental and cultural vitality and prosperity' (Kivulini Heritage Trust 2011). Kivulini was the main avenue through which TCF received grant applications and project information from community groups in Kenya and distributed grants to them in turn.

Kivulini was a key connector between WTL and TCF. It helped WTL write grant proposals, visited the local groups they worked with, and worked as a general advisory organization. Hussein maintained a close relationship with Hassan. Although Hussein was not from Beliqo (he was born in another village in the region), much of his extended family lived in Beliqo village, where his brother was considered an elder. Most of my interlocutors in Beliqo knew of Hussein and spoke of him with respect and admiration.

iv. The Christensen Fund

The Christensen Fund is a charitable foundation based in San Francisco, named after its founders, the Christensen family. Although the Christensen family took a far less proactive role in the foundation than the Aga Khan does in his, Diane Christensen, the daughter of the original founders, was on TCF's board at the time of research. It was founded in 1957 with a focus on the acquisition and promotion of 'non-European' art. In the 1980s its mission expanded to include the preservation of not only artistic expression but also the landscapes that play a key role in artistic production, and from 2003 the Fund has focused on promoting biocultural diversity. TCF's spacious San Francisco office accommodated over a dozen employees, though a small number of TCF staff members, notably many of their programme officers, were based in the Fund's countries of operation.

My interlocutors at TCF included its then-executive director **Ken**, as well as **Wolde**, the Oxford-based then-programme officer for the East Africa region (active until 2014), as well as **Yeshi**, a grant associate at TCF, and **Jeff**, director of grant-making until 2014. TCF is a global foundation: though its offices are in San Francisco, when I visited its office its grant-making programmes spanned Central Asia, East Africa, Melanesia, Northern Australia, the US Southwest, and the San Francisco Bay Area, as well as a global programme of encouraging international institutions, conferences, and leaders to promote biocultural diversity. TCF was above all a grant-making body—unlike AKF, TCF was *not* an implementing or operating foundation overseeing its own programmes. The focus of the grant-making was on biocultural diversity and indigenous knowledge, and the role that indigenous knowledge and cultural traditions play in biodiversity and environmental conservation. Although TCF emphasized its non-prescriptive role in making grants, it expected grantees' projects to fit within the framework of the fund's mission, and thus could not avoid influencing the kind of projects and ideas grantees engage in.

v. Country Context

Why Kenya and Kyrgyzstan? The two countries, and in particular the two semi-pastoralist communities that make up the local nodes in each network, have both intriguing parallels and critical differences. While the Kyrgyz Republic is the smaller of the two both in land area (close to 200,000 km^2 compared to Kenya's 581,000 km^2) and in population (just over 7 million to Kenya's 52 million), both countries have a similar GDP/capita in purchasing power parity (around US$7,000), with Kyrgyzstan having a slightly higher human development index at the time of the research. They were both in the medium range of the Gini coefficient of inequality at the time of the research (since then, Kyrgyzstan has moved into the low Gini range). However, beyond these statistics lie far more interesting contextual details that are important to understanding the case studies and the relationship between them. The next section both sets the scene and outlines a few selected historical, cultural, and political details that figure prominently in the chapters that follow.

d. Violence, Democracy, Ethnicity, and Isolation

Geography, particularly the geography of physical isolation and political marginalization, is important in both case studies. In Kenya, this is the geography of the country's north, which is the site of both Isiolo, home to Waso Trustland, and Beliqo village. Isiolo is a frontier town in the literal sense: it is on the edge of Kenya's northern districts, the part of Kenya that was once administratively labelled 'The Northern Frontier District', yet the *matatus* (minibuses) and the paved road from Nairobi still reach it. It was once where the paved road ended, but thanks to a state contract with a Chinese company, the pavement has been extended northward, pushing into what is referred to in Nairobi as 'upcountry'. It is a dusty and busy place, with a mix of ethnic groups (Samburu, Meru, Somali, Gabbra, and Borana) both in residence and passing through, herders moving flocks of goats, and lorries thundering through loaded with cattle and people. The town of approximately 80,000 is the capital of Isiolo County, with concrete and brick government buildings tucked away from the main road, home to the elected county council and the array of agencies and offices dedicated to the 'development' of this arid, pastoralist-based, and drought-prone land.

Many residents of northern Kenya feel themselves to be ignored by Kenya's government, a marginalization that in the opinion of the people living in the north emerged first out of a purposeful policy of the British, and then out of the Shifta War between the secessionist north and the Kenyatta government. Beliqo, a six-hour bus ride over a rutted, unpaved road north from Isiolo, is a living example of the still-simmering resentment towards this history and its legacy. Although the community of Beliqo receive a number of state benefits, many of the Borana feel marginalized by the Kenyan state. This marginalization stems from a combination of a lack of infrastructure and social services and a history of conflict and exclusion of the north by both the colonial and the post-independence leadership (Arero 2007).

The crux of this historic tension was the 1963–1968 Shifta War. The Shifta War pitted secessionists of the north (largely the Somali population and some, though not all, of the Borana) against the Kenyatta government (Dahl 1979, Whittaker 2015). In response, the government used measures including forced sedentarization into villages that functioned as concentration camps and confiscation or slaughter of herds of cattle (Whittaker 2012). The Borana see this as the first and most brutal step in a long history of political and economic exclusion and marginalization, crediting the roots of their current impoverishment to these policies and continued neglect by the state (Arero 2007). However, this is changing, both with Kenya's 2010 constitution, which has inspired much lip service and some real policy changes in the north, and with the economic opportunities promised by the then-newly independent and oil-rich South Sudan, which in the 2010s stirred talk of building a pipeline through northern Kenya. These were double-edged plans for local residents: they promised economic and infrastructural development, but they also inspired fears of land-grabbing and exclusion of local communities from new-found wealth.

Similarly to Kenya, the Kyrgyz Republic too has a north–south division. In this case, it is the north that is the seat of political and economic power in Bishkek, the capital, with a more cosmopolitan, homogeneous, and Westernized culture. The south, separated from the north of the country by the mountains of the centre, is far more religious and less urbanized, and is also beginning to be increasingly influenced by Islamist groups from Uzbekistan's Fergana valley. The south of the country also feels politically neglected and divided from the north. The seat of political power there is in Osh, the south's regional and political capital. This is the Kyrgyz Republic's second largest city, laid out around a river and filled with Soviet apartment blocks and administrative and university buildings. Most of the Kyrgyz Republic's Uzbek minority is based around Osh,[2] and it was here that the violent ethnic clashes in June 2010 between ethnic Kyrgyz and Uzbeks took place. The worst of the violence occurred between 9 and 16 June in the cities of Osh and Jalal-Abad; the numbers of dead and injured have never been verified but are likely to be in the thousands, and the numbers of displaced people in the hundreds of thousands. The source of the conflict is contentious, but it is clear that the Kyrgyz police and security forces to some extent took part in and colluded with the violence. These devastating clashes were still fresh in people's minds during my time there in 2013, including in the village of Saro-Kamush. Although it is entirely Kyrgyz, Saro-Kamush is not far from where the violence took place.

In a parallel fashion, the pastoralist north of Kenya has long struggled with violence between ethnic groups, and the early 2010s were a time of recurrent violent cattle-raiding and competition for pastureland between different ethnic groups, which was exacerbated by the 2011 drought. In both countries, this localized ethnic conflict over resources took place against a backdrop of suspicion about government corruption and broader political violence. In Kenya this was the 2007 post-election violence, starkly demonstrating the tensions between ethnic divides and over ethnically linked political privileging (Brown & Sriram 2012). In the Kyrgyz Republic, political violence erupted during the Tulip Revolutions of 2005 and 2010 (as well as more recently in 2020), both of which were popular movements protesting corruption and crony-capitalism in the political system, both forcing the resignation of then-acting presidents in the country.

[2] The population of the Kyrgyz Republic is 73 per cent Kyrgyz and 14 per cent Uzbek, who are the country's biggest ethnic minority.

V. Historical and Political Background

Despite some of these political and social similarities, Kenya and Kyrgyzstan emerge out of very different historical and geopolitical contexts. While both could be said to have emerged from colonial rule, the Soviet regime, especially in its later, developmentalist forms, was different in character from British colonial and settler-colonial rule in Kenya. Kenya also achieved political independence far earlier, in 1963, compared with 1991 for the Kyrgyz Republic. There is widespread nostalgia in the Kyrgyz Republic for the Soviet Union, nostalgia less frequently heard in Kenya for British rule. Kenya also has far older and more widely developed connections to international development institutions and global civil society, dating from the developmental state of the 1960s to the current plethora of state-registered, internationally recognized civil society organizations working on development issues. Yet there is a good deal of cynicism amongst Kenyans about the propensity to start groups as a way to receive money from the government or international organizations. This scene is far newer in the Kyrgyz Republic. During the Soviet regime, associational life was rigidly controlled and happened within the purview of the Soviet state through women's councils, cultural and sports groups, and membership in local Party organizations. Civil society organizations interested in engaging with development, particularly with issues of democratic representation, environmentalism, poverty, and women's rights, began to emerge in the late 1990s (Buxton 2011). However, even now there is far less international attention and aid aimed at the Kyrgyz Republic—the most visible international aid agencies and foundations in the country were USAID, GIZ (the German aid agency), Norwegian Aid, and AKF, while in Kenya the list would be too long to enumerate.

Both Saro-Kamush and Beliqo are villages of semi-nomadic pastoralists, and thus in both cases environment and natural resource use, particularly of pastureland and water, were topics of frequent discussion and contention. This was heightened by exposure to natural disasters, which were linked to climate change by the international development organizations in both case studies. In Kenya, this was the severe drought of 2011. My fieldwork in Beliqo took place during the drought, which had decimated many of the cattle herds of the village residents and left three-quarters of the village reliant on food aid. Not only was the drought a recurrent theme in conversations and interviews and a useful starting point for eliciting opinions about environmentalism and environmental change, but the staff at Waso Trustland explicitly linked the drought with climate change, and their work with Beliqo and its forest with drought mitigation, as well as adaptation. In a parallel way, natural disasters were a frequent theme in Saro-Kamush. Because of its position in a mountain valley, the village had repeatedly suffered mudslides and flooding due to glacial melts—only a few months before my time there, half the village was flooded. This was true throughout the Kyrgyz Republic and was brought up not only in many of the different villages I visited but also by MSDSP and AKF Kg. Both the staff of the climate change adaptation project and the working group in the village explicitly linked this experience with climate change.

Besides drought and floods, both communities were highly concerned with the conditions of and access to their pasturelands. Land rights form a particularly sensitive topic in the north of Kenya, where most of the land is communal land open to use and grazing by the pastoralist communities that survive off it, and held in trust by the elected county council. The CFA in Beliqo claimed that the forest they aimed to protect was being logged and burned for charcoal by other ethnic groups. At the same time, this also engendered scepticism and anger towards conservation efforts in the region, which had transformed some pasturelands into national parks and game reserves. This was reflected in the controversy caused by the efforts of a Kenyan NGO, the Northern Rangelands Trust, to set up a community conservancy in the grasslands around Beliqo. Although the conservancy claimed to include pastoralists, who in theory would be able to use the land and its springs freely, many in the community and in Isiolo (including Hassan of Waso Trustland) were deeply suspicious of the organization. This suspicion was rooted both in a history of land dispossession in the name of conservation and in ethnic distrust—Northern Rangelands Trust was started by a white Kenyan (himself the owner of a private game reserve) and run largely by people from the Samburu ethnic group, who have a history of conflict with the Borana.

Likewise, since the fall of the Soviet Union and the end of collectivized agriculture, pastureland in the Kyrgyz Republic has been accessible to communities through traditional use rights, with families paying a 'tax' to the government based on the number of animals they keep on the land. Overgrazing has become a major issue in the Kyrgyz Republic and was mentioned repeatedly to me in Saro-Kamush. Many residents believed that others kept far too many animals for the pastures to support, in a classic tragedy-of-the-commons scenario. Besides pasture and glacial melts, another frequent topic of environmental concern in the 2010s was the Kumtor goldmine. The mine was fully owned and operated by a Canadian company at the time of research (more recently, the Kyrgyz government has tried to nationalize the mine), and was accused of propagating a variety of environmental and social ills, from corruption to polluting the Naryn River to causing the melting of nearby glaciers. Local media frequently discussed the mine (and the possibility of other foreign-owned mining operations), keeping the environmental dialogue around it alive in people's living rooms.

In both communities, the state was seen as having largely failed to engage with these environmental issues. In Kenya, the Kenyan Forest Service and the Kenya Wildlife Service were responsible for preventing logging and poaching—and, as will be discussed in more detail in the chapters to come, both the staff of Waso Trustland and the residents of Beliqo saw them as having failed to do so. Hassan also blamed the state for an inappropriate response to the 2011 drought and for not ensuring just use of natural resources—both the trustlands of the north and the water of the Waso Niro River. However, the organization was making use of the 2005 Kenya Forests Act, which, in a tacit acknowledgement of the government's failure, allowed community control and supervision of local forests. The residents of Saro-Kamush expressed a similar level of distrust for the state, which they understood to be colluding with the environmental abuses of the Kumtor mine and refusing to engage with the issue of overgrazing. As noted, both the 2005 and 2010 revolutions in the Kyrgyz Republic stemmed from popular disenchantment with the corruption and cronyism of the political system. Thus both communities perceived themselves as marginalized and dissident in relation to central authority and state power. In short, the case-study sites—despite being located in countries that are rarely mentioned in the same breath—share a variety of contextual features. These overlaps, as well as the remaining differences, will repeatedly serve to broaden the discussion in the chapters that follow.

3
Knowledge at the Grassroots

> If we only knew deeply the importance of trees, we wouldn't cut them down. But circumstances [of the drought] force us to some extent. [To reconcile this] I'm against taking the whole tree—should take a branch, not the whole tree . . . CFA [Community Forest Association] brought this knowledge and ideas to many . . . CFA educated us by giving seedlings to plant, by caring [for the forest]. (Hadija, shopkeeper, livestock trader, widow, and sole provider for six children; member of Bismilahi Women's Self-Help Group, Beliqo)

> I've heard of the climate change adaptation project, I went to two days of their workshops . . . because the village elder told us to come. They told us about ecology, changes, floods, strong winds. Also about a project, something to do with the canal, and saving the school by building an embankment. There was something about climate change, but I don't remember what . . . (Maksut, livestock-owner, Saro-Kamush)

This chapter will trace the way epistemic connections created by networks of development institutions can reach parts of the world where few other global connections are so prevalent, direct, and knowledge-focused. The argument here is that networks of development organizations can deeply affect the way people think, act, and understand the world around them: be it their relationship with the state, with the environment, or with each other. Yet at the same time, local activists and organizations too hold agency and power to change the epistemic content of such networks, both by overtly pushing for their own interests and, more frequently, by reinterpreting the content of these networks to suit local ideas and needs. This complicates the development literature and rhetoric around participation and control: in practice, participation in development projects often entails an iterative process of grassroots organizations repackaging local interests and needs into the epistemic framing of intermediary and global organizations, while at the same time nudging such organizations towards alternative framings and ways of doing and understanding development.

Civil Society Knowledge Networks. E. Fouksman, Oxford University Press. © Elizaveta Fouksman (2026).
DOI: 10.1093/9780198943723.003.0003

The argument here is thus two-sided: it teases out the ways in which local communities are affected by being a part of epistemic civil society networks and at the same time play a role in constituting these networks. To trace the dynamics of both of these processes, this chapter first focuses on understanding the ways in which being part of global knowledge networks via development institutions changes the epistemic, political, and even spatial geography of each village in our case studies. In other words, this chapter explores the impact of such networks on the connectedness—spatial, technological, epistemic, economic, and political—of local communities. While the scholarship around the sociology of globalization has largely focused on consumer culture, markets, and technology as the key ways that both epistemic and cultural connections and shifts occur around the globe, I trace the way civil society connections also play a key role in forging connections between different spatial geographies. In particular, this chapter will expand the concept of a *network society*, which otherwise is largely focused on the links forged by information technology (Castells 2005, 2023), connecting it with broader scholarship on transnational activist networks to demonstrate the way development institutions can and do forge connections—epistemic and otherwise—where a technologically based network society fails to reach. In so doing, the chapter looks at political incorporation via civil society networks, delving into development debates around good governance and the depoliticizing nature of development institutions, arguing that civil society *can* be a source of political incorporation rather than depoliticization, though in highly delimited ways (an argument I will continue to develop in the chapters to come).

Building on the argument of institutionally facilitated connectedness, the chapter then looks in detail at the epistemic content of these connections. In particular, the focus here is on the interaction between knowledge, discourse, and practice (or action) in the two villages in the case studies. Strikingly, in both Kenya and the Kyrgyz Republic it was not only (or even largely) ecological knowledge and practice that was formed and spread by different nodes in the case-study networks. Indeed, far more prevalent were *process-focused ideas* about participation, inclusivity, local agency, and local knowledge. The central question here is how ideas, both about the content of ecologically focused interventions and about the participatory processes of these interventions, were taken up, disputed, ignored, and reshaped by the village communities in the two countries, in both cases demonstrating surprising agency and savviness in the ability of grassroots movements and activists to channel ideas and knowledge circulating through the networks towards local needs and desires, and thus both extending and building on existing critiques of participatory or bottom-up approaches to development.

As Arun Agrawal has argued in *Environmentality* (2005b: 3), 'new environmental subject positions emerge as a result of involvement in struggles over resources and in relation to new institutions and changing calculations of self-interest and notions of the self'. This chapter and the ones to follow demonstrate precisely the ways in which politics, resources, and identities are shaped, co-opted, and intertwined via individual and community involvement with civil society networks. In particular, this chapter will introduce arguments around the way such networks reshape communities' and citizens' relationship to the state, the way that political, cultural, and social power is built though the deployment of 'authenticity' in transnational networks and spaces, and the way development discourses both travel and transform across the interaction between communities and different development organizations.

The two epistemic networks examined here approached knowledge propagation, implementation, and grassroots participation with significant differences in emphasis and priorities. Both the differences and similarities between the two case studies point out the underlying mechanisms that constitute the way civil society knowledge networks form and function. Although the villages of Saro-Kamush in the Kyrgyz Republic and Beliqo in Kenya were both communities of semi-nomadic pastoralists at the spatial, economic, and political peripheries of their countries, they were quite different in their existing national and international connections, the extent to which they participated in a variety of civil society organizations, and their expectations from and knowledge of national and international development organizations. These very differences allow us to tease out the ways knowledge, values, and rhetoric are transferred, contested, and reshaped between the global, the intermediary, and the grassroots, furthering the case that it is civil society connections that pull such communities into national and global epistemic currents.

I. Building Civil Society Connections

a. Beliqo

i. From Civil Society to the Network Society

The village of Beliqo is a particularly effective prism for examining the inner workings of civil society-based knowledge networks. This is because of the simultaneous remoteness—physical, geographical, technological, and political—and interconnectedness of the village when I was conducting research there in the early 2010s, as well as the richness of its associational life. While Beliqo was of course not entirely isolated or spatially separate (Gupta & Ferguson 1992), it faced geographic, technological, and even political disconnection—and yet forged multiple and often tight-knit civil society connections. The nearest major town to Beliqo is Isiolo, and to reach Beliqo one either had to endure a crowded seven-hour bus ride over a boulder-strewn unpaved road, timing the journey to coincide with the fact that the bus travels only every other day, or, if like most of Beliqo's residents the journey is far too expensive, pay less to hop on top of a lorry carrying cattle. This journey was not undertaken lightly, even by local residents. To get from Beliqo to other villages or small towns in the area, one can crowd into the back of a flat-bed pick-up truck, which were notoriously prone to accidents. During my time at Beliqo, a very select number of people left the village to head to other villages or towns (as opposed to those who left on a regular basis to herd animals). Mobility was linked to disposable income and a higher level of education—and as will be discussed in detail below, most who were able to leave either held government jobs or leadership positions in active civil society organizations.

This remoteness was not simply physical; it was also technological. Without a mobile network and electricity at the time of the research, Beliqo might at first glance seem to be outside of a 'network society' that is built on mobile phones, the internet, media, and 'forms of socialized communication' (Castells 2005, 2023). The lack of a mobile network was a recurring complaint in the village. Amina, a busy middle-aged woman running a small shop, discussed out-migration from the village and the draw of town life, part of which was 'stimulation' in the form of 'TV, radio and phones'. Chief Dima, one of the two village chiefs, also repeatedly brought up the lack of a mobile network and the many schemes he was considering to bring a network to the village. Asana, a young woman who was one of the few in the village pursuing secondary education, spoke vehemently about leaving the village so that she could have access to television and phones and be aware of events in the outside world. This ties into Castells' own assertion that the network society, while spread across the globe, is uneven and more people are excluded from it than are included. For Castells, this is a question of the 'penetration' (2005: 5), rather than the breadth, of a global network society. In Castells' view, Beliqo would be a part of the globe that had not been penetrated by the social, political, and cultural networks made possible by new technology. Yet, as will be discussed below, Beliqo *was* connected in vital ways through its role in civil society networks. However, there was one more aspect of disconnection in Beliqo that must be discussed—perceived political marginalization.

The people of Beliqo saw themselves as isolated from broader national and transnational communities not only technologically and geographically but also politically and historically. As discussed in the previous chapter, the Borana were involved in the Shifta War between the Kenyan state and secessionist movements in the north of the country shortly after independence (Whittaker 2015). Many older Beliqo residents remembered parents or grandparents being interned in the camps set up by the Kenyan government during the war, and having cattle, a major source of Borana wealth, confiscated or slaughtered by the state. Ibrahim, a 30-something livestock-owner who was also the organizing secretary for Beliqo's Community Forest Association, argued that the Borana people who live in the north are not recognized by the government as Kenyan—that the government 'doesn't bother with us'. He told me that it was the government that was to blame for Borana impoverishment—that the Borana once had 'plenty' of animals and that they were either killed by the government during the Shifta War or killed by the lack of good grazing, which Ibrahim also attributed to the government. Ibrahim's grievance with the state was both historical and contemporary, both with the larger Kenyan state and the local county council, which he saw as complicit with the current state. His sense that northern Kenya was not simply neglected but actually robbed by the Kenyan state was echoed repeatedly in my conversations in Beliqo.

This political marginalization could be understood as a struggle for citizenship. Manby (2009) has written about the treatment of pastoralists and residents of Kenya's northeast in her depiction of the Kenyan state's uneven apportioning of ID cards. The same people who fought for autonomy now fight for inclusion in the state and its provisions. Yet it was not primarily ID cards but rather the lack of resources from the state, together with a history of conflict and deprivation, that I heard about repeatedly in Beliqo, echoed by everyone from the chief to the water pump attendant in the village. Guracha, a young livestock-owner and youth activist, talked about how the Borana of the region have been 'marginalized, left behind since the 1960s', when people were put in camps and their livestock taken. In his view, since then 'we have been neglected, and schools have passed us by' and it is due to state marginalization that the community does not have money to collect rainwater in a cistern (a major concern for Beliqo residents). Abdi, a middle-aged herder whose livestock had been wiped out by the 2011 drought, told me that for the past five decades the people of the region have been forgotten, and that the poverty of the region was brought about by the government. This is a powerful collective narrative of victimhood, one that emerged out of real grievances (Dahl 1979; Arero 2007), but also portrayed the Borana as people in need and thus helped convey these grievances and attract attention from civil society institutions.

Coupled with this narrative of marginalization was a feeling that the state was failing at any attempt to rectify the situation, or indeed to control what happened in the north. This was evident when I asked people in Beliqo their opinion of the role and work of the Kenya Forest Service (KFS) and the Kenya Wildlife Service (KWS). What I heard was largely derision, with many residents insisting that KFS 'doesn't care about us' and 'abandoned the area'. Beliqo's grievances with the Kenyan state fit into broader themes around governance and state capture by particular groups, questions that are outside the scope of this work. What is essential here is that the perceived neglect by KFS and KWS was not only a reflection of the neglect by the state of the region and the Borana people but also demonstrates the response to such state neglect: the ever-more-prevalent role of civil society organizations, both local and external. Indeed, while Beliqo could be understood by certain metrics to be on the geographic, technological, and political periphery, it was connected—often in the same realms that demonstrate Beliqo's remoteness—in a very substantial way through networks of civil society organizations.

Despite the many ways in which Beliqo was characterized both by its residents and by outsiders as 'remote', this characterization was too simple. Beliqo had a rich civil society landscape with multiple connections to organizations outside the village, not only regional organizations (such as Waso Trustland Project) but also national and international organizations and funding sources. These organizations brought not only epistemic currents and connections but also bridged the physical, technological, and political barriers experienced by Beliqo residents. The minority of Beliqo residents who were able to overcome Beliqo's geographic remoteness and physical disconnectedness from urban centres were enabled to do so by their connections to government or civil society. These included the village chiefs, the chairman of the Community Forest Association, and to a much smaller extent other members of the CFA executive committee, such as Habiba, my host in the village and the secretary of CFA. When these members of the community left the village, the expense of it was largely underwritten by government or civil society institutions—for instance, Waso Trustland Project (WTL) paid for three members of CFA to come to Isiolo to attend WTL's partners meeting.

Civil society organizations were not only a route out of the village but also a major reason outsiders (non-family members) came to the village. Because Beliqo has such a rich landscape of civil society connections, a variety of civil society actors from without—ranging from workshop leaders to project initiators to funders—visited the village. These organizations will be detailed below, but they included staff members from regional, national, and international organizations, including WTL, Kuvilini, and The Christensen Fund. Thus it was unsurprising that everyone I spoke with in the village was sure that I was working for or somehow connected to an outside NGO or charitable foundation; that I was there to bring funds or identify problems. Not even having WTL's director Hassan introduce me to the community as a researcher could convince residents otherwise.

In the same way, civil society was the most frequent antidote to the technological and thus informational and media isolation in the village. Indeed, as a result of these networks, the people of Beliqo were far from technologically excluded. Many owned mobile phones, useless though they were in the village, and some, like Chief Dima or some of the secondary school-educated young people, had email addresses. They used mobile networks and the internet whenever they were able to leave the village, and in fact I received a number of emails from Chief Dima after leaving Beliqo. Thus utilization of communication technology was interlinked with geographic mobility, which was facilitated by civil society involvement. Internet use was even more strongly tied to civil society participation: outside civil society organizations like WTL did a lot of internet research and emailing on behalf of grassroots groups in the village to help them search and apply for funds. As Halkano, a young man who worked as a forest scout for CFA, stated, 'we have no access to internet, but via WTL we can be heard elsewhere'.

More generally, civil society networks connected the village with broader news, happenings, and events and brought the possibility of involvement in Kenya's wider political and economic processes. Indeed, this was one of WTL's mandates—to hold workshops in remote communities regarding both national and regional news around resource and land rights and general political developments. Crucially, the civil society connections were also the way that Beliqo was embedded in networks of gossip, rumour, and information about what was happening locally, be it news about 'drilling for oil by Chinese nearby' or 'tree logging'. Indeed, much of the local news around resource use in Beliqo was an echo of what I heard discussed at WTL's office—for instance, Hassan mentioned the drilling of oil by a Chinese firm, and this rumour seemed to reverberate through the village.

Of course, civil society is not the only source of connection in the village—a couple of the wealthier people had petrol-powered generators, I spotted one battery-powered television during my time in the village, and it was also possible to use hand-held radios (though I did not see any while living there).

The same is true for the difficulty of physically reaching Beliqo. Residents *did* make the expensive and exhausting (and to some even dangerous) trip to Isiolo and other urban centres. Yet it is predominantly civil society networks that provided reasons and ways for people to become integrated into broader spatial and geographic networks, and for outside organizations like WTL to bring in news, rumours, and gossip, and to bring out local concerns to regional, national, and global institutions.

Beliqo demonstrates that even pockets of the world that are outside of the reach of electricity grids and mobile networks remain integrated, albeit indirectly, in 'horizontal' 'self-directed mass communication' (Castells 2005: 13) precisely because civil society networks can allow people access to socialized communication either directly or through an intermediary acting on their behalf. Civil society knowledge networks can thus widen Castells' network society frame, from a technologically based network affecting but not penetrating the majority of the globe to epistemic networks that might be technologically facilitated but is ultimately based on social structures in which the interlinking geographies of civil society play a vital role. In these pockets of the network, civil society organizations can be crucial in linking the local with the national and global—not only through the dispersal of knowledge and information, as the bulk of this work argues, but also through creating forms of connections that overcome geographical, technological, and even, as discussed below, political isolation.

ii. Inside the Anti-Politics Machine: Good Governance Debates and Political Incorporation

Civil society knowledge networks can not only incorporate communities such as Beliqo into the network society but also act as conduits for (certain, delimited) forms of political incorporation. Indeed, whether development-focused civil society democratize or depoliticize has been a long-running debate within the development studies literature. This debate asks: do development programmes and projects facilitate and enable grassroots encounters with the state, or rather divert citizens' energy and attention away from the state and towards 'aidland' (Mosse 2011)? The debate was sparked in the early 1990s by two nearly simultaneous publications. First came the World Bank's report 'Governance and Development' (1992), which promoted what became known as the 'good governance agenda'. The good governance agenda posits that civil society institutions plays a key role in ensuring a society has well-functioning markets, wide-reaching social services, and a responsive state (Lewis 2002). Looking to the role of associations and grassroots movements in the collapse of the Soviet empire, proponents of good governance argue that the state is just one organization of many that fulfil particular roles or needs (be they provisioning schools or building infrastructure), and that citizens (like consumers) can put pressure on the state by exercising choice via civil society organizations. In this view, civil society writ large is a key counterbalance to the power of the state, helping both with accountability and wide-ranging democratic participation. Indeed, this vision of the state as tamed and made accessible and accountable via associational life and civil society dates back to de Tocqueville's *Democracy in America* (1835). Proponents of the neo-Tocquevillian view that the associational nature of civil society can act to mediate the power of the state range from James C. Scott's (1998) view that a weak civil society enables the rise of authoritarian state power to Mary Kaldor's (2003) argument that global civil society can defuse and counter conflict and war.

Yet alongside this interest in the links between civil society and democracy in the global South came its critique. This was most famously voiced by James Ferguson in *The Anti-Politics Machine* (1994). Ferguson argues that development-focused civil society does not ensure a responsive state but rather the opposite—it is 'an anti-politics machine, depoliticizing everything it touches, everywhere whisking political realities out of sight, all the while performing, almost unnoticed, its own pre-eminently political operation of expanding bureaucratic state power' (1994: xv). In this view, civil society does not politicize but rather politically disempowers the communities and citizens it works with.

A host of critical scholarship has followed in Ferguson's footsteps (see, for instance, Abrahamsen 2000; Grindle 2004; Lewis & Mosse 2006; Matanga 2010). Abrahamsen, for instance, has argued that good governance discourse becomes another mechanism for the Western donors to impose a retreat of the state, and that while the good governance agenda claims to 'empower ordinary people' (2000: xii), it is instrumentalized to shrink the state. Yet the longer I spent in Beliqo, the more I came to realize that despite the almost universal feelings of abandonment and marginalization by the state, the civil society landscape of the village wove in the mechanisms and institutions of the state. Perhaps the most obvious example was the use of the 2005 Kenya Forests Act to set up CFA. The Forests Act reflected a broader move across the global South in the early 2000s to decentralize and increase local participation in environmental governance (Agrawal 2005b; Mogoi et al. 2012). It devolved the protection of Kenya's forests to local communities and gave communities the legal mandate to set up local organizations to protect forests from unsustainable exploitation by both outsiders and community members. Without WTL being aware of changes in national laws and opportunities afforded by such legislation, and without Hassan and Liban integrating this awareness into their work with Beliqo's civil society groups, Beliqo residents could not have known about the legal mandate provided by the state to protect the local forest from logging. Once more, we see the centrality of civil society in creating networks that connect different geographies of knowledge. And it is outside civil society organizations like WTL that bring in the savvy needed to work with state mechanisms—despite WTL's overt distrust of and antagonistic position towards the state. It is WTL that told Beliqo residents about the Forests Act, and even facilitated exchange visits to other CFAs to observe the way they were taking advantage of the Act's provisions. Becoming part of civil society knowledge networks was a key part of what Agrawal calls 'the constitution of environmental subjects—people who have come to think and act in new ways in relation to the environmental domain being governed' (2005b: 7).

Thus the state was still essential to both Beliqo residents and, as described in the next chapter, to the NGOs they work with. Indeed, the fact that the state retained a central role, even if in a negative sense, in the conversations I had in Beliqo points to the limits of the role of civil society and the continued reliance on and expectations of the state. This both echoes and nuances the criticism that Chandhoke (2003) levels against the good governance model (explored in more detail in Chapter 4 on NGO intermediaries). Chandhoke has argued that development-focused civil society depoliticizes by becoming a subcontractor of the state, fulfilling the state's promises and responsibilities without giving its citizens the opportunity to protest or make demands on the state. Thus 'state institutions network with other organizations that were formerly contained within the non-state sphere of civil society' (Chandhoke 2003: 2960; see also Jayal 1997). State responsibilities are subcontracted to civil society organizations until the state becomes a pluralized networking polity. And as subcontractors of the state, civil society organization can no longer be oppositional or mediating actors but rather become co-opted into the state's agenda.

The reality in Beliqo was more complicated—and more mixed. It was knowledge of state mechanisms such as the 2005 Kenya Forests Act (not to mention the various legal mechanisms around creating state-recognized civil society groups such as registered community-based organizations (CBOs) and NGOs) that formed the basis of CFA, and more broadly to participate in and make use of the 'governmentalization of the environment' (Agrawal 2005b). At the same time, it is also this kind of knowledge that allowed the residents of Beliqo—with WTL encouragement and support from The Christensen Fund (TCF)—to circumvent the state, to bypass the neglect of the KWS and the KFS. This simultaneous and contradictory relationship of criticism, reliance, and autonomy is a theme that weaves itself through this case study. The good governance agenda is often concerned with representative democracy and its mechanisms, and indeed has been critiqued for the shallowness of such concerns (Abrahamsen 2000). To deploy Nancy Fraser's famous delineation in a new context (Fraser 2020), our case studies are focused less on *representation* (either substantive or symbolic) and more on *redistribution* of (and access to) resources via the state.

Besides the village school and the two chiefs, it was the civil society organizations in the village that utilized the state most heavily. This included not simply state legal mechanisms but also having the know-how to tap various state agencies for resources. For instance, the chairman of CFA was away most of the month I spent in the village, trying to receive funds for CFA from regional government offices. The Ewaso Niro Development Authority (ENDA) gave CFA roots and seedlings for its tree nursery, while Arid Lands, another government agency, gave another civil society organization in the village a water pump. The pump broke and was never repaired or replaced, which was rather telling about the fragility of government support. Most importantly, this sort of government aid came not to individuals or even to the local government of the village. Instead, it went to formalized, registered civil society groups, often through the help of other civil society intermediaries like WTL. This demonstrates Chandhoke's argument that the state subcontracts services to NGOs and other voluntary groups; 'state structures have been loosened, they have been disaggregated, and they have spanned out' (2003: 2959). This is precisely what seemed to be happening in Beliqo—residents felt neglected and isolated by the state and turned to civil society instead, and the state itself willingly utilized civil society groups to replace or augment its role. Civil society could not do so entirely, and its 'emancipatory potential' (Rieff 1999) is curtailed both by its continued reliance on some state mechanisms and by the limits of its inclusiveness. Yet civil society and its development interventions is more than a depoliticizing 'anti-politics machine' (Ferguson 1994). In the case of Waso Trustland and Beliqo, civil society became a strategic way to engage with and prod the state and gain access to its resources.

iii. Participation and Its Discontents: Pragmatism and Socioeconomics

Despite its small size and relative remoteness, Beliqo had a rich associational landscape. This included not only a number of associations ignored by external development agents, such as the village mosque and madrasa, as well as government-facilitated groups such as the district peace committees, but also organizations formally registered (with the state) as community groups that can receive aid from external NGOs. Indeed, there were a number of outside NGOs, big and small, that ran programmes in the village. These include not only Waso Trustland and the Northern Rangelands Trust (which funded and helped run the Beliqo-Bulesa Community Conservancy) but also the Merti Integrated Development Programme (MID-P) and Vétérinaires Sans Frontières Belgium (VSF), both based in Merti, a larger village about a two-hour bus ride north.

The village also had over 20 home-grown grassroots civil society organizations, most registered as Community Based Organizations. These groups ranged from the funded and well known to those that existed in name only. Indeed, most were without funding and yet carried on, trying to involve participants in everything from savings groups to cultural workshops, and hoping that funding would someday come. Fatuma, a middle-aged woman who runs a store on the main road, gave me a detailed history of the appearance and growth of such groups in the village. According to her, one of the first groups in the village was Jabesa, a women's group started in the mid-1990s at the urging and with the support of the global NGO Action Aid, which at the time had an office in Merti. When the group started, Action Aid gave each of the members a small loan, which they used to start a small business trading in livestock as well as to purchase a plot of land in the village on which they built a house which the group now rents out as the offices of the Beliqo-Bulesa Community Conservancy. Other groups formed when they saw the success and support given to Jabesa. The group carried on, despite the fact that Action Aid left and funding ended in the late 1990s. In an interesting aside, Fatuma noted that Action Aid's work in the area was handed over to the Merti-based local NGO MID-P. Fatuma told me that MID-P had let down local groups like Jabesa by failing to continue Action Aid's programmes and by failing to respond to Jabesa's proposals. Fatuma told me that this was because the organization had 'gone in the hands of Africans', as opposed to Action Aid, which she understood to be run by foreigners. This shows a high level of trust in foreigners and the tendency by locals to privilege global civil society institutions over local or regional ones. Ironically, while global and national organizations laud local agency and knowledge, several of the people I spoke with in Beliqo idealised foreign interventions. A similar sentiment was expressed by Quocha Naka, a 73-year-old man who told me that all the 'good' or 'successful' projects seem to him to have Westerners involved.

When I asked residents why they participated in civil society groups, they cited a mix of pragmatic and idealistic motives. Dida, a young woman who is a member of two groups, stated that 'where we expect fruit, we join' and that groups are created to 'make the capital needed to uplift one another'. Jamila, an assistant schoolteacher and a member of both a women's group and a youth group, stated that the former was started so that women could 'help themselves', and that she joined the two groups so that she was looped into what was happening in the community and could possibly access extra funds. Muhammed, an elderly man with a heavy limp, told me that he participated in a group for disabled people together with several others because he did not want to sit idle, and wanted to make sure that if one group fails, he has others to aid him in improving his livelihood. Thus CBOs seem to be new collective forms replacing older forms of shared social security. Indeed, the activities of most of these groups were focused on income generation. Although members of almost every group told me that they hoped for external funding, most acknowledged that this funding might never come. Many functioned as de facto savings associations. The livelihood focus was evident even in groups whose overt mission was not economic. For instance, members of the cultural group Bada, whose stated aim is to preserve cultural traditions, told me they hoped to one day benefit from cultural tourism.

Despite a richness and diversity of grassroots civil society organizations in Beliqo, my interviews, which cut across socioeconomic class, age, education, and even geographic location of residence in the village, pointed to a distinction in the level of participation in civil society based on economics and age (though not gender). The very elderly, as well as those who seemed to be visibly economically disadvantaged or described themselves as such, were much less likely to be a member of civil society groups or even to have much knowledge about the possibility or opportunity to be involved. For instance, Kule, one of the oldest residents of the village, told me that she never joined a group because 'elders like me are not invited', and that she is never told about the existence of groups or the possibility to join them. This sentiment was echoed by the majority of the very elderly people I spoke with. And economically disadvantaged residents of Beliqo often (but far from always) felt unable to join because of a lack of time. As in the Kyrgyz case discussed below, time (and attention) is a major commodity of the local, and time poverty is a key barrier to participation in development programmes (Blackden & Wodon 2006). Malicha, who herded his livestock himself (as opposed to slightly wealthier members of the village, who can pay others to look after their animals), was often gone from the village with the herd, and thus simply had no time to be part of a group.

Such exclusion on the basis of socioeconomics and age points to the transformatory limits of civil society: despite rhetoric of community decision-making and community participation within CFA, 'community' itself is a highly differentiated entity, and participation is to be limited to those with time and social capital in the village. Indeed, this observation on the limits of the emancipatory potential of grassroots civil society is tied to critiques of participatory approaches to development (Robinson 1998; Gaventa 2004; Hickey & Mohan 2004). My time in Beliqo demonstrated even the most superficial forms of participation in civil society (simply being a member of a civil society group) is fraught with exclusions. This reflects many of the critiques of participatory development approaches that centre on the way these reproduce and even amplify existing social power dynamics (Cooke & Kothari 2001). In the case of Beliqo, participation was clearly connected to gradations of both economic and time poverty in the village, as well as age and social status.

However, though participation in civil society in Beliqo was in some dimensions limited or closed, awareness of civil society activity and the effect of such awareness on knowledge and values was nearly universal. This was particularly the case with CFA, which was very active and thus a very prominent part of the village. Awareness of CFA activities was prominent even amongst people who seemed, for economic or social reasons, to be on the fringe of the community. For instance, Dahabo, a young woman who only moved permanently into the village eight months before I spoke with her (before this she had been following her family's herds out in the grazing lands), and who herself was not involved in any of the village's groups, knew of CFA because she 'saw them planting trees' and constructing a tree nursery. Quocha, a 73-year-old elder who lived on the edge of town, told me that the elderly do not engage with 'groups' but rather 'stay as we are, remembering past life'. Yet at the same time she spoke about a group she noticed planting trees—therefore demonstrating the prominence of CFA activities, even to those removed from or not active in the community life of the village. While participation in civil society within Beliqo was fraught with exclusions, the reach of the network within the local was not bound to participation alone. Awareness—and from awareness, ideas—could also spread outwards throughout a non-participating community.

iv. Material Incentives, Ideological Motivations, and the Implementation of Development Rhetoric

Residents of Beliqo who *did* participate in civil society were often driven by material motivations. For instance, not only did CFA give paid work to its field officer, Habiba, and to three youths who worked as forest scouts, but members of CFA also told me of hopes that tourists would eventually come to camp in the forest and see the wildlife. CFA also wanted to integrate an income-generating aspect to its activities in the years to come, and outlined this in the new grant proposals they brainstormed with my and WTL's help. These included starting a beekeeping operation and setting up fish ponds. These activities seem outside CFA's stated aims of conserving the forest, but to the members of the organization (as well as to WTL staff), making the community more economically self-sufficient was a natural part of any civil society project. This view reflects the broader connection between civil society participation and livelihood described above.

Yet such immediate, material reasoning is only a part of the story, and idealistic motivations played a role as well. When I asked about the reasons to conserve the forest, some community members added nostalgic or aesthetic explanations—such as the desire for one's children to see the forest or the animals that reside in it. Of course, this has a material dimension as well—the practical desire for one's children to be able to make a livelihood from the natural resources of the forest in the future. Indeed, the latter reason to preserve the forest is connected to what I will argue is a key contribution of civil society to ecological thinking in Beliqo—that of enabling a shift in time frames from immediate concerns to more long-term thinking.

At times, these pragmatic and idealistic motivations were able to coexist comfortably side by side, and at others they were in tension with one another. One example of these tensions were the several farming groups in Beliqo, who were a part of the CFA umbrella, and yet had cleared trees in the forest not far from the river in order to plant a small number of crops within reach of water. Dabaso, a village elder in his 60s and a part of a farming group called Befi, was frank:

> We were cutting trees, and [CFA] told us not to. We explained our problems to them, we combined [organizations], and now we plant more trees together . . . Circumstances forced us to cut trees before for the farm. We knew trees were important, but had no choice.

He did not try to dismiss the contradiction between clearing trees for farming and saving trees for the forest. For Dabaso, this was simply the tension that one had to straddle between what one wished to do in the ideal case and what one had to do when forced by need and circumstances. Dobaso was enthusiastic about the impact of both groups, but while he admired CFA for their commitment to the forest, he also dwelled on the fact that CFA helped Befi acquire a new water tank.

Indeed, a pragmatic emphasis was evident in what CFA *did* in the community rather than what they talked about or claimed on grant applications.

The three key actions that CFA was known for throughout Beliqo was 'planting trees' from a tree nursery they formed, 'building a social hall' for the community's use, and 'catching loggers'. Many of the trees grown in CFA's tree nurseries and planted by CFA were fruit trees rather than indigenous trees (though indigenous trees were also planted), revealing the emphasis on material gain together with ecological conservation. The social hall was a clear material gain for the village, largely unrelated to conservation objectives. The loggers, who were widely rumoured to be outsiders, were understood to be taking away the material resources of the village—when they were caught, they were not prosecuted, but their wood was confiscated and used to build a new madrasa. When I asked why CFA's work in conserving trees was important, Beliqo residents thought the answer was obvious, even elementary—as one resident put it, 'without vegetation there is no life'. I was told that the forest provided building material, protection from wind and erosion, and fodder for browsing animals. Indeed, most of the people I spoke with credited their ability to survive through the severe drought that summer to the existence of the forest, where their goats could browse, while the cattle died off due to lack of grass. Reliance on the forest for current survival was also mixed with the practical desire for one's children to be able to make a livelihood from the natural resources of the forest in the future.

Such materially based ecological reasoning belies post-materialist understandings of environmental activism, such as Ronald Inglehart's (1971, 1981, 1995) argument that environmental awareness and activism are luxuries available only to societies that have already ensured the basic material needs of their citizens. What I heard in Beliqo contradicted Inglehart's argument, and points to the many critiques and counter-examples to this idea that have developed despite the dominance of this view (Guha & Martínez-Alier 2000). The ecological concerns of the people of Beliqo, both those involved in CFA and conservation activities and those observing CFA's work, were materialist—they repeatedly stated that as pastoralists they depended on the ecology that surrounded them for their livelihood. Indeed, CFA grew out of the grassroots group REAR-Charri, whose explicit goal was the 'reclamation' and 'exploitation' of natural resources. Authors such as Reimann (2005) assume that civil society organizations that adopt such a materialist-based approach are focused only on personal gain. Yet the idealistic and pragmatic reasons behind ecological conservation coexist in Beliqo and in CFA. This observation of pragmatic and ideal is echoed in the literature on African civil society by authors such as Harbeson (see Harbeson et al. 1994). Thus Beliqo residents have their own unique goals in the civil society knowledge network and yet connect with the global by participating in the overarching discourse of the network as a whole. One of the mechanisms that enable this connection is the uptake and use of development rhetoric, particularly by members of CFA.

The development parlance I heard most often within CFA meetings, on CFA grant applications, and when talking to CFA members was that of participation, inclusiveness, and financial sustainability. It was clear that CFA was aware of some of the key ideas and approaches valued by donors and foundations, and how to utilize these process-orientated terms to extract resources while pursing local needs and interests. As David Mosse (2001) has argued, the practices and rhetoric of, for instance, participatory development act as a 'system of representation' in the interactions between communities and other development actors. In Beliqo, such rhetoric was formed through the help of outside NGOs, and in particular WTL, as discussed more in Chapter 4—but, with their help, was adapted to suit the interests of local groups within a system of representation legible to donors. While Mosse has argued that such rhetoric can have little influence on the sorts of projects and material actions that actually take place within development, in this case CFA was able to utilize these systems to achieve local aims. A clear instance of this was CFA's use of the language of financial sustainability. As argued above, CFA's conservation work driven by an interest in promoting livelihood in the village. Waso Trustland Project was able to present these hopes for income generation very concretely in grant applications as a way for projects to eventually be financially 'self-sustaining'—not inherently through their conservation activities, which WTL did not expect to generate any income, but through side projects that would generate income for the village. Part of this income would then somehow (through a mechanism that WTL never made explicit to me or on the grant applications) be reinvested in conservation efforts. Thus with WTL's help CFA could transform its livelihood aims into the language of financial sustainability, despite a weak connection between livelihood activities and conservation.

This use of the rhetoric of financial sustainability was coupled with a particular attention within CFA's structure to the demands of participation, bottom-up development, and inclusiveness, again echoing the systems of representation prized by many global development actors but also pragmatically building coalitions and spreading resources through the village. CFA has been able to generate a broad base of support from most of the other civil society actors in the village because of its structure. CFA has a four-person management committee, made up of members of REAR-Charri, the group out of which CFA was born, and then 17 more members, each one a representative of a civil society group in the village. As such, only one or two groups had no representatives in CFA. Speaking to these representatives and other members of their groups, I heard mixed views. Some said that the representatives told their groups nothing about the goings on of CFA, and some representatives hinted that they did not really have any say in CFA, and most decisions were made via CFA's executive committee and Waso Trustland. Yet many praised CFA for being open and inclusive, involving a range of actors throughout the village. For instance, Muhammed, a talkative and enthusiastic pump attendant who was one of the original members of REAR-Charri but not on the management committee itself, spoke of the 17 representative members of CFA as having 'voice' and that at the general meetings of CFA 'anyone can share ideas'.

However, at the CFA general meeting that I attended, these 17 members were silent. Abdi, chairman of a youth group in the village, had quite scathing and impassioned words for CFA, claiming that there is no consultation with community members and no transparency about CFA decisions. But his view was in the minority of those I heard. The consensus seemed to hover somewhere between the two, with almost all interviewees being aware of three of the most visible CFA activities—tree planting from their nursery, constructing the social hall, and catching loggers in the forest—and that members of their respective groups were on the committee, but not knowing much about the group and its decisions or aims beyond that. But because of its structure, it could claim to be inclusive and participatory—its members often referenced the wants of the 'community' and the good of the 'community', as if representing the monolithic thoughts and desires of the entire village (Cleaver 2001). Thus CFA was able to build on existing ecological understandings in Beliqo, its own activities, and the use of broad development rhetoric to fit CFA's work into the broader biocultural diversity discourse of the civil society network.

b. Saro-Kamush

i. Forging Civil Society Connections

Compared to Beliqo, the village of Saro-Kamush was far less technologically, physically, and politically remote. Mobile phones worked (though intermittently and in patches) in the village, electricity was in almost every house and cut no more than one or two times a week, and every family I visited, even the poorest, had a television. While smartphones were not yet ubiquitous when I was there in 2013, Maksat, my translator, once mentioned the possibility of getting a computer and a mobile internet connection, and I met one family—one of the wealthiest in the village—whose visiting eldest son sat in front of a laptop tinkering with an internet dongle. While the connection did not actually work during my visit, and this family was certainly the exception rather than the rule, the internet was not entirely unheard of in the village.

The village nestles in a high mountain valley and is at the very opposite side of the country from Bishkek, yet while Saro-Kamush lies on the geographic and political periphery of the Kyrgyz Republic, it is far less technologically and spatially isolated than Beliqo. It is not prohibitively difficult to leave the village, at least to travel to the nearest administrative centre. This is Kara-Kulja, itself considered (administratively) a large village, and the seat of both the local government for the area and, significantly, the local office of the Mountain Society Development and Support Programme (MSDSP). Getting to Kara-Kulja from Saro-Kamush is a mere 20-minute car ride, and though there is no public transport and a ride is not always easy to find, it is possible for residents of the village to occasionally make the trip, though this was still considered expensive. Maksat, my translator, travelled to Kara-Kulja at least once a week, but she was quite well off, and multiple people (such as Eliza, my host) depicted this rate of travel out of the village as surprising or even excessive. In contrast, Eliza never once left the village in the month I spent there (she once complained bitterly to me of this), and her mother-in-law left once (to visit her daughter in Kara-Kulja).

Saro-Kamush also had a very different organizational and civil society environment from Beliqo, both in terms of local civil society organizations and connections to external ones. The Aga Khan Foundation's climate change adaptation project was the second or third externally funded non-profit programme in the village's history: Save the Children had run a disaster risk reduction and awareness programme for the village schoolchildren a few years previously. Before the Aga Khan Foundation, this was the sole international NGO involved in the village. ARIS, a regional NGO, had partly funded a project to build a public bathhouse in the village,[1] but during my time there the project was at a standstill because of a misplanned heating system. Although there was much talk about collecting money from the community and finishing it off, the project seemed to have foundered. As will be analysed later in the chapter, these delays were a significant indicator of the crucial role of external civil society institutions in both propagating and promoting collective projects in the village, in contrast to the self-perceived inability (often in fact belied by reality) of the village to self-fund and organize its own civil projects.

[1] A community bathhouse was vital to Saro-Kamush, as no one had running water in the village.

As well as few external development organizations, Saro-Kamush had far fewer local civil society organizations than Beliqo—at least the kinds of civil society organizations that are recognized by the state and by large reginal NGOs. A number were remnants of institutions from the Soviet era, such as the Women's Council, the Women's Committee (the former was made up of older women and advised the latter), and the Youth Committee. Others were part of a slow burgeoning of local CBOs, most of which took the form of savings/micro-credit groups. One of these was Saraul, an active local organization run by Burmat, the village nurse, which consisted of eight families she invited to join and was a micro-credit, savings, and women's handicraft group. However, most of the village residents I interviewed were not a part of any externally recognized local group. Most people told me that they 'never heard about them' and 'had not been invited to join'—indeed, unlike Beliqo, the few groups that did exist seem to be heavily based on family networks for membership. My respondents often added that they did not have the time, or that they were in a group already but that it was inactive because of a lack of leadership and interest.

In large part, the difference in the civil society landscape between Beliqo and Saro-Kamush can be explained by the difference in their histories. The aid and development industries have been present in Kenya for far longer than in the Kyrgyz Republic (Matanga 2010; Buxton 2011). Indeed, the density of civil society organizations in a village as far removed from urban centres as Beliqo, particularly organizations that are well equipped to suit the tastes and needs of donors and NGOs, points to a long history of interaction with and savviness regarding development institutions. In the Kyrgyz Republic the Soviet state not only organized and controlled any civil society organizations but also provided services and prevented any other international or non-state actors from doing so. As a result, development aid in all of its ubiquitous forms has appeared in the country only in the last three decades, after the fall of the Soviet Union (Buxton 2011).

The current existence of *any* grassroots civil society organizations in the village demonstrates a kind of knowledge transfer in itself, an organizational form that arrived with international aid and development organizations. Prior to the breakup of the USSR, the Soviet Union had very different ideas of the forms that civil society should take, if any—most were 'party sponsored and dominated organizations' (Weigle and Butterfield 1992: 9; Evans 2006), such as cultural and sports clubs or women's committees. While some of the grassroots organizations in Saro-Kamush still mirrored the Soviet model, new organizational ideas were slowly creeping in. Such a transformation was partly encouraged by the Kyrgyz state, which since the 1990s has had a formal registration process for CBOs which enabled donors to make donations and set up programmes via such organizations. The Climate Change Adaptation Working Group that is the focus of this case study is itself yet another organizational form, a conceptualization and embodiment of ideas about the way civil society should work and be structured, as thought up by international consultants and brought by a regional NGO (MSDSP) to the village.

However, the relative newness of the kinds of civil society organizations acknowledged by the state and by international and national donors did not mean that the village lacked a rich associational life. Both the mosque and the school were hubs of social interactions, celebrations, and social debate. Indeed, the village *did* have a history of pulling together around a couple of community projects—namely, a small new mosque in the village, as well as a new kindergarten building for the village children. Neither of these projects were funded by external development institutions, but rather in part by the village residents and in part by a major donation from a wealthy community member no longer living in the village. Thus civil society is not limited to simply state-registered groups that can be partnered with NGOs like MSDSP or donors like the Aga Khan Foundation.

Yet despite the obvious examples of the mosque and the kindergarten, the residents of Saro-Kamush perceive such internally motivated projects as extremely rare and unlikely. When I asked what problems the village faced, in particular ecological problems (the focus of the climate change adaptation project), there were plenty of answers. Some were very similar to what MSDSP focused on in climate change training: droughts, heavy rains, flooding, mudslides, and a lack of infrastructure to deal with this. Others were new: pasture degeneration and the pile of trash in the village that was never picked up. I asked residents why external organizations like the Aga Khan Foundation were necessary in the village—why the village residents did not self-organize and fundraise to fix their infrastructural and social problems. The most common answer was that the village lacked the cohesion and leadership needed to do such a project: that the problem was 'internal dissent' or 'all talk and no action' or 'laziness'. I was told time and time again that external organization and help was necessary to create momentum and lead such a project. The mosque and kindergarten school were seen as the exceptions rather than the rule: they benefit most of the village residents evenly and are therefore less political than, say, pasture management which would involve self-sacrifice, or the building of infrastructure that might benefit some but not others. In fact, the climate change adaptation project's canal project *does* only benefit one side of the village, which validates the village's self-diagnosis of needing external motivation to mobilize around certain types of projects.

This perceived need for strong leadership points to a pre-existing expectation of the way social projects in the village unfold—either through the force of particular individuals or through the intervention of outside agents.

The climate change adaptation project run by MSDSP and the Aga Khan Foundation is one of the first and certainly the widest in scope and ambition of externally run projects in the village. In contrast to Beliqo, it was the only development project during the time that I was there. Yet much like CFA in Beliqo (which Waso Trustland evolved out of REAR-Charri), MSDSP's project manager Pirjan very purposely decided to align the project in Saro-Kamush with an already-existing CBO, building on local institutions and connections. This already-existing CBO was Zhalgiz Alma (Single Apple), a savings group started by Nurmat, my host in Saro-Kamush and a man in his 30s who had the reputation in the village of being an activist. Besides working as the physical education teacher in the village school, he had served as the elected village elder[2] and had run for the local council (and lost). He had started Zhalgiz Alma nearly a decade before, and had even registered it as a CBO with the state. Both he and other members of Zhalgiz Alma told me that it was once a thriving and active group under Nurmat's leadership. Indeed, even people in the village who had never been part of the group would bring it up when I asked about civil society in the village. However, while it was once very effective and popular, when Nurmat left to work in Bishkek and abroad, it disintegrated (though it was never formally disbanded). The person who took over from Nurmat mismanaged and embezzled some of the organization's money. When Nurmat returned, Zhalgiz Alma remained inactive, though it was still registered with a list of members with the state.

The formalized nature of the organization and its recognition by the state made Zhalgiz Alma the obvious way for the climate change adaptation project to deliver money and an infrastructure project to the village. It is another way that state mechanisms such as the registration of civil society institutions play a key role in the formation of epistemic development networks, in large part because of their importance to intermediary NGOs and donors. During the first part of the Climate Change Adaptation project, which focused on the delivery of knowledge around climate change and adaptation, Nurmat was not involved at all—indeed, he actually did not attend any of the workshops or trainings around climate change and adaptation, and during my conversations with him could tell me very little about either. He became involved with the programme much later, at the stage when

[2] A local government position equivalent to a village chief, but elected for a limited term. Although called an elder and mostly filled by elderly men, age and gender is not a requirement for the position.

all the training was done and the working group for the mini-grant project was formed. It was then that the members of the working group asked him to get involved because of his knowledge of running a CBO—knowledge that included managing money, recruiting members, and registering projects. Simultaneously, Pirjan was on the look-out for a pre-existing state-registered CBO in the village to use as a vehicle for the mini-grant, making the transfer of money and control of the project far easier. In Saro-Kamush, Nurmat and Zhalgiz Alma fit the bill—and thus Nurmat became the de facto leader of the mini-grant project of the climate change adaptation project in the village, despite the fact that he had entirely missed the formalized environmental knowledge transfer aspect of the programme.

ii. From Participation Signalling to Local Institutions

This process illustrates the role of both state mechanisms and knowledge of local social and power dynamics in the way the climate change adaptation project is implemented. Yet at the same time, it also illuminates the role of Pirjan's own acquired knowledge of the local communities he worked with—of village politics, existing institutions, and inter-personal dynamics in the village—based on building personal relationships. The dynamics of this history echo long-standing critiques of participatory approaches to development, particularly the argument that it is not 'participation signalling' through mechanisms such as workshops and mapping exercises but rather long-term involvement and close knowledge of contextual social and political dynamics of communities that facilitate involvement and inclusion (Hailey 2001). Indeed, the way in which Nurmat became the central character in the work of the climate change adaptation project in Saro-Kamush is emblematic of the way civil society epistemic networks form connections with the grassroots. These connections are both *structurally pragmatic* (building on existing structures and relationships) and *ideologically idealistic* (focusing on methodological ideologies of participation and accessibility in their rhetoric, if not practice). They rely on building knowledge of and connections with local communities, without which Pirjan could not have discovered the existence of Zhalgiz Alma and Nurmat. Although the programme is structured in such a way that wide participation is encouraged, and the programme *proposal* pays particular attention to involving youth, elders, and women, in practice Pirjan makes strategic decisions about who to involve—and to what extent—in the project.

While Pirjan's initial approach in each village where he ran the programme was to connect with the village elder, in the weeks I spent with Pirjan he often expressed his frustration with this tactic, as frequently very few people showed up to the programme's workshops, and even fewer came to more than one of the sessions. I was able to see this first hand during the time I spent with Pirjan in the small town of Naryn in the centre of the country, where Pirjan ran a two-day adaptation-planning workshop in surrounding villages.[3] In both of the villages we visited together attendance was sparse, and very uneven between the two days of the workshop. In both cases Pirjan blamed the village elder, and told me that he generally attempted to not rely on the elder exclusively but also to speak to the 'most active people in the village'—who are the schoolteachers, village nurse, councilmen, and water management committee or pasture committee members.

Pirjan did exactly this in Saro-Kamush. Besides speaking to the village elder, Pirjan spoke with the principal of the village school—and it was she who gathered the most participants for the project. The school became a central node in spreading information and interests about the programme: most attendees of the workshops that I spoke with told me that they had been told to come by a member of staff of the school, and every person involved in the project working group, almost everyone attending the programme sessions, and nearly everyone that knew about the climate change adaptation project was in some way connected to the village school, be it through the janitor, the lunch ladies, or the teachers. The school was also the physical as well as the social centre of the project—meetings and trainings of the project, both those by Pirjan and the mini-project working group, were held in the school's empty classrooms.

The school thus became the climate change 'knowledge node' of the village, and this underlies the high participation rates in Saro-Kamush relative to the villages I visited around Naryn, where there was no physical or institutional hub for the programme. This was related both to history and to individual agency: not only has the school received the attention of international NGOs before, but several of the teachers have a reputation for being 'activists' in the community. In sum, though Pirjan took advantage of very particular institutional forms of civil society that are recognized by the state, he also built on his knowledge of the local to engage with associational life in the village that was outside both these formalized local institutions and state actors such as the village elder—knowledge he gained not via workshops or participatory mapping exercises but rather via conversations, gossip, and time spent in the village.

The result was that while the climate change programme's design and proposal explicitly use the rhetoric of participation, the reality of the way the

[3] These villages had already had the initial assessments and the first climate change information session.

programme was run was more deliberate, more serendipitous, and less open and flat. As will be demonstrated by the following chapters, global and intermediary organizations of both case studies echo the assumptions of mainstream participatory development in assuming that local agents are *eager* to participate, but are stymied by hierarchical or other barriers unthinkingly erected by the programme design. However, both Beliqo and Saro-Kamush demonstrate that people can lack time, interest, or energy to get involved in development programming, and must be persuaded either by the programme or by powerful figures in their social circle. Pirjan seems well aware of this barrier. Cooke and Kothari (2001: 6) argue that participatory approaches and rhetoric presume communities which are 'homogeneous, static and harmonious units within which people share common interests and need'. Yet the way that Pirjan implemented the climate change adaptation project in Saro-Kamush points to a far more nuanced understanding of power and influence in the village, an understanding based on detailed knowledge of the local. In villages such as Saro-Kamush, where Pirjan had an awareness of local politics and people, the programme draws far more people than in those where he was unable to connect with local institutions. Thus while the rhetoric and methodological approaches of participatory development might be spread by civil society knowledge networks, they are pragmatically altered by interacting with the knowledge that intermediary organizations hold of local politics and social dynamics. This leads to a pragmatic model of development practice, where the rhetoric of participatory approaches (discussed more in the chapters to come) is layered onto knowledge of local social and political dynamics.

II. Knowledge and Practice in the Villages: An Environmentalism of the Poor?

a. Ecology, Tradition, and Action in Beliqo

i. Pre- Existing Ecological Awareness

As discussed earlier in the chapter, much of the focus of CFA's practice was linked with livelihood. However, CFA presented their work, both within the village and to the outside world, in the rhetoric of ecological engagement and cultural tradition. A large part of this presentation was the result of the efforts of Waso Trustland Project, discussed in Chapter 4. But WTL was only able to create this discourse on the basis of ecological rhetoric and understandings that already existed in the village. These included oral ecological histories of degradation and climatic change in the region along with already-existing interest in conservation, both of which CFA and WTL were able to fit into the ideas and global discourse around biocultural diversity and indigenous knowledge. This discourse was not purely instrumentalized: affected the actions and projects of CFA, which in turn influenced ecological attitudes and actions in Beliqo more broadly. This became a two-way, iterative cycle with both idealistic and pragmatic elements.

During my time in Beliqo, I was struck by the homogeneity of the discourse around the region's ecological history. The stories that people told focused on an idealization of the past and despair about the present. Almost all my interlocutors described the past as an ecological ideal that has progressively deteriorated, especially in regards to forest cover, pasture quality, and rainfall. This narrative recurred across ages and levels of civil society involvement. For instance, Wako, the 37-year-old chairman of CFA, told me that '20 years ago we had rain come twice a year, but now all has changed'. Sophia, a young woman in her early 20s, told me that the rains have nearly stopped coming, and said she noticed this radical change five or six years ago, 'when people started cutting down the trees'. Quarfa, a 90-year-old woman who lived on the fringes of the village and did not participate in any village civil society, told me that 'the world has changed' because in her youth the forest was rich with indigenous fruit trees that kept the people and animals fed, and now the forest has shrunk and 'all the fruit trees have turned into poles that don't even give shade'.

Such ecological histories were prevalent through the village and reflect the assertions of scholars such as Crate (2008), Salick and Ross (2009), and Lauer and Aswani (2010), who argue on the basis of such awareness that indigenous cultures often have a heightened knowledge of climate change—arguments that, as demonstrated later in the chapter, were reframed by The Christensen Fund into ideas around biocultural diversity. It is possible that climate change was not the primary reason for the decline of the forest and pasture but that this decline was linked to patterns of use and increasing numbers of people and animals (Beinart 2003). Yet the ecological awareness of a changing climate and forest echoes metaphors of organic intellectuals and citizen scientists, demonstrating that knowledge is not necessarily held or created by acknowledged experts, despite the assertions of some of the epistemic community literature (Haas 1992).

This ecological narrative was reinforced by a frequent refrain that 'trees bring rain'. This was a claim echoed throughout my interviews. When I asked where this idea came from, I was told it was 'taught to us'—taught either by civil society organizations or, for a few younger and more privileged members of the community, by the schools. Indeed, the words had the ring of rote repetition, and the idea that trees bring rain is an old one—it was widely discussed in Europe and the US at the start of the 19th century (Kutzleb 1971; Kollmorgen & Kollmorgen 1973) and is perhaps a holdout of colonial science and environmentalism, and colonial knowledge production more broadly, as it can now be heard in communities throughout the African continent (Eguavoen 2013; Ikeogu et al. 2013). To my surprise, despite connecting trees and rain, very few of the people extended that connection to drought. Nevertheless, this connection between trees and rain was an ecological awareness that CFA could utilize to justify its activities both in the village's eyes and within the broader network under the conservation category. The clear sense of climatic change over time, often tied to a perceived history of progressive degradation and an idea of the connection between forest and climate, provides a link between the attitudes of Beliqo residents and wider views of climate change and biodiversity loss. Even though the outward language of climate change was not spoken in Beliqo, the residents of the village were aware of a climate that changes, and linked this awareness with loss of forest.

This link between climatic change and ecological degradation was often framed with a discussion of conservation within the Borana cultural tradition. For instance, Chief Dima told me that the Borana have 'traditional taboos against the cutting of our trees', and Jarso, the village shopkeeper, said that 'our tradition forbids aimless tree cutting. It's a great sin for Borana [people] to cut a big acacia tree'. This framing places the understandings and discussion around the environment in Beliqo squarely within the bounds of biocultural diversity discourse and its assertion of the link between cultural and biological diversity. Although this framing underscores Borana-specific traditions, I also heard it within Muslim religious rhetoric. Halima told me that cutting trees was a sin, and that the drought was God's punishment for the logging. She described killing trees as a loss of respect for Borana society. Such sentiments neatly fit into the rhetoric of biocultural diversity that was implemented by The Christensen Fund, CFA's main funder, with its emphasis on indigenous knowledge, religious practices, and the role of sacred spaces in traditional modes of conservation.[4] Indeed, it strikingly echoed TCF's insistence that conservation and ecological action can be based on local traditions and custom.

Residents of the village described cutting trees as a modern phenomenon introduced by ethnic outsiders. As Habiba stated, 'Merus come here with power saws and cut our trees for timber. Finally the community said *no*,

[4] See, for instance, Maffi 2005; Negi 2005; Wild and McLeod 2008; Pilgrim et al. 2009.

brought timber [confiscated from caught loggers] to the community to build the madrasa. We've gotten Merus to stop cutting now: very few do, especially after [the activism of] CFA.' This story linked modernity, symbolized by the power saw, with xenophobia, a loss of tradition, and ecological degradation, fitting into the biocultural diversity discourse by privileging traditional practices as ecologically aware (Berkes et al. 2000; Ifejika Speranza et al. 2010). Thus CFA had the fertile ground of a local ecological narrative in the village on which to build a connection between their work and wider environmental concern, despite an underlying focus on livelihood. CFA was also able to do this through cultivating an awareness of broader development terms and practices and incorporating them into their internal lexicon and the way that the group was run—thus fitting their work into the expectations of the global donor community.

Towards the end of every interview, after talking about trees and the forest and the importance of both to the community, we would discuss the then-ongoing drought. I would ask whether it was particularly bad that year, why the person I was speaking to thought this was, and if and why droughts in general had been getting worse. These questions were typically answered with an incredulous look or a smile, as if I was asking the sort of obvious question no one needed to answer. The responses would be something along the lines of 'it's God's case' and 'only God knows the reason behind the drought' or 'only God knows why'. When I asked what could be done about the drought, whether to stop or mitigate it, I would receive a similar reaction, with the answer either being 'nothing, only God can make rain' or 'we can only pray'. This was striking in the face of CFA activism as well as the simultaneously widespread belief that trees bring rain—despite hearing this phrase repeatedly, no one told me that planting trees could stop future droughts, or that the current drought was linked with deforestation. No one thought to connect the 'trees bring rain' refrain to deforestation and droughts. The production of knowledge is not undifferentiated or static—as this chapter demonstrates repeatedly, ideas are accepted and internalized to various and different degrees. While the presence of CFA and other ecologically focused civil society groups had certainly affected the way that people understood, talked about, and acted towards the environment, it had done so much more in the immediate micro scale rather than a wider, more macro understanding of climate change. Indeed, the relationship between local ecology, environmental action, and climate change was never brought up by the active members of CFA, other than the chairman, Wako.

Perhaps the most complex and telling conversation I had about religion and ecology was with the local imam, who was a proud member of CFA as well as the village preacher and a teacher of the village children in Beliqo's one-room after-school madrasa. Sheik Muhammed echoed many of the ideas around the importance of the forest voiced by most community members. He went even further, explicitly stating that the forest is good for the weather due to a connection between trees and stopping the winds. He also explained that part of his religious understanding and religious teaching is that 'it's bad to destroy nature, because nature is part of God's creation' and that the Koran explicitly speaks of conservation, arguing that God made the natural world good, and it is the devil that leads to misuse of nature. Indeed, he echoed much of Waso Trustland's land-rights rhetoric by stating that 'nothing is valuable or durable except land, other than knowledge—nothing is more durable than resources'. Yet at the same time he insisted that the rain is in God's hands and the drought a punishment for the lack of fearing God. When asked if anything could be done by people to stop or soften the drought, he initially surprised me by firmly stating that yes, indeed there could. He then went on to describe a mass prayer that could be undertaken as a community, which by apologizing and imploring to God would lift the drought. He created a bridge between the secular cosmology of 'trees bring rain' and the religious fatalism of 'it's in God's hands', presenting an activist vision of ecological intervention that nevertheless retains the crux of the idea that nature and weather are beyond human intervention other than by supplication. His approach does not connect easily with the secular, humanist perspectives of international foundations, even with The Christensen Fund's lauding of biocultural diversity. Yet it is also a view that reflects an evolving process of fitting together religious, ecological, traditional, and activist ideas from a variety of sources, civil society networks amongst them.

ii. Ecological Values and Actions: Ownership and a Shift in Time Scale

The creation and adoption of a common discourse was critical to Beliqo's ability to participate in this civil society network. However, this adoption was not merely instrumental: I would argue that CFA's participation in the network had in several essential ways changed how people in Beliqo understood and interact with the environment. These changes entailed not only the obvious redirection of attention and resources towards conservation but also more subtle shifts in the way people understood ecological ownership and responsibility and the time scales with which they evaluated ecological behaviours.

My respondents in Beliqo frequently referenced ecological ownership and described it in a historical arc—something that once existed, then was replaced by state mechanisms such as the KFS, and now has returned once more thanks to CFA, and through CFA, WTL. Dabaso, an elderly farmer, told me that the Beliqo community has 'learned from CFA' that 'we are owners of the trees', and after this realization agreed to jointly care for them. This ownership was presented in stark contrast to the policies of the state, which before the 2005 Forests Act simultaneously took away the impetus of ecological caretaking from the community and failed to fulfil this role. Adan, a younger herder in the village, told me that people used to think that the forest belonged to the government, in care of the KFS, but that 'the KFS has ignored local problems'. Adan argued that since people thought the environment was government property, they felt free to destroy the forest for personal gain. (Adan was one of the few Beliqo residents I spoke with who did not place the blame for logging on ethnic outsiders.) He made the case that now the community has 'learned ownership' from CFA and now sees that the forest 'belongs to us'. In this narrative, the government's claim to ownership and control over the local ecology undermined the Borana traditions which in the village's communal memory held people responsible for preventing the destruction of the natural world. It is then the knowledge passed on through the civil society network that precipitated a resurgence of a sense of ownership and a motivation for action—ironically enough by making use of the state, as argued earlier in this chapter, by working with a new mandate given by the government in the 2005 Forests Act. It is striking that in creating a sense of ownership of natural resources, the civil society network lowered the expectations of the state (much as argued by Ferguson or Chendhoke), and yet greater autonomous resource management was in fact enabled by new state mechanisms.

Along with inducing a renewed sense of ecological ownership, the civil society network encouraged a shift in time frames from immediate concerns to long-term thinking. For instance, Hadija explained that the cutting of trees was a problem because the drought made people desperate and forced them to think about immediate survival. Hadija argued that though people might acknowledge the necessity of trees, CFA enforced 'deep' knowledge of their importance, forcing people to overcome 'circumstances' and to think differently about resource use—her example, echoed by many others, was the shift between cutting one branch of a tree rather than the entire tree, be it for charcoal or for building.

Although material reasons for preserving the forest existed before CFA, CFA's work and visible presence encouraged (by growing and distributing seedlings) and enforced (by policing the forest and catching loggers) a shift in values and culture of privileging the future of the forest over the immediacy of material necessity. This shift in values and actions was less visible than CFA's overt efforts to catch loggers and plant trees, but it is a significant outcome of CFA's presence in Beliqo. Once again, this echoes some of the writings around indigenous knowledge and conservation, particularly the work of Berkes (2004, 2007), who writes about the advantages and difficulties of community conservation efforts. He acknowledges a plurality of objectives and argues for involving 'networks and linkages across various levels of organization' that use pluralistic frameworks, 'acknowledg[ing] processes at multiple levels' (Berkes 2007: 15188, 15192). Indeed, Berkes' argument around the complexity of institutions and objectives that coexist in community conservation efforts in a 'globalized world' (15188) is precisely what the ideas and actions of CFA and Beliqo residents demonstrate.

b. Ecological Knowledge in Saro-Kamush

i. Pre-Existing Attitudes and Knowledge: A Moral and Political Cosmology of Ecological Degeneration

Just as is the case in Kenya, the ideas brought by the climate change adaptation project to Saro-Kamush were far from entirely new there. Indeed, the residents of Saro-Kamush were well aware that the climate has changed over recent decades. In particular, most of my interviewees who were over the age of 30, whether they were participants in the climate change adaptation workshops or not, noted long-term changes in seasonal weather patterns. They spoke about 'far colder winters' when they were children, back when they could skate on the frozen river—as opposed to now, when the river did not freeze at all in the winter. They also spoke about the ways that the rains had changed—the usual narrative was that the rains were once far more predictable, both in frequency and intensity—and that now 'there is either too much or too little rain: uneven distribution.' 'Now the rains were far more intense', I was told, causing frequent flooding, but at the same time they came too rarely. Some, such as Chinara, the school director, also told me about the melting glaciers in the mountains surrounding the village.

When I asked the reasons behind the change in climate, most of my informants simply stated that they did not know. Others echoed my interlocutors in Beliqo in attributing the changing climate to God. However, a significant minority did have a theory. They told me that society and people have degenerated over the past two decades—people have become greedy, individualistic, and selfish with the disintegration of the Soviet Union—and nature or the environment has mimicked the same degeneration. When I probed for the causal factor in this connection, asking if this was because people treated the environment more carelessly or because of some other behavioural change towards the environment, the answer would be no. People either said that nature mirrors humankind through some sort of undefined (or perhaps supernatural or mystical) mechanism, or they would directly attribute it to God. While there seems to be an implicit critique of the capitalist world system which the Kyrgyz Republic entered with the fall of the Soviet in this view, no one made the connection explicit. Indeed, Saro-Kamush residents were silent on the appearance of international and national NGOs just at the time of the collapse of the Soviet Union and the start of this moral and ecological degradation. I was left wondering if this was a deliberate, self-censored silence, a 'hidden transcript' (Scott 1990) linked to residents' perception of my own association with the Aga Khan Foundation (AKF) and MSDSP and to some extent as another 'development expert'.

This view of social and individual decay after the end of the Soviet Union could also have been part of wider-spread post-socialist nostalgia (Nadkarni & Shevchenko 2004; Yurchak 2006). Yet I would argue that it was more than this: the perceived link between disturbances in the social and ecological sphere echoes those made in other societies at moments of crisis. It suggests an underlying level of understanding of ecological issues as integrated into a broader human system and affected by political, economic, and social change, and it points to a moral cosmology that connects ecological degradation with personal and social degeneration.

The climate change adaptation project thus fit into a social logic in Saro-Kamush about the relationship between nature, society, and individuals. Yet this broader perspective was not an intentional part of the programme design. MSDSP and AKF were uncritical of larger systemic factors behind ecological change, and certainly did not attempt to engage with them through the climate change adaptation project. Indeed, the contrast between the apolitical or pro-government position of MSDSP and the politicized and structurally aware perception of the residents of Saro-Kamush and other villages was also evident in another common topic of conversation in my interviews: Kumtor. When I would ask about ecological degradation and climate change, many of my informants would talk to me about the ecological impact of the Kyrgyz Republic's main mine, the then-Canadian-owned goldmine of Kumtor. Both in the villages around Naryn, which is close to the mine, and even in Saro-Kamush, which is on the opposite side of the country, many people would bring up Kumtor and their worries about ecological degradation resulting from the mining, ranging from pollution in the Naryn River to the movement and melting of glaciers in the mountains around the mine. Aizada, the climate change adaptation project officer in the Naryn office, complained to me in exasperation that villagers kept on talking to her about Kumtor when she wanted to talk to them about climate change without understanding the difference between the two.

This is another example of a kind of 'anti-politics machine' like the one discussed earlier in the Kenyan case, of MSDSP and AKF Kg's preference for engaging in apolitical ecological interventions. Climate change adaptation does not threaten or even engage with any state policies, and indeed the programme overtly attempted to work alongside local government. Engaging with the ecological implications of the Kumtor mine, though this was something the villagers were highly concerned about, would have been too politically contentious, in clear opposition to AKF's goals of working alongside and enhancing the functioning of the state. In an echo of Ferguson's (1994) argument, this depoliticization of ecological and civil society engagement was presented as an apolitical position. However, as was the case with CFA and WTL in Beliqo, involvement in development-focused civil society did not entirely remove the political. It was certainly true that civil society organizations in both case studies moved away from deeply controversial, contentious issues, such as land rights or mining rights. Yet, as discussed earlier and in more detail below, engagement with civil society organizations demonstrated pathways to accessing state resources and state attention, which itself was a politicizing process, a 'pro-politics machine' in a different sense.

Besides a perception of ecological degradation that coincided with the fall of the Soviet Union and the rise of capitalism, and concerns about the ecological degradation caused by Kumtor, some people in Saro-Kamush were also aware of man-made ecological degradation that had occurred in the area in the last 50 years. The most frequent concerns that I heard about were the erosion caused by the widening river and the degradation of the communal pastures. Those who complained to me about the ever-widening river—which had eaten up arable land[5] and forced the village to move up to the top of the bluff overlooking the river canyon—either did not know why the river had changed so dramatically or blamed the Soviet regime. One of my interlocutors, a middle-aged herder and livestock-owner, told me that it was the fault of the Soviet state, which had dammed the river to build a cement factory, causing it to widen out and eat into its banks. The promised

[5] During the late Soviet period, rice had been grown on its banks.

employment opportunities of this factory also ended up being a lie, as it was built shortly before the transition to capitalism, and ended up closing not long after it began operating. Indeed, this man described the ecology of the valley before the arrival of the Soviets as a 'paradise' and told me that it was the Soviets that ruined it with overgrazing, due to the explicit Soviet policy of dramatically increasing meat production in Central Asia.

Although this perspective echoes historical work on Soviet environmental policy (Josephson 2007; Josephson et al. 2013), such an explicitly historical and political perspective was in the minority. While overgrazing and the degradation of communal pasturelands was a frequent topic of conversation when I would ask people in Saro-Kamush about their ecological concerns, most of the village residents talked about this as beginning after the fall of the Soviet Union. They told me that overgrazing was caused by selfishness and greed, the equivalent of the tragedy of the commons: while land is still held communally by the village, everyone started to think only of themselves and increasing their wealth once the Soviet restrictions on property ownership were lifted. This echoes the perception of interlinked ecological, social, and moral degradation in the post-Soviet period discussed above: even those who acknowledged that the Soviet regime caused ecological degradation still stressed the destructive selfishness in present-day overgrazing on communal pastures.

The village has institutions that were created to engage with the issue—like nearly all Kyrgyz villages, there was a grazing committee, whose main duty was to see that everyone paid the appropriate level of taxes on their use of the communal land,[6] but which was also responsible for the general oversight of pastureland. However, when I asked village residents why the pasture committee did not control the overgrazing, people would shrug their shoulders and tell me that the committee was not interested, or was corrupt, or was only interested in collecting taxes. When I asked members of the pasture committee why they could not stop overgrazing, their response was that they did not have the power or authority, or that it was outside their responsibility, or that there needed to be stronger laws. This is a classic tragedy of the commons narrative (Hardin 1968), which saw the only solution as a stronger central (state) authority with enforcing power. Yet residents also complained that people were apathetic, that the village lacked activists and leaders, that no one was organized enough, and that everyone was too selfish. The belief implied that strong community ties and moral rules were what were both lacking and needed to control ecological

[6] Since the land is held communally, the level of tax depends on the number of animals on the pastures.

degradation, echoing Elinor Ostrom's view of collective action and social dilemmas and her revision of Hardin's argument (though Ostrom does argue that such ties and rules generally exist—see Ostrom 1990; Ostrom et al. 2002; Ostrom 2007). The residents of Saro-Kamush seemed to think that while community ties and moral rules once were strong enough for ecological governance, now this had degraded to the point that external agents—be they organizations like the Aga Khan Foundation, the government, or stronger legal structures—needed to intervene in the village to fix communal problems.

ii. From Climate Change to Disasters: Trainings and Epistemic Transformation

The climate change adaptation project by its very nature circumvented the ecological issues that most people in the village discussed with me—and thus any danger of politically contentious politics or campaigns, be they grazing rights or mining. Because the programme was about adaptation, not mitigation, and climate change, not ecological degradation more broadly, it was designed to exist in a neutral, politically disconnected space. Yet the result of such political neutrality was that most people in the village failed to realize that the programme had anything to do with the environment at all. My expectation in coming to Saro-Kamush was that the programme and its workshops would have shifted the way people understood the environment in predictable ways—that it would make them aware of and engaged with the implications of climate change. Yet while the presence of the climate change programme certainly changed people's ideas, knowledge, and actions, it did so in far less obvious and predictable ways.

Even though Pirjan had run three multiple-day workshops in the village, all of which included lectures on climate change and on adaptation, the direct message did not get across. Few of the people who attended the workshops could tell me anything about climate change, or about adaptation—even when I used different terms, or began explaining the concepts. When I asked what the workshops had been about, nearly everyone told me the same thing: disasters. The general perception was that the programme was about disaster risk reduction. My interlocutors came away with the sense that disasters, especially water-related ones such as mudslides, floods, and droughts, were increasing in frequency and intensity, and this was corroborated by their own experience. Their sense was that the Aga Khan's programme engaged with these increasing disasters in some way. This fit neatly onto the previously discussed moral cosmology of many village residents that linked the increasing individually focused post-Soviet political economy with social, moral, and ecological degeneration. Yet one of the stated goals of the programme—increasing awareness of climate change as a pre-condition for increasing people's adaptation to its effects—was certainly not taking place, as shown not only by my interviews but also by MSDSP's own monitoring surveys, which concluded that 'the main parts of the [climate change adaptation] plans are related to social and DRR [disaster risk reduction] problems not the climate change issue itself'. This was linked not only with the ways in which the programme was structured and run, and the way knowledge was transmitted (or not) in climate change workshops, but also the conceptual, removed, and global scope of climate change concepts, as opposed to the much more material and immediate understanding of disaster (Beinart & Brown 2013).

Yet if people in Saro-Kamush were not learning about climate change or adaptation through the programme, what were they learning? During my interviews, it became clear that the programme was transforming the thinking and ideas of the people in Saro-Kamush—only in terms of neither climate change nor adaptation. In practice, the climate change adaptation project became a disaster risk reduction programme—interestingly enough, something the Aga Khan Foundation was very interested in and that they were doing explicitly in other parts of the country. This foreshadows the argument of the next two chapters: both NGO intermediaries and global foundations act pragmatically, and are skilled at taking up new knowledge and rhetoric while still integrating their original aims and programmes. Thus the workshops and trainings *were* transferring knowledge—but the knowledge was far less conceptual and far more pragmatic than the way these workshops were originally planned. Instead, the greatest transformative potential of these workshops lay in the fact that they demonstrated a route for residents of the village to engage in constructive collective action, and to access both the material and the epistemic and organizational resources needed to execute a physical intervention in the village. It was a matter of knowing how to get things done—not *why* or *which things* needed to get done.

This was reflected in the fact that everyone in the village knew about and was committed to the mini-project part of the programme—even those who did not know about the programme in any other way. Those who attended the climate change adaptation project's workshops rarely shared any of the information that Pirjan had formally taught with their family, friends, or neighbours. Mukai, a middle-aged builder who had attended four days of climate change adaptation workshops and found them both well taught and interesting, told me that he did not discuss what he learned at the workshops with anyone else, and that he did not see 'the use' of doing so. Yet everyone I spoke with in the village knew about 'the canal project'. This is the climate change adaptation mini-project that is the final component of the climate change adaptation project. In the case of Saro-Kamush, this is a project to clean out and rebuild a canal, together with laying a pipe and a road over one portion of it. Not only did everyone I spoke with in Saro-Kamush know about the project, but everyone was highly supportive and invested in it, both rhetorically and in fact financially. Because the project was only partially funded by MSDSP (they contributed US$4,000), everyone in the village was expected to financially contribute to the canal (in proportion to the number of people in each family).

Everyone I spoke with told me that they were happy to do this, that they either had already given the money or were about to, and that the chance to fix the canal 'was the best part of the AKF project'. This was true even of families whose fields were on the side of the village that did not benefit from the canal project, who explained that the canal would be a communal good, and that water is a key resource that must be ensured to the village. Thus when it came to the actual project, the programme had no problems getting buy-in and commitment from Saro-Kamush residents. Such buy-in was not only due to the pragmatic, material benefits of the mini-grant, though these are certainly there: a middle-aged man named Satarov told me quite frankly that 'civil society can only change people's minds through money—that's our mentality'. Interest and commitment were also there because the project built on the existing moral cosmology of social and ecological degeneration (via the focus on disasters) and both provided external motivation via access to resources and capitalized on Nurmat's leadership abilities.

Indeed, the programme was far more effective at mobilizing village residents around the mini-project than transferring knowledge about climate change and adaptation per se. Much of the mobilizing happened outside of the programme's formal structures: village residents learned about and agreed to the canal project at village-wide meetings held and organized by Nurmat, which were not a part of MSDSP's programme at all. The case of Saro-Kamush thus demonstrates the ways in which civil society-based epistemic networks enable collective action, not only through material but also through epistemic resources. Part of this process is one of framing: of enabling collective problems to be reframed in ways that fit into the interests—and knowledge—of development institutions (Joachim 2003; Carpenter 2007b). But it is also about the agentive possibilities of local actors, who can bend the interests and ideas of development institutions to fit local needs. Environmental concerns are just one possible vehicle for this process, but a particularly flexible one—both ideas of conservation (and indeed, biocultural diversity) in Beliqo and climate change adaptation in Saro-Kamush are able to be utilized to promote livelihood, infrastructure building, or disaster risk reduction.

iii. Knowledge in Practice: From Climate Change Adaptation to Infrastructure Building

In the words of Gasper (1996, p. 166), 'many projects fail in terms of their stated objectives while being more successful in terms of unstated agendas', and the climate change adaptation project in Saro-Kamush demonstrates the kinds of transformations which both knowledge and practice can undergo between the rhetoric of global movements, the designs of intermediary organizations, and the knowledge and practice in villages where the programme was run. As argued above, it was the mini-project that captured the imagination of most of the residents of Saro-Kamush. Indeed, much of the original structure of the project that was put in place by AKF Kg and MSDSP Kg seemed to fade away in practice. For instance, the design of the climate change adaptation project specified that the working group in each village should create an adaptation plan based on the discussion of the participants in the Pirjan's workshops, integrate the plan into the village development plan, and keep working on the plan over time. Yet few of the members of the working group in Saro-Kamush knew anything about the climate change adaptation plan that they were supposed to draft and update—only when I brought up the last training session run by Pirjan and the chart that all of the participants created there (which is meant to be a draft of the adaptation plan that the working group would build on) would working group members remember something about any such plan. None of them saw their role as developing the plan or updating it—most told me that they were part of the group to support and supervise Nurmat's work on the canal-building mini-project. In short, the intent of NGO intermediaries such as AKF Kg and MSDSP to transform knowledge about climate change into climate change adaptation plans in practice shifted to an emphasis on the actual mini-project, which itself was infrastructure- and livelihood-focused.

However, the execution of the canal-building mini-project *did* develop new concepts and experiential knowledge in the village—even if these were not climate change or adaptation. The project required community knowledge, involvement, and mobilization. Everyone in the village had to agree to put money and labour into the project. This required village meetings to talk about the project, convened with the help of the village elder, as well as members of the working group (organized by Nurmat) to go door to door to collect monetary contributions for the project from village residents. MSDSP was not involved in any of these processes—and thus part of the knowledge transfers of the programme ended up being local community organizing skills. As discussed earlier in the chapter, many village residents were deeply sceptical about their ability to instigate and run a community project, and the execution of the mini-project required just such an ability.

To execute the mini-project, Nurmat also had to wade into the local politics and power dynamics of the village. In the case of Saro-Kamush, because it was the village school rather than the village elder that had become the heart of the climate change adaptation project, the village elder, while vaguely supportive, did not take an active role in the project. Nurmat complained bitterly about this when it was time to work on the canal. Although everyone in the village that I spoke with told me that they would contribute labour, no one actually showed up on the first morning of work—and Nurmat attributed this to the village elder's neglect at mobilizing the men to work. In fact, that first morning of work was done by Nurmat and the people he *could* easily mobilize—senior boys from the village school who were Nurmat's PE students! Nurmat vowed that this could not happen again, and indeed the second day of work was carried out by a team of village men. Yet it demonstrates that negotiating village politics was a key part of transforming ideas into action—a part that NGO intermediaries such as MSDSP left to local actors, ignoring local politics and power dynamics within their rhetoric of local agency and bottom-up development (Cook and Kothari 2001). This often led to frustrating moments like the one described above, but also was the most deeply 'participatory' aspect of the programme. And it was not just local politics that played a role in transforming ideas into action—a core aspect of the epistemic impact of the project was the connections it created with the Kyrgyz state.

iv. Building State and Civil Society Connections

Just as in Kenya, the residents of Saro-Kamush spoke to me extensively about their perception of the Kyrgyz state. Although their views emerge from a radically different history, they echoed many of the views of Beliqo residents. I was told over and over again that the Kyrgyz state was corrupt and unreliable with 'no power or strength', that it did nothing for the village, and that village residents cannot count on it to provide even the most basic services. Examples of state failure ranged from the lack of trash pick-up[7] to the absence of aid after the flooding that had been happening regularly for the past few years. Most people explained such neglect by saying that the state was corrupt, that

[7] Village residents dumped their trash down the side of the cliff that marked one of the village boundaries and then burned it.

it did not care about the people, and that those who went into government were greedy and did so for their own gains—that 'the government doesn't want to hear from simple people, only rich people or those with money'.

However, almost everyone in the village knew that the state *was* in fact helping—even if minimally—with the canal project. The local government promised to lend the project an excavator and some petrol, and under pressure from Pirjan even signed a contract to do so.[8] This state involvement was intentionally brought about by MSDSP and the programme design, which explicitly included state involvement. While the other state-focused aim of the programme—to integrate the climate change adaptation plan into the village and regional development plan—was largely unheard of and unknown in the village, the physical contribution of the state to the canal mini-project was widely acknowledged and appreciated. Just as in Kenya, this route to accessing state resources was an epistemic contribution of the project and the civil society network in itself. The canal mini-project did not simply replace the functioning or responsibility of the state (as argued in Chandhoke's model of the networked state), but simultaneously demonstrated alternative route to access state resources.

State resources were not the only thing village residents learned to access because of the canal mini-project: they also learned about tapping into the resources of development institutions and 'aidland'. While Beliqo residents were already aware of the ways that aid, information, and resources could be sought from external development institutions, this knowledge was still slowly making its mark on Saro-Kamush. The climate change adaptation project played a big and purposeful part in this learning. The programme demonstrated both the sort of resources and connections that such institutions could bring, as well as the utility of having pre-existing, state-recognized, development-focused civil society organizations in the village. Most interestingly, the programme explicitly taught and encouraged village residents to look for the resources and involvement of other development institutions besides MSDSP and the Aga Khan Foundation. Pirjan not only taught residents how to write a project proposal (which they had to do to apply for funding for the mini-project) but also told them about other grants that could fund the mini-project should MSDSP decide not to do so. No one in the village had applied for development funds before the climate change adaptation project. As Irlean stated, 'we do hear of international organizations, we just don't know how to get access to the funds'. After the

[8] As noted earlier, Pirjan came up with the idea of the contract due to the experience of a mini-project in another village, where local officials were rescinding on promised government funding for the work.

project, the village residents became more ambitious. Chinara (the school principal and a member of the working group) said to me that 'if the [mini-project] is successful, we will write more project grants'. Nurmat told me that he was thinking of applying for a grant from the Norwegian Development Agency. His decision to seek resources from other international development institutions demonstrates a conceptual shift: national and international development institutions are now alternative pathways to resources and aid beyond the perceived failure of the Kyrgyz state.

III. In Conclusion: Local Agency within the Networks

The power dynamics within civil society knowledge networks might at first glance seem obvious. International donors, plugged into global epistemic communities around ecology and environmentalism, set the agenda—be it climate change adaptation or biocultural diversity—and both NGO intermediaries and grassroots activists follow the money, so to speak. Yet the two network case studies presented here and in the next chapter suggest far more complex relationships. While global development organizations wield power by virtue of controlling resources, both grassroots nodes pursued their own objectives by generating, filtering, and reshaping knowledge. Indeed, as will be argued later in the book, this knowledge is needed by global development institutions to legitimize their work in their internal quest for authenticity. As such, the grassroots too wields epistemic power, though often in indirect and unacknowledged ways.

It is clear in the Kenyan case that the residents of Beliqo were not simply subject to Waso Trustland, Kivulini, and The Christensen Fund's ideas. It is only those ideas that could be reshaped to speak to local concerns and secular and religious cosmologies (particularly around the relationship between social factors and ecology) that were adopted and implemented in the village. This adoption and implementation ranged from using the legal power and structures granted by the 2005 Kenya Forests Acts despite deep distrust of state mechanisms, to deciding that forest ownership lay with the village residents, to declaring that logging and burning trees for charcoal was no longer acceptable in the forest. Yet tensions existed in the subjective and selective ways these ideas were implemented and ignored—for instance, members of a farming group in Beliqo echoed CFA's conservation discourse, and yet admitted that *some* trees do need to be cut down to make clearings. And while the biocultural ideas that drove The Christensen Fund and Kivulini might lead them to imagine that the tree nurseries planted by CFA were of native species, in fact many of these were fruit-bearing trees such as mangos that could supplement income or food security. Thus neither CFA members nor others in Beliqo were simply recipients of the knowledge that external civil society organizations attempted to impart or impose. While their ideas and worldviews were changed by their interactions with other civil society organizations, they also adapted or adopted knowledge to suit their interests and needs, fusing these with local needs, approaches, and concepts.

Likewise, the residents of Saro-Kamush were still able to exercise power and agency within the climate change adaptation programme, shaping it to their own desires and interests and fitting it into their own understanding of the political, the communal, and the ecological. They were able to do this not only in the material sense with the canal mini-project but also by adapting and adopting the rhetoric and structures of the climate change adaptation programme to fit with their social relations and community structures. Indeed, it is the programme that must in implementation adapt itself to the local realities, power dynamics, and social structure of the village—as demonstrated by Pirjan's use of the school community and of Nurmat's leadership and pre-existing CBO in Saro-Kamush. It did so not through the trappings of participatory development (such as mapping exercises or community workshops) but rather through the building of close social bonds and detailed knowledge of existing structures and personalities in the village. Even without explicit pathways for knowledge to move from village residents to the reginal and national organizations involved in the programme, locals could shape the way the programme was implemented and used in Saro-Kamush. Becoming part of civil society networks also provided new routes and pathways for residents of the village to present their concerns and desires to both the state (in ways that are simultaneously de- and repoliticizing) and to development institutions. It is through these indirect mechanisms and delicate power negotiations, through the complex interplay of local interests and desires, intermediary organizations' previous practice, and global epistemic attention, that the epistemic content of the civil society knowledge networks shifts and changes to incorporate local knowledge and perspectives.

4

NGOs

Networks of Knowledge Intermediaries

> We don't go [to village communities] deliberately to teach, but to do anything you must know something: every task requires knowledge . . . We teach ways to package thoughts: we are *not* building capacity to get more grants, but rather to understand the environment, the bigger picture. (Hussein, director, Kivulini Trust)

> . . . we want to give people more knowledge [about climate change]—so they know background causes and future projections, what to expect ahead. There is very little information and knowledge in the Kyrgyz Republic—our goal is to spread it, and teach how to plan for [climate change-caused] events. (Pirjan, climate change adaptation project manager, MSDSP Kg)

If the overarching argument of this work is that development institutions of all scales form epistemic networks that create, dispute, and enact knowledge, then the core argument of this chapter is that intermediary organizations in the networks are essential in not only accessing, selecting, and reshaping the ideas of the global nodes of the network but also in having privileged access to the knowledge and the needs of the grassroots nodes. This chapter thus argues that NGOs, large and small, act as *idea intermediaries*, connecting the global and local scales of knowledge and action while filtering and reshaping the ideas of both. The word 'intermediary' does not mean that these organizations are 'mere conduits or tools' (Fechter and Hindman 2011: 4)—they are intermediary in their position between the global and the local, but they are 'mediators' in their ability to 'transform, translate, distort, and modify the meaning . . . they are supposed to carry' (Latour 2005: 39). An essential part of the argument is that these intermediaries are heterogeneous in their aims and interests, and they both filter and reformulate ideas into their own ideologies and worldviews, which then influence the functioning of the network as a whole.

Civil Society Knowledge Networks. E. Fouksman, Oxford University Press. © Elizaveta Fouksman (2026).
DOI: 10.1093/9780198943723.003.0004

Such idea intermediaries can have widely disparate goals and organizational cultures, as demonstrated in the Kenyan case, or can be more tightly knit together as in the Kyrgyz Republic. In either case, these organizational 'nodes' in the knowledge network forge relationships throughout the network through two simultaneous processes. First, these idea intermediaries implement the ideas and rhetoric of global movements to align themselves into one coherent knowledge network that facilitates the transfer of knowledge and resources and the transformation of ideas into action. Yet at the same time, these organizations and the individual actors within them create ideology and knowledge themselves. The disparate goals and cultures of each organization are not forgotten or subsumed—in fact, these differences deeply affect the *ways* in which knowledge is transferred and transformed in the network. Nor, as argued throughout this book, do the ideas flow one way: the intermediaries do hold power and influence over both international foundations and global movements, not simply by legitimizing and enacting the goals of the former, but also by contributing to the creation of the latter. One key way they do so is by claiming *authenticity* for their ideas by asserting that they are close to and thus reflect the needs of the grassroots.

Intermediaries wield power in these civil society knowledge networks through the ways they choose patrons and sponsors, as well as through their capacity to transform ideas into plans for action. NGOs help to define and designate expertise and authority, linking back to knowledge gained in seats of power in the global North but also validating experience gained in the global South. I argue that this designation of expert and expertise—seen particularly in the case of the Kyrgyz Republic—not only gives in-country NGOs legitimacy with powerful Northern actors, but also helps align the individual aims and goals of each node into a cohesive set of ideas that echoes the aims of global movements. Yet, at the same time, these intermediary organizations are able to forge a connection, though sometimes a very surface-level one, to grassroots action and needs.

This chapter makes the case that NGOs and other intermediary organizations forge their connection to the grassroots using the very mechanism that gives them legitimacy on the level of international foundations and global movements. This mechanism is another global discourse, already discussed in the preceding chapter: *participatory development*. In both Kenya and the Kyrgyz Republic, it is through adopting the rhetoric, ideas, and (to some delimited extent) practice of participatory development that NGOs find the point of engagement with the grassroots. Yet both case studies point to the adoption of this practice more as a point of entry with the local rather than deep or long-term engagement. To echo Mosse (2005), participatory approaches become a way to legitimize development interventions, and discourse becomes the end rather than the means of development. In both the projects in Kenya and the Kyrgyz Republic, the participatory element is at times difficult for intermediaries to maintain, though it is far deeper in the Kenyan case. Indeed, it is exactly the structural differences between the two that lead to the different enactments of participatory development. But both case-study networks use participatory approaches to development, or claims to knowledge about the grassroots, to legitimize connections both to local and global actors. Thus participation itself becomes more of an idea rather than a practice, an epistemic tool used and spread within the network that in turn facilitates connection between the nodes.

These networks of idea intermediaries do not exist in a vacuum—factors ranging from global advocacy movements to universities and academic knowledge production to local interests and desires all influence the network and provide opportunities for intermediaries. This is perhaps most effectively demonstrated in the way that these development organizations pointedly engage with the state. Indeed, in both Kenya and the Kyrgyz Republic, deliberate engagement with the state and government institutions demonstrates the ways NGO intermediaries seek to both supplement the functioning of the state, and to utilize state power and resources to bolster and sustain the main aim of the intermediary actors: the process of transforming ideas into action.

I. Disparate Nodes, One Network

The organizations in each network had a variety of goals and aims, both stated and demonstrated, not to mention very different institutional cultures. This heterogeneity has been largely ignored by conceptualizations of global civil society or activist networks, though it has been pointed out by some writing on the processes of global connection and the sociology of globalization (e.g., Anderson 2005). Yet such disparate organizational cultures and aims were nevertheless able to provide coherent bridges for projects or partnerships across different institutional levels. This chapter will argue that this is not purely a result of strategic compromise, or materially focused mission drift towards global aid resources, but largely a function of the very process of the transfer of knowledge and ideas, of engaging with global movements and adopting their ideas and discourse: in other words, the process of *organizational learning* (Brown & Duguid 1991; Dodgson 1993; Argote & Miron-Spektor 2011).

a. The Kyrgyz Republic: AKF Kg and MSDSP

i. Expats and Locals at AKF Kg: Power and Hidden Knowledge

Although Aga Khan Foundation Kyrgyzstan (AKF Kg) is in name a branch of a foundation, it functioned more as a semi-autonomous development NGO, albeit with vast access to the resources and international clout of AKF. When I was there in the 2010s, it competed for funding from intergovernmental organizations and private foundations, sometimes in its own name and sometimes in the name of MSDSP Kg, and ran programmes in partnership with MSDSP Kg. AKF Kg termed the latter their 'implementing NGO', though in fact the implementation seemed largely collaborative. Because of its relationship with the global Aga Khan Foundation (of which it was nominally a branch office) it was guaranteed internal funding for certain programmes—funding which was internally referred to as 'His Highness' funding'. Yet it functioned in many ways like an independent NGO, with two-thirds of its funding coming from external funders. Indeed, AKF Kg was constantly on the lookout for new sources of funding, and new projects or programmes as well as ways to expand the organization's current programmes, though it was simultaneously constrained by both the mandate of the Aga Khan Foundation and the joint strategic plan of AKF Kg and MSDSP Kg, which was meant to be jointly decided on an annual retreat.

One of the most striking things about the offices of AKF Kg when I was there was that expats held the three top positions in the organization: Karl, a German, was the CEO; Jack, a Canadian, was in charge of fundraising and grant-writing; and Nicolle, an American, was head of the research and monitoring and evaluation unit. All three were development veterans, having worked for many years in development organizations in Africa or Southeast Asia before coming to AKF Kg. The culture of the organization was thus dominated by expat authority and by the distinction between the expats and locals working in the organization. When I asked Karl how most of AKF Kg's decisions are made, in particular those around creating programmes for new grant applications, he said that this was done by Jack in conversation with himself and Nicolle. Karl was not the only one who said this: during my interviews, most of the Kyrgyz staff members at AKF Kg stated that Jack was the one creating ideas around programming. As will be shown later, this is to some extent untrue (and Jack himself largely denied this), but there is a strong sense that a particular culture of expats, all with years of experience working in the development sector, made decisions in Bishkek.

Expats and locals worked closely together in AKF Kg, yet there was a strand of division and at times competitiveness between the two groups that points to underlying power dynamics. Expats at AKF Kg complained about the material rather than idealistic motivations of the Kyrgyz staff, stating that 'they are there for the salary'. This was tied to the broader issue of the way work in the development sector is conceptualized: local staff members saw working for AKF as a stable, prestigious, and reasonably well-paid career, rather than an idealistic or altruistic way to effect positive change. After the collapse of the broad bureaucratic apparatus of the Soviet state, foreign-funded civil society became one of the few paths into a stable administrative career (Buxton 2011). Yet the salaries of the expats were far higher than that of the Kyrgyz staff. Expats (or locals with excellent English skills who were educated abroad) were largely in the positions of (managerial and decision-making) power at AKF. They were the 'development experts'—but what their complaints seemed to indicate was that their authority stems not simply from expertise but from a claim about altruistic motivations.

The expats at AKF Kg highlighted the divisions between the two groups, particularly around knowledge sharing and creation. They were simultaneously resigned and frustrated at the lack of knowledge sharing with and input from local staff members—both those at AKF Kg and at MSDSP. Jack told me that 'local staff members that go for training outside [of the Kyrgyz Republic] don't use the knowledge they gain . . . Staff are implementers, not researchers'. Nicolle echoed Jack's worry: 'knowledge moves up, not down, because of communication barriers and language . . . knowledge moves up to donors or to the Geneva office, but staff on the ground don't know *why* they're doing what they are doing—there's no ownership'. Both Jack and Nicolle diagnosed a lack of 'ownership' by the local staff as a failure of epistemic connection, a block in the networks of idea flows. Thus while Mosse (2011) has written about the ways development experts see global knowledge as 'standing above' particular contexts, both Jack and Nicolle were worried precisely about such decontextualization and a lack of connections. To them, the lauding of indigenous or local knowledge within development policy has translated into a kind of one-way knowledge extractivism from local staff members by global development institutions. Yet implied was an assumption that the responsibility for this lay with in-country staff as much as international institutions.

While Nicolle complained of new ideas failing to reach local staff members, she also painted a picture of stymied bottom-up and grassroots knowledge: both of programmes that fail and of grassroots needs. In her words, 'failures are not communicated—due to fears of losing one's job or funding . . . MSDSP has strict reporting protocols, but not on failure'. Information that is *not* spread through the network points to the power dynamics within and between the two organizations. Indeed, this silence on the subject of 'failures' can be read in light of a 'hidden transcript' (Scott 1990) of resistance to the power wielded in AKF Kg's overt organizational hierarchies. Not only do these hierarchies dictate what information and ideas are created and communicated, but the circulation (or lack thereof) of ideas could itself be a way of quietly resisting the overt organizational hierarchies in the network.

ii. Pragmatism and Representation at AKF Kg

One of the outcomes of an organizational culture dominated by expat 'development nomads' (Chambers 2005) is that the overall aims and goals of AKF Kg seemed largely pragmatic. This could be seen in the breadth and variety of its programmes and funding sources, which mirror the great diversity of interests of the global Aga Khan Foundation, ranging from education to civil society, from disaster risk reduction to natural resource management, from livelihood to health. As the primary aim of AKF Kg was to find and secure funding and then to satisfy donor requirements, the staff there were largely concerned with four things: what programmes His Highness' funding would cover (and how staff at the AKF headquarters in Geneva will perceive the fulfilment of the programmes); what new programmes could be created in response to calls for tenders or grant applications that would still be within the organizational mandate; how ongoing programmes could be re-imagined—or re-depicted—to fit new funding opportunities; and finally how programmes that were carried out were to be depicted to donors. In Karl's words, 'it is donors who have power over ideas—they have their own ideas about issues, and know the system', and Nicolle echoed this when she told me that 'new ideas come externally'.

Thus AKF Kg is largely concerned with what David Mosse terms 'systems of representation as much as operational systems' (2006: 940). For example, AKF Kg applied for and received funding from The Christensen Fund (TCF) for a kindergarten project. (That TCF funds some AKF programming is serendipitous, though connections such as this one demonstrated the expansive nature of these networks: they are not isolated chains, but also have crosscutting connections, ultimately pulling an ever-expanding number of actors into such networks.) AKF pitched the kindergarten project to appeal to TCF's interests by asking for funding to preserve local Kyrgyz folktales and teach them to children (thus helping preserve and continue local cultural diversity and heritage). When telling me about this, Jack was frank: 'we just wanted funding for our kindergartens; preserving local folk tales is not the point'. This is not necessarily cynicism or manipulation; rather, it demonstrates that AKF Kg's role becomes exactly what Mosse (2005, 2006) describes as endemic to development projects: the need to defend as well as create systems of representation that fulfil the expectations and needs of global donors. These donors are themselves, as will be demonstrated in Chapter 5, closely intertwined with global movements and development trends.

This pragmatic, representational approach is itself a way of knowing and understanding development—an epistemic stance. The ways in which AKF Kg discussed and understood the climate change adaptation project demonstrate such pragmatic epistemics. The climate change adaptation project was something of an outlier in the Bishkek office. This was demonstrated by the difficulty AKF Kg has had in characterizing the programme and 'placing' it in an established programmatic division: at the time, AKF had no programme area dedicated to the environment or for climate change (since this book was research, AKF has added a 'Climate Resilience' thematic area of focus to their portfolio), and in its three iterations the programme drifted between the Civil Society/Local Governance division, Natural Resource Management (which in fact mostly focuses on agriculture), and a division called 'Built Environment'—which encompassed agricultural infrastructure, disaster risk reduction, and climate change adaptation. The programme shifted through these divisions in its three iterations as the staff members at AKF Kg and MSDSP who wrote each of the three proposals struggled with the way that the programme would be conceived internally and represented externally.

This representational struggle reflected AKF Kg's resistance to engaging with new ideas and categories that the organizational networks they were part of have not yet accepted and internalized. According to Laurie, the consultant hired by AKF Kg to develop the climate change adaptation project, AKF Kg was influenced by AKF Geneva's then-'traditional' ideological stance in focusing on livelihood, health, and education rather than environment or ecology. Indeed, Laurie termed The Christensen Fund 'unorthodox' and 'avant-garde' for their focus on biocultural diversity—echoing their own radical self-image.

Yet while AKF Kg engaged in a representational struggle to align their programming with its 'traditional' (in Laurie's words) focus, it had to represent the aims of the network to donors in such a way that the funding focus would seem a perfect fit for the programming. This can be seen in the rhetoric of the first climate change adaptation project proposal (to the Interchurch Organization for Development Cooperation), which while nodding to 'the impact of . . . climate change' spends much time talking of 'environmental hazards' (i.e., disasters, which will be discussed more below) and 'socio-economic vulnerabilities . . . [and] livelihoods' (AKF Kg 2010). It treads the fine line between trying to align with donor calls and the ongoing focus of AKF Kg on livelihoods and disaster prevention. Indeed, the wide-reaching influence of this representational challenge is echoed in Jack's description of the climate change adaptation project, when he stated:

> Donors like the bottom-up approach, so we've started to formulate community-based input more. At the beginning of the [climate change adaptation] programme we did a participatory rural appraisal, but didn't use the information.

The emphasis here is on formulation, not implementation. Pathways for knowledge input from local communities are imagined, but not used. Nicolle echoed Jack's focus on formulation in frankly stating:

> Needs are not formally communicated [to field staff] . . . There is no innovation in this—all [of AKF's projects include community] training, but there is no follow-up, no one asks what people's *need* is. People know what NGOs want—that we're looking to fill indicators.

The focus on systems of representation is thus tied to the ways knowledge flows are stymied within the network of organizations and communities. At the same time, Nicolle gestures to a self-awareness of how widespread this representational logic is—in her eyes, even communities know and fulfil this need.

AKF Kg's engagement with donors demonstrates pragmatic, utility-maximizing aspects of AKF Kg that at times seemed in tension with its representational one: Karl, the CEO, declared in a meeting that AKF Kg should work on climate change because this is where the money and the donor interest is, *and* because it is becoming an increasingly important focus area in development. Jack's comment about the kindergarten folktale programme funded by TCF shows a similar struggle between representation and pragmatism. This tension helps explain the contradiction between AKF's reluctance to label the climate change adaptation project as environmental or ecological programming and the fact that the second iteration of the project (the one this work examines most closely) was funded by the Prince Sadruddin Aga Khan Fund for the Environment (PSAKFE). However, compared to the overall programme budget of the main Aga Khan Foundation, the Fund was in fact quite small. Resources reflect ideology and engagement—both the size of the fund and the sidelined nature of the climate change adaptation project and its ambiguous and shifting categorization were a reflection of the tenuous relationship of both the international Aga Khan Foundation and AKF Kg in Bishkek to global environmental movements and ideas.

iii. Conservation of Ideas at MSDSP KG

The network of intermediary institutions in the Kyrgyz Republic contrasts with the network in Kenya in that its disparate parts or nodes could not function as independent entities with entirely different connections. The Mountain Society Development Programme Kyrgyzstan (MSDSP Kg) was registered as a Kyrgyz NGO that could independently apply for funding and theoretically create and execute its own programming, had almost entirely Kyrgyz staff members, and was strategically based in the city of Osh on the opposite side of the country. Yet, in reality, MSDSP was structurally integrated into the Aga Khan Foundation, particularly the Bishkek office. Talant, the then-director of MSDSP, was in Bishkek at least three or four times a month for meetings at AKF Kg, and many of the department/programme heads as well as the reporting officer were also frequently in Bishkek. All reports produced by MSDSP Kg were filtered through AKF Kg in Bishkek, and the programmatic decisions came from Bishkek. Key MSDSP staff members were also hired and fired by AKF Kg. Unlike the Kenyan case discussed below, this was an overtly hierarchical system, where roles were clearly defined—and the stated role of MSDSP was *implementation.*

The staff members of MSDSP were the ones that had to get a programme up and running, and as a result they had conservative views about what they wanted to do and how they wanted to do it. These views were not expressed directly or vocally, but rather in the way programmes are implemented. If AKF Kg was pragmatic in searching for funding, MSDSP was pragmatic in seeing their expertise as existing in a few areas, and reformatting the actual implementation of each programme into one of these established areas. Thus AKF Kg's pursuit of a wide variety of funding opportunities did not lead to mission drift in MSDSP's programming because the actual areas of implementation by MSDSP remained largely constrained to what it already knew and did.

In the case of the climate change adaptation project, this meant that although the programme certainly contained elements focused on teaching the meaning and impact of climate change and the concept of adaptation, once two village-level training sessions had been completed, the programme shifted to creating and implementing an infrastructure project. In the case of the project in Saro-Kamush, this is the upkeep of a canal, while for other villages this could be a bridge over a river, or digging wells or water reservoirs or a pit for dead animals. These kinds of projects all fell within MSDSP's areas of expertise and established practice. Despite the participatory and community-based rhetoric of AKF Geneva (discussed more in Chapter 5), MSDSP seems to have taken over the post-Soviet state's 'high modernist project' (Scott 1998). MSDSP has extensive expertise in infrastructure projects such as canal-building—they even had an in-house civil engineer to design their infrastructure projects. Pirjan, the manager of the climate change adaptation project, suggested 'best practices' to village residents during adaptation training and planning sessions, guiding them towards creating infrastructure-based projects of the sort that MSDSP feels most comfortable in delivering. Talant also made a similar point, stating that 'earlier we were already doing [similar programming to the climate change adaptation project]—in 2005–6 we were rehabilitating canals to improve water management and crop production'. Talant supported Nicolle's comment that people know what NGOs want when, in response to my query about responding to local needs and knowledge, he mentioned that 'people do come to MSDSP with ideas—mostly around infrastructure rehabilitation'. Talant is implying that not only is infrastructure MSDSP's area of long-term expertise but also people know this is what MSDSP does, and have come to predict that this is the kind of development work MSDSP will be willing to engage with. Thus the 'needs' of local people are shaped by their perception of what intermediary organizations could offer (Mosse 2001).

Yet the climate change adaptation project staff who were based at AKF's Bishkek office (Laurie and Rahat) insisted that the adaptation ideas could and should be creative and original, and even carried out on a family level, not just on the village level. However, as discussed in Chapter 3, once the programme shifted into the 'mini-grant' phase, neither climate change nor adaptation were referenced any longer—instead the focus was very much on executing the project. This echoes the pragmatic approach of AKF Kg, but without the added representational focus. Because AKF Kg took care of representing the programme to donors, MSDSP could focus on reformatting and integrating the climate change adaptation project with their existing interests and knowledge—of shifting the epistemic focus of the programme to something they already knew and valued.

At the same time, sharing ideas via 'trainings' was a core part of MSDSP's work. For MSDSP, trainings were the key tool for formalized knowledge transfers to the grassroots. Several people at MSDSP told me that trainings, workshops, and 'communicating information' were a large and standard part of MSDSP's work. Talant even complained about the fact that trainings were undervalued in the communities where MSDSP works:

> People ask to decrease [time spent in] trainings [because] people don't see the effects of behavioural change, they see only physical changes. A balance between physical and behavioural changes is needed, so we still do trainings, because

> problems come out of behaviours. For example, in pasture management [people need to learn to value] quality over quantity. We do lots of training because behaviour influences the physical [realm].

Talant here explicitly acknowledged the role of knowledge transfers in changing the way people act in the world, and emphasizes their transformational potential. Yet while Talant blamed beneficiaries for wanting to decrease training time, Laurie, in discussing the same thing, put the blame on MSDSP. She stated that 'MSDSP isn't fantastic at engaging in the field: for instance, they cut village resilience assessments [for the climate change adaptation project, which consists of small group discussions] from three days to one day . . . they lost nuance'. Yet shortening the assessments could be reinterpreted as MSDSP's responsiveness to local needs. As shown by Talant's statement above, time is a key local need and bargaining tool. It is NGOs that must battle for the sustained time and interest of local residents, an aspect of programming not readily acknowledged in grant applications or participatory rhetoric. Indeed, cutting the programme from three days to one could be MSDSP acquiescing to village-level demands for time and efficiency—and thus in fact responding directly to local needs.

Some of Talant's rhetoric justified Laurie's critique: earlier in our conversation he dismissed the very same trainings he praised, saying that 'people just show up for the free lunch' and that in the climate change adaptation project there is 'little effect on people post-training—they shift to a more practical approach'. Yet despite these contradictions and moments of scepticism, trainings remained the key tool that MSDSP employs to formally transfer knowledge and ideas. I would argue that this is both because MSDSP ultimately understood its programming to be as concerned with knowledge and idea transfers as with physical changes and investments, and because trainings were the most obvious and easiest way to attempt to spread ideas and concepts.

Yet trainings ended up transferring not only the epistemic content championed (or dictated) by the global nodes of the network. They also spread the ideas and expertise of intermediary organizations such as AKF Kg and MSDSP. The climate change adaptation trainings themselves focus on natural disasters and disaster risk reduction through the entry point of climate change, rather than climate change per se. Most of the examples and discussions in the trainings I attended were of floods, droughts, mudslides, extreme winds, and even earthquakes. MSDSP and the AKF network more broadly had wide experience running different types of disaster risk reduction programmes, and linking climate change closely with disaster risk reduction is another way for MSDSP to reshape programmes to fit their areas of expertise around infrastructure development and disaster risk reduction.

MSDSP did indeed deliver material to villages about climate change and adaptation—material developed by Laurie—and thus did spread knowledge of climate change adaptation, though with varied success. However, the end outcome of the programme seemed more focused on disaster risk reduction, particularly through the completion of the infrastructure-focused mini-project, rather than the very fact of climate change adaptation. I had a revealing conversation with Talant after I had returned from fieldwork in Saro-Kamush. After discussing some of my preliminary findings, Talant, who was one of the original creators and writers of the climate change programme, wondered out loud whether the climate change adaptation paradigm is useful, and whether it might not be better to simply run an infrastructure or disaster risk reduction programme in villages without bothering to talk at people about climate change and adaptation. He went on to justify this position by admitting that he was not surprised to hear that understandings of climate change and adaptation did not seem to be spread effectively amongst the local community by the project. Talant ultimately saw infrastructure/disaster risk reduction ideas as the key epistemic contribution of the programme, and thus the mini-project as its end good. He believed not only that it would be more effective and efficient to focus on what MSDSP has long done and has expertise in but also that tangible *things* or *results* (such as a new canal) rather than intangible *ideas* or *processes* (such as learning about climate change or formulating a plan) were more central to MSDSP's work.

This implementation-focused approach was particularly visible in my observations of Pirjan's work at Saro-Kamush. Once the workshops and trainings were finished at the village, Pirjan saw the remainder of his work as getting the mini-grant project off the ground and executed. This consisted of meetings with the working group and Nurmat to sort out logistics and give and receive updates on the work, without further discussions of its relationship to the climate change adaptation plan or the role that the working group should take within the programme. Yet both the grant application of the climate change adaptation project and Laurie, who designed the programme, insisted that the end goal is not to have the working groups successfully implement a mini-project but rather to educate people about climate change, to empower locals to tackle problems, and most importantly to create a 'living' adaptation plan that would be repeatedly updated and referred to in the village and local government when planning any sort of development projects for the village. Laurie's ultimate vision was to capture the *sustained interest* of local communities.

Laurie disagreed with Talant's perspective, insisting that knowledge of climate change and adaptation was central to the project, as knowledge in itself is empowering. This disagreement is indicative of the different aims of AKF Kg and MSDSP Kg. AKF Kg's combination of pragmatic and representational aims meant it focused more on the interests and ideas of the donor community, global movements, and international development discourse, while MSDSP's implementation-focused role underpinned its aim of carrying out the interventions in which they have established expertise, within the framework of whatever the overarching project happens to be. At the same time, MSDSP was very good at adapting the discourses and the new ideas of the programmes created by the AKF office in Bishkek. Although Pirjan was focused on getting the mini-grant off the ground when in the field, in interviews he echoed both Laurie and the climate change adaptation project material by insisting 'there is very little knowledge in Kyrgyzstan, and [the programme's] goal is to spread it'.

One factor behind this adaptability was the wide-ranging experience of MSDSP's Kyrgyz staff in the development sector. Kyrgyz staff members of organizations such as MSDSP were as much 'development nomads' as the expats, or even more so—but within the Kyrgyz Republic. For instance, Erkin, the project manager of the first iteration of the climate change adaptation project, pursued a career in the military when Kyrgyzstan was still part of the Soviet Union, and then transitioned to working for the Kyrgyz government in the Ministry of Emergency Situations. His experience there enabled him to move into the aid/non-profit sector, specializing first in disaster risk reduction and then climate change. He spent a year working on the climate change adaptation project for MSDSP, and once the contract ended began working for another environmentally/climate change-orientated NGO. Likewise, Pirjan was a biologist by training with the equivalent of a doctoral degree. He worked as a lecturer and biologist in an Osh university, but then switched to the non-profit world (in part because it paid more). Although he called himself an environmentalist, his work had been in quite a few different areas in the Kyrgyz development sector. At one time he was running the national school debate programme funded by the Soros Foundation; at another he freelanced as a civic activism trainer. He also co-founded an environmental NGO. Both of these men's careers point to not only the growth of the development sector in the Kyrgyz Republic over the last few decades (and the fact that it is one of the most viable career options in the Kyrgyz Republic for people with a university degree uninterested in business) but also the structural factors of 'the era of short-term, project-based aid work' (Fechter & Hindman 2011: 7) that enforces such variety and nomadism. Many staff members both in MSDSP and other non-profits were hired for a specific project lasting a few years, and once the length of the particular project or the funding is over, they would switch to working for a new project and in many cases a new organization.

The fact that the Kyrgyz staff in this network had a wide range of professional experience in the Kyrgyz aid community and that there was continual movement between organizations and programmes created a cohesion of organizational cultures throughout Kyrgyz development-focused civil society. Because of this breadth of experience and exposure, Kyrgyz staff members were well versed in the discourses and ideas of global movements. Unlike the AKF Kg staff, their experience was limited to the former Soviet world, but, especially since the early 1990s, this has become porous to international development discourses.

This musical-chairs pattern in NGO staffing was enabled by a marginal role for distinct ideas and ideology in Kyrgyz organizations—if most organizations function with the same general ethos, moving between them becomes far easier than having to adapt to new ideas and worldviews. As demonstrated by Pirjan, MSDSP staff members were able to find the thread between MSDSP's drive to continue doing the activities where they already have expertise—such as infrastructure building—and adapting this expertise to a variety of new ideas and discourses, such as climate change adaptation. When I pressed Pirjan on the epistemic links between climate change and infrastructure building, he had no problem justifying any of the mini-projects:

> Canal-building is climate change adaptation, and mitigation too: it will stop mudslides from carrying off soil from the hillsides, and will provide water for watering, so it's an instrument against drought. [The project] will also give access for vehicles/technology over [the canal's] bridge to fields—which will help increase yields.

Yet at the same time, in a candid moment during an interview Pirjan admitted that 'the mini-grant *motivates* [people]—they forget about climate change but the grant keeps them stimulated'. Once again, acquiring the buy-in and the time and energy of the local is a central concern for intermediary actors.

Pirjan was able to juggle the on-the-ground realities with both the interests of MSDSP in continuing infrastructure building and the focus on AKF Kg on climate change. Pirjan was able to execute this balance perfectly in large part because of his previous experience as a trainer and from working on civil society building projects. He began the project in 'trainer' mode (learned through previous experience running training projects and working as a university lecturer) to build engagement with new ideas and information, but once this was accomplished, he switched to a pragmatic focused on getting the programme executed and a community-based action off the ground (helped by his earlier work with non-profit projects and local civil society groups, and urged on by MSDSP's pragmatic stance).

iv. Aligning the Network: Tools of Consensus Building

Thus far this chapter has argued that the case-study network in the Kyrgyz Republic (as we shall see, much like in Kenya) comprised organizations that pursued disparate goals, ones that did not necessarily align with the overarching aims of the global movements or even with the stated aims of the programme itself. Yet these organizations were still able to function as one cohesive knowledge network that created, utilized, and most importantly transmitted ideas and knowledge within itself and to and from the local and the global nodes. In the Kyrgyz Republic, unlike in Kenya, this ability emerged in part out of the tight-knit structure of the network of intermediaries: AKF Kg is officially a branch of the global Aga Khan Foundation, MSDSP Kg was created specifically to serve as AKF Kg's implementing organization, and in Saro-Kamush both the working group and Zhalgiz Alma were created or revived by the climate change adaptation project specifically to help implement and connect the programme to the village. As each organization was to some degree an offspring of another, they were forced to align themselves to one another to a certain extent, both in their rhetoric and in their programming. Yet the organizations were also able to align by conceptualizing their different aims as part of one unifying rhetoric. I argue that this was fostered by precisely a process of knowledge creation and knowledge transfer between different parts of the network.

In the Kyrgyz Republic this happened through a number of techniques implemented by AKF Kg and MSDSP. One of these was the use of trainings and workshops. This means not only the training around climate change, adaptation, and development-project creation taught by Pirjan in villages, but also training and workshops for the staff members of the climate change adaptation project. Pirjan, Aizada (the programme specialist based in Naryn), and other MSDSP and AKF Kg staff attended several workshops around climate change and adaptation, both run by and open to other non-profit development organizations. This included a multi-day workshop on climate change run by GIZ (the German development agency) in Bishkek, which was open to other NGOs, and a climate change workshop in Almaty, Kazakhstan attended by Pirjan. Thus transnational knowledge held by the 'experts' of the global climate change adaptation and mitigation movements was purposely injected into the network through workshops for the intermediaries. (I could find no signs of intermediaries running workshops for the global nodes in either of the case studies.) In this way, intermediaries became part of larger epistemic communities, participating in, enlarging, and spreading transnationally held ideas (Adler & Haas 1992).

AKF Kg scouted out and paid for staff attendance to these workshops, showing the organization's awareness of the need to facilitate such transnational knowledge transfers. AKF Kg also held frequent workshops for its own and MSDSP staff, mostly run by its expat staff members (pointing to delineations of expertise that will be discussed further later in the chapter), on topics ranging from Excel to report-writing. Workshops and trainings were used by global foundations and organizations as a formal way of aligning the intermediaries with their global knowledge and aims: AKF Kg and MSDSP staff members were flown to Switzerland to receive training at the AKF head offices in Geneva. At the same time, flying Kyrgyz staff to international workshops and conferences allowed AKF to put the face of local staff members onto the approaches and ideas of the head office. It can also be read as a form of patronage, both as a perk and a reward of working for MSDSP.

As Finnemore and Sikkink (1998: 905) point out, 'professional training does more than simply transfer technical knowledge; it actively socializes people to value certain things above others'. Thus a shared knowledge commons (Hess & Ostrom 2007) was created throughout the network, enabling intermediaries with a variety of institutional cultures and aims to align and communicate both on the basis of commonly held rhetoric and language. Indeed, there was 'development lingo' I encountered repeatedly at AKF Kg, at the three MSDSP offices where I spent time, and in AKF Kg's and MSDSP's programme materials. These range from 'beneficiaries' to 'local governance' and 'civil society', from 'livelihood' to 'participation', not to mention the constant use of 'climate change' and 'adaptation' amongst specific programme staff. This development lingo was in Kyrgyz, English, and Russian, and was particularly striking to hear it translated or sometimes, when no appropriate translation could be found, even transliterated into Russian. The diction of development thus slipped across languages and created familiarity and organizational cohesion around key ideas and their expression.

This does not mean that the workshops or transnational knowledge transfers smoothed away the disparate aims discussed above: knowledge consists of 'the particular dynamics that animate nested communities of practice within larger social groupings' (Marchand 2010a: 3). Thus each intermediary in the network is its own 'community of practice', with its own institutional culture, preferences, goals, and organizational priorities. But these communities are 'nested' in the larger grouping of the network, and held together in part by the workshops and trainings that serve as 'pathways to knowing' (Rapport & Harris 2007), creating common pools of knowledge that link the network to transnational epistemic communities.

The network of intermediaries was also dependent on formalized mechanisms that are intended to gather and pass up knowledge as to what happens at the local level: the mechanisms of monitoring and evaluation. In the case of the Kyrgyz Republic, this was the only *formalized* way that the villages where programmes are being run are able to transfer concerns and information through the network. These systems were largely put in place by AKF Kg to fulfil their representational role: donors want and expect accountability systems such as impact assessments or surveys to demonstrate that the programme is indeed running the way it should. Indeed, donors need such knowledge of what happens on the ground to buttress their own legitimacy by demonstrating the importance and necessity of the programmes they fund—and thus their own existence (Ebrahim 2003). The knowledge creation of programme monitoring and evaluation was thus an existential necessity for multiple nodes of the network.

Nicolle, whose position as head of the Research, Evaluation and Learning Unit at AKF Kg made her responsible for overseeing most of the monitoring and evaluation for both AKF Kg and MSDSP, argued that AKF and MSDSP conducted surveys or ran impact assessments largely to fulfil their donor requirements, rather than to lean about or improve their programming. Indeed, despite the name of the unit, she claimed that there was little learning going on through such formal mechanisms. This was also emphasized by the fact that despite utilizing the rhetoric of participatory needs assessments (as discussed earlier in the chapter), both Jack and Alibek (one of MSDSP's monitoring and evaluation coordinators) told me that MSDSP carried out needs assessments *after* a programme was approved and received funding, not before. Thus programmes—including the climate change adaptation project—were justified post hoc as part of carrying out the programme design rather than as part of the programme creation. Others at MSDSP, such as Talant and Kambarbek, the natural resource management programme manager at MSDSP, gave more measured responses, seeming to take it for granted that monitoring and evaluation is an effective way to keep track of programmes. However, many of the staff members saw monitoring as a chore necessary to pacify donors.

Yet despite earlier criticisms of the ineffectiveness of its monitoring and evaluation systems, some of the expats at AKF Kg insisted that 'MSDSP is the only [Kyrgyz] organization trusted in donor community'. This is in part because regardless of impact on actual programmes, monitoring, and evaluation gave the entire network of intermediary organizations an *evidence-based shared narrative* of what was happening on the ground. Although programming was rarely changed on the basis of this monitoring and evaluation, it did unite the different goals and organizational cultures of AKF Kg and MSDSP around a set of shared understandings, both of the achievements and the shortfalls of their work.

In the case of the climate change adaptation project, Alibek conducted surveys and focus groups (designed by Laurie and Nicolle) and found several weaknesses in the programme. Yet this did not result in changes or a deep reassessment of the programme. Both Laurie and Talant seemed to hold the perception that it was too late, and that the monitoring was done less to change the current programme than to inform the organizations' understanding. When both MSDSP and AKF staff gathered to discuss the third iteration of the programme, Alibek's report did not lead to any major changes in the programming, but rather was received as a background understanding of what shape the current programming was taking on the ground, pointing to certain weaknesses to look out for in the next round. In short, formal monitoring and evaluation was used for representational rather than corrective ends.

The ideas and knowledge of MSDSP's field staff—the staff members in the field offices of MSDSP that had the most contact with the communities where programmes were run—thus had no mechanisms through which they could be shared across the network. Indeed, there was a striking dissonance around the topic of field staff expertise. While staff in AKF Kg's Bishkek office praised the expertise and commitment of the staff in MSDSP's field offices, multiple staff members at MSDSP argued that the views and perspectives of the field staff had no impact on the way the programmes were run because they were focused on the details of executing the programme rather than the bigger picture. Kubanich, the head of the MSDSP's Kara-Kulja field office, complained bitterly to me that the field office had many programme ideas and knowledge from the ground, but that this was ignored by those above him. In short, the intermediary organisations in the Kyrgyz network *did* have mechanisms to learn and spread knowledge of what goes on in the communities where they work, but this information was used to create a pool of common understandings that aligns the network rather than impacting the way programmes were created or run on the ground. Indeed, this can be broadly attributed to the mechanisms the network of intermediaries has created to forge connections to the grassroots: having field offices and staff that were deeply engaged with communities and carrying out monitoring and evaluation can both be understood to be ways of attempting to align the different actors involved into a shared understanding and rhetoric of overarching programmatic aims.

Because of the close institutional connections and hierarchies between AKF Kg, MSDSP, and the local organizations they themselves set up in the villages where they work, the 'image' of the network in the Kyrgyz Republic was cohesive and controlled. This was also in part due to the history and background of the Kyrgyz staff—Talant once stated that MSDSP staff members 'look to the top for all decisions, which is a Soviet relic of organizational culture'. Yet part of this was also the structural factors of the AKF network. Outside of grant proposals, tenders, and donor reports, which are quite another matter and fall into the representational categories already discussed, MSDSP and AKF Kg were both succinctly summarized on the global AKF website, and published one annual report. Nominally this was the MSDSP Annual Report, but as AKF Kg had no other and as MSDSP activities were closely coordinated by AKF Kg, the report represented both organizations. Indeed, the report, as well as all other public output of both AKF Kg and MSDSP, were under the purview of one person: Mavluda. Although technically a MSDSP staff member, Mavluda sat in the AKF office in Bishkek, demonstrating the interknit nature of the two organizations and the interlinked way in which they presented themselves. Mavluda took over whenever there was any need for visibility, including interacting with the press at any MSDSP location (I ran into her leading local press around in the Naryn office).

Because there is one person controlling the messaging, the public message was uniform: as noted above, MSDSP's annual report briefly mentioned climate change adaptation, though the focus was very much on the themes of livelihood, education, civil society, and health set by the global Aga Khan Foundation, and mirrored the then-structure of the global AKF website. The same was true of MSDSP and AKF Kg's annual strategic plan (developed collectively and approved by AKF staff from Geneva). The plan stated that 'improving climate change resilience will remain a cross-cutting theme', and after this nod to climate change, the rest of the document was focused on 'interventions in natural resource management, education, and health, [which] converge in villages and are implemented in collaboration with and between community-based groups and local government'. Thus the intermediaries sent a univocal external signal: climate change adaptation was important and noted, and thus a part of their rhetoric and approach, but the overarching focus lay in the core programme areas of the global Aga Khan Foundation. This was another way of forming coherence in a network of different organizations with different aims: since the network had one coherent externally orientated message, this becomes a knowledge commons in itself, a shared set of ideas for the network as a whole.

v. Beyond the Networks: Relationships with the State

Relationships with the agents and organizations of the state permeate both of the case-study networks. Indeed, there were startling similarities in the way intermediary organizations engage with the state both in the Kyrgyz Republic and in Kenya: both Waso Trustland in Kenya and MSDSP in the Kyrgyz Republic did so in an explicit and goal-orientated way. Also parallel is the level of distrust and ambivalence towards the state at the local level, already discussed in Chapter 3, and the way that intermediary organizations in the network fail to appease this distrust but do manage to *teach* the villages how to tap into the resources and promises of the state. However, both motivations and methods vary between the two. In Kenya, Waso Trustland is highly suspicious and disdainful of the state. In the Kyrgyz Republic, both MSDSP and AKF Kg did not voice any reservations about the state, and made state inclusion and utilization an overt goal. In both cases, the engagement of civil society networks with the state both illustrates and nuances the good governance critique by Chandhoke (2003) that the state itself was becoming networked and pluralized through its reliance on civil society actors.

Waso Trustland's relationship with the state was central to its work and self-perception, and thus is woven into the sections below. However, while AKF Kg and MSDSP had a coherent stance on their relationship with the state, building this relationship was delegated to particular programmes and people. Both AKF Kg and MSDSP were explicit about wanting to work with the state and to incorporate state structures and state resources into their programming. AKF Kg cultivated strong ties with the Kyrgyz government, helped by the Aga Khan Development Network (AKDN) office in Bishkek:[1] I sat in on one meeting in Bishkek where Karl and AKDN staff discussed meetings with parliamentarians and the parliamentary perceptions of AKF's work. Talant told me that 'AKF has a good relationship with the government, including at the national level'. This is because, in his words, 'MSDSP has continuity [in its programming], it doesn't have to follow the money the way most NGOs do—the government appreciates this'. Indeed, AKF Kg and MSDSP understood themselves to be aiding the state, particularly local government institutions.

[1] This is something like the embassy of the Aga Khan, with the overt role of maintaining diplomatic relationships between the Aga Khan's various agencies and businesses and the countries they work in.

MSDSP ran projects under the umbrella of local governance that were specifically designed to work with the Kyrgyz government on the local (village and village-district) level. Although the local governance programme had its own staff in Osh and in the field offices as well as dedicated projects, the MSDSP strategy document stated that it was an overarching theme addressed throughout all of MSDSP's programming (MSDSP Kg & AKF Kg 2011). Not only was the aim of working with government structures integrated throughout the work of the two organizations, but it was also interwoven with MSDSP's work on civil society development—indeed, both local governance and civil society are bundled into the same programme with the same staff members working on both. Arslan, the local governance programme officer at MSDSP, said that the goal of the programme was 'to increase potential of local governance and civil society and link with local population, to involve them. [The programme] works *both* with local government and civil society'. Thus, although the programme aimed to strengthen local government institutions, it also created bridges between these institutions and local civil society organizations.[2] It was telling that programming dealing with local governance and with civil society was so closely interwoven and interlinked. AKF Kg and MSDSP's view of the role of civil society is not to question or critique but rather to work with and aid the state.

A large part of the local governance programming focused on workshops and trainings for local government officials. For Arslan, MSDSP created a link between people, civil society, and government by promulgating and spreading ideas. Arslan stated that:

> There is a lack of trust for government, and thus it's very difficult to mobilize people, to get *information flowing*... [but MSDSP] tries to create links between all sides, *links of information*. We get government to give information to the people and to create participatory governance linked with people and civil society . . . *MSDSP pushes for the government to take people's opinions into account*.

For instance, this could involve encouraging local government institutions to hold public hearings when developing the local development strategy – which also tied into MSDSP's interest in local participation. Talant echoed Arslan, saying that MSDSP 'addresses the miscommunication between government and people'. The underlying assumption was that providing information was a way to build trust in the state. Running workshops for local

[2] Civil society in this usage is narrowly defined by MSDSP (both in documents and by staff in everyday usage) as registered CBOs, for instance savings or water-management groups.

government officials was also a reflection of MSDSP's power and influence—workshops are, after all, a claim of superior expertise.

The climate change adaptation project was a clear example of MSDSP's two-way influence on both state and local civil society organizations. The project's initial proposal stated that the project will 'enhance the capacity of local authorities, and government representatives' (AKF Kg 2010). When I asked Arslan what climate change adaptation had to do with local government, he told me that the first iteration of the programme was 'oriented on building relationships . . . and the potential of local government in dealing with climate change'. Indeed, in her initial report on climate change adaptation for AKF Kg, Laurie wrote that one of the goals of AKF Kg/MSDSP's climate change adaptation strategy would be to 'share climate change adaptation experience and lessons learned to encourage replication and *influence policy*'. As such, a major part of the project was making presentations about climate change adaptation and local impact assessments to government officials on the village and village-district levels, in the hopes of influencing local policy. A central aim of the project was to get villages' climate change adaptation plans to become part of the village-districts' development plans.[3] At the same time, it is through the programme that MSDSP has become a member of the Kyrgyz Republic's Climate Change Network, a collection of civil society bodies lobbying and engaging with the state. Most importantly, examining the programme in practice demonstrates the way it relies on and interweaves the role of local officials—and to some extent national ministries such as the ministry for emergency situations—in the way it functions.

The climate change adaptation project is also an excellent example of the way that AKF Kg and MSDSP's programming (both within and outside of the local governance programme) explicitly aimed to access the state resources. Because the programme explicitly involved local government institutions throughout—for instance, by running workshops on climate change adaptation for local officials—once working groups started implementing the adaptation mini-project, MSDSP was able to utilize state resources to help the project—and through this process demonstrated to working group members how state resources can be accessed. Pirjan told me that when approving the mini-project, MSDSP showed the plan to local government officials and pressured them to agree to help in various ways: for example, the local council agreed to lend Saro-Kamush their excavator for the project and to provide gasoline.

[3] Every village-district (Ail-Okrug) is supposed to have and be following an economic and social development plan.

Accessing state resources was not always easy: a neighbouring local council promised sizable financial assistance to another climate change adaptation mini-project that involved building a bridge over a flooding river. When it came time to hand over the money, officials balked at doing so. After this, Pirjan declared that from that point on he would put all such promises in writing. For Saro-Kamush's mini-project, he asked for written and signed promises to lend the excavator and provide gasoline. As discussed in Chapter 3, locals are deeply distrustful of the state and see it as neglecting its responsibility, but learn through this process how to access state resources. MSDSP is aware of this process and is attempting to create 'links of information' between government, civil society organizations, and locals.

Through this process, the state itself becomes pluralized and networked in the ways discussed in Chapter 3: its responsibilities are fulfilled not simply through its own operations but also through organizations such as AKF Kg and MSDSP, who ultimately teach local residents how to take on responsibilities in the areas where the state is inadequate or remiss. This echoes but also furthers and refines the good governance critique. As noted earlier, proponents of good governance argue that the state is just one organization of many that fulfil a particular role or need (such as protecting forests or digging canals). The good governance agenda posits that civil society plays a key role in insuring a society with well-functioning markets, wide-reaching social services, and a responsive state. Critics such as Abrahamsen (2000) or Chandhoke (2003) argue that this blurring of the line between state and civil society becomes a problem because of the lack of accountability and representation. Citizens can theoretically protest the negligence of the state through votes and demonstrations, but are unable to do so when the same responsibilities are transferred to NGOs, who are not democratically elected and thus not directly accountable to citizens.

Yet the civil society organizations in both case-study networks were not simply handmaidens of the state—they decided on their own agenda. Often this agenda was indeed to bolster the areas where the state had failed, and in the case of MSDSP's local governance programme, local state institutions were actually asked how MSDSP could help them. At the same time, intermediary civil society organizations were able to create connections between the local and the state, giving both ways of accessing the other. Arslan claimed that 'MSDSP pushes the government to take people's opinions into account'. Thus beyond simply acting as nodes of the networked state, organizations such as MSDSP and Waso Trustland had a key role in spreading knowledge about both state services and resources *and* local needs and desires. This not really about democratic engagement at all but rather engagement with local officials and civil servants to access the already present mechanisms of the state, and to make concrete resource-based demands.

However, these programmes were also intimately tied with the desires and interests of the international funders—and their global movement of choice—who underwrite the intermediaries, as well as the intermediaries' own goals. When I specifically brought up the good governance critique to Talant at MSDSP, his response was that:

> Time matters—the government can't do many things because of resource limitation, constraints . . . Funding the government directly is ineffective because of low-quality government workers, poorer human resources. NGOs *are exposed to something new, [through] international exchanges we have exposure to information*.

The crux of Talant's argument was that intermediary NGOs such as MSDSP were able to innovate in a way that the government could not—not only because of a lack of resources but specifically because of the ways that MSDSP was linked to flows of ideas and knowledge. In this vision, NGOs become the research and development wing of the state; state and civil society are not in opposition (Ferguson 2006), but neither is the development-focused civil society in this case simply a handmaiden of the state. In this framing, AKF Kg and MSDSP do more than fill the functions of the state—they redefine these functions in light of external ideas and approaches that state officials might either have little access to or choose to ignore.

b. Kenya: Kivulini Heritage Trust and Waso Trustland Project

i. The Kivulini Heritage Trust: Fostering Biocultural Diversity in Nairobi

The Kivulini Heritage Trust played two vital roles in forming biocultural diversity discourse—and thus ecological knowledge flows—between Beliqo, Waso Trustland, and TCF. First, Kivulini helped other organizations (such as WTL) and local communities package their problems and project proposals to fit into the grant requirements of TCF. Second, Kivulini enabled TCF to understand what is happening on the ground, to get a sense of the 'indigenous knowledge' that they valued, and thus to develop their sense of legitimacy and purpose. Indeed, Hussein, the founder and director of Kivulini, was acutely aware of Kivulini's role as an intermediary. Not only did Kivulini act as an intermediary in passing up grants proposals and passing down funds from

TCF, but the organization also sparked and then shaped ideas on the community level into a form palatable to TCF: in Hussein's words, it 'teaches ways to package thoughts'.

Kivulini's purpose statement was in many ways an echo of TCF's in the 2010s: to support 'communities' endeavours to sustain environmental and cultural vitality and prosperity'. Both the formal vision and mission statement of Kivulini echo this dual emphasis on both culture and natural environment. Yet while the main aim of Kivulini was the broader one of biocultural diversity, Hussein linked Kivulini's work with broader, global environmental concerns. Hussein saw biocultural diversity not as Kivulini's sole focus but as a way to engage with the challenges of northern Kenya's pastoralist population around ecological and cultural degradation. At the same time, Hussein extrapolated from the tie between culture and local ecology to broader, global environmental concerns such as climate change, for instance in conversation linking climate change with changes in flow levels of the Ewaso Niro River that flows through Beliqo. In the words of Hussein, Kivulini's broader aim was to 'solve big problems through the right routes'. One began with 'empowering the communities themselves, giving them voice', which would enable them to engage with institutions bigger than themselves, whether the state or transnational organizations. In Hussein's view, this was done by making sure that communities are 'proud, both of their culture and themselves'. This pride did not in Hussein's view mean a rejection of Western culture or Western knowledge. These communities can 'use Western culture to enrich [their] own culture' by no longer self-labelling their own culture as 'primitive' but rather embracing both 'their own knowledge and Western knowledge at the same time'.

Hussein argued that this is the route to sustainable management of natural resources, a type of management where people do not become the 'enemy of nature and wildlife' (as in the fortress conservation approach) but instead are able to 'utilize their environment, the land and soil' while still ensuring its survival. Hussein's example of this was sacred sites, where communities cannot kill animals or cut trees because of the cultural value of a space. Thus Hussein saw Kivulini's main contribution to the communities with which it worked as highlighting the relationship between culture and nature via the promotion of indigenous knowledge: in his words, one must have a sense of the 'bigger picture to protect smaller details'. The link between culture and environment seemed almost obvious in Hussein's terms: 'nature acts on culture, and impacts us' just as people act on nature. Examples could be it the ritual use of plants, the relationship between the honeyguide bird and the people that depend on it, or the relationship between wild and cultivated plans and livestock. Indigenous knowledge was the way in which this relationship was highlighted and acknowledged—Hussein referred to community elders who 'have [their] own way of addressing ecological issues, [which are] deeper, more relevant, and stem from experience, examples, and proverbs'. Hussein had a sophisticated awareness of his own role in promoting this view. Indeed, he headed off a critique of romanticism without me ever voicing it, stating flatly that 'we preserve pastoralism *not* out of romanticism, but for survival of people'. Indigenous knowledge and its link to cultural and ecological preservation were thus existential necessities in Hussein's view.

Yet Hussein made it clear that indigenous knowledge combined with civil society alone was not enough. Political involvement and innovative approaches and new ideas were also vital. When talking about what was needed to strengthen pastoralism, he told me that it was necessary to 'add value, through new technologies and tools' as well as through better 'marketing of animals and animal products' from the pastoralist communities of the north to the rest of the country. He pointed out that a focus on biocultural diversity preservation could bring tourist benefits but these are dependent on not only protecting cultural and natural diversity but also on transportation infrastructure—in his words, 'tourism needs roads'. Roads are dependent on the state, and thus politics. Thus biocultural diversity did have an instrumental value to indigenous communities, but one that relied on markets, new ideas, and infrastructure provided by the state.

At the same time as Kivulini privileged indigenous knowledge in their discourse, outside knowledge was also valued, and indeed depicted as crucial. Hussein described Kivulini's role in knowledge spread as 'dropping an idea in front of the community, and the community takes it up'. Hussein acknowledged the tension between the discourse of indigenous knowledge and participation as one of the essential aspects of Kivulini's identity, and the fact that Kivulini acts as a filter for groups, choosing groups on the basis of seeing if they would invest TCF money 'in the way we want, in the way we will help them'. If Kivulini saw a community or a need they thought would be translatable into the discourse (and practice) of biocultural diversity, then, in the words of Fatuma, 'Kivulini encourages CBO formation and registration' so that they could financially support programmes. They also worked with already formed groups, as long as the groups were willing to be tweaked or even transformed to fit the grant requirements.

This position of vetting and guiding CBOs implies the exercise of external authority, which lay in tension with the overt valuing of local knowledge and agency in the rhetoric of Kivulini. Kivulini thus takes on the role of 'filtering' local perspectives through the sieve of its shared discourse of the global. Yet Hussein insisted that Kivulini was not a gatekeeper but rather an upward link:

> We teach proposal writing, and make people understand the importance [of their concerns]—they don't *make the link to global importance*, so we link local to global . . . We sit for hours until vision comes out of [locals]. *We're not teaching, but sharing some relevant information, knowledge*. For instance, we don't talk of emissions, but of the fact that flowers are being farmed upriver [which pollute or divert the water] or dams are being built. We choose what to talk about, we're realists.

Throughout our conversations, Hussein repeatedly refused to see his role as that of teaching or telling people what to prioritize, but rather as a conduit of knowledge and languages. Yet here he was acknowledging the power inherent in this translator role, which creates the issues that both communities and global donors engage with. This reflects John Meyer's (1999, 2010) argument of civil society organizations as 'consultants' and 'advisors' manipulating the knowledge and direction of actors through advice and input from the sidelines. In Meyer's work, these actors tend to be states, but I would argue that this is a case where Kivulini as a civil society 'consultant' is shaping both actors on the ground and the actors controlling resources in the global node. Yet Kivulini's role goes beyond giving advice: Hussein does not lack agency and action but rather straddles the insider–outsider divide, partly because of his background, discussed in more detail below, of being both from a pastoralist community in northern Kenya and Western-educated.

There is some ambivalence in Kivulini's view of and relationship with local community-based organizations. Hussein acknowledged that local civil society groups were instrumentalized as a way to gain income and employment, pointing out that groups were formed if it was clear that there was the possibility for funding for a project. This was not brought up as a critique but more as the reality behind the proliferation of CBOs in Kenya. While Hussein did critique some CBOs for being no more than 'just activities backed by NGOs', the implication was that this was the NGOs' fault, and that 'CBOs shouldn't be used as field assistants by NGOs, should know *why* what they're doing is important'. To this end, 'Kivulini asks why, and creates a vision for CBOs, be it [one of] equality, or environment'. Thus Hussein acknowledged Kivulini's role in pushing an agenda and a long-term vision while at the same time engaging both individual interest and the entire community.

One of the words that was most commonly repeated throughout the series of conversations I had with Hussein was 'vision': its importance, the fact that many communities and even civil society organizations in Kenya lacked it, the importance of Kivulini's and TCF's vision, and the tension between emphasizing a community's own goals, vision, and participation and bringing in Kivulini's values. Hussein engaged with this tension by stating that:

> We don't go deliberately to teach, but to do anything you must know something: any task requires knowledge . . . [Kivulini] teaches ways to package thoughts, *not* for building capacity to get more grants, but rather to understand the environment, the bigger picture. Kivulini asks the bigger picture questions . . . by sharing a vision with the community, we bring it higher.

Thus Kivulini did teach, but it taught how to 'package' ideas so that they link to bigger, often global questions and issues. Hussein's conception of the usual pattern of interaction between international or national-level organizations and local communities was that 'people with money have the bigger vision' (in his examples, environmental protection or global warming) and they give money to Nairobi-based organizations with a smaller environmental vision (for instance, planting trees), who in turn give money to CBOs to act as 'labourers' carrying out the activity in question, such as planting trees. Hussein sees Kivulini as unique in 'challenging' CBOs and communities to have a broader vision of their own, as otherwise 'they are themselves limited by the donor's vision'.

Hussein is very open about the fact that Kivulini did not have the capacity to be on the ground, and in his perspective, if Kivulini was to encourage communities to take up a project, Kivulini must make it 'the community's proposal'. Hussein conceptualized this collaboration between the community and Kivulini very much as a use and a *valuing* of local knowledge, with ideas 'community proposed' and then 'Kivulini enriched'. This kind of relationship was of course an ideal, communicated to me in conversation rather than seen in the field. But the way that Hussein spoke of the relationship between local-level organizations and Kivulini was a large part of understanding the role that Kivulini played in linking the local into the global, in particular in bringing in biocultural diversity values and understandings, while at the same time encouraging local ownership of the projects through a process of valuing local knowledge.

Despite having a strong sense of its unique role in 'empowering' communities, Kivulini was very much aware of its connection to and reliance on The Christensen Fund. Hussein did admit that TCF required community projects to combine biodiversity and culture. Hussein's view of Kivulini as translating TCF's vision of biocultural diversity into the projects adopted by the communities seemed to lie in tension with his insistence on allowing the communities autonomy, a tension he never resolved directly. Hussein made no secret of the ways in which Kivulini's and The Christensen Fund's ideas and values aligned—he stated directly that 'the line between TCF and Kivulini is very thin'. At the same time, members of Kivulini argued that one 'can't push values downwards' onto communities, that organizations such as Kivulini 'must build off what's there'. Like MSDSP, Kivulini implicitly acknowledged that a project must capture the sustained interest and attention of a community, and to do so must build on local values, perspectives, and interests.

This is the closest Hussein came to the rhetoric of participation or bottom-up development. At the same time, Kivulini clearly had an acknowledged top-down role to play. In one conversation Hussein spoke of Kivulini's role as being to 'create the cause', achieved by his method of going out in his car to disparate communities in northern Kenya, spending an entire day with each of the groups, eating, sitting, and 'walking through the landscape' together while having discussions about the value of the place and the traditions of the people. He always brought what he termed a 'portable office'—a laptop, camera, and portable printer—and wrote up a grant proposal then and there. After this a project was, in Hussein's view, mutually constructed between the community and Kivulini. In other words, Hussein directly described his role as 'teach[ing] proposal writing in order to make people understand importance', whether the importance of certain cultural practices or of landscapes and ecologies. Kivulini thus saw itself as not simply finding or even creating community level projects that fulfil its own and TCF's vision but also as being part of the creation of values in these communities.

Hussein framed Kivulini's aim as 'validating' and 'streamlining' indigenous knowledge into 'current' or more widely accepted ways of understanding. In his words, recognizing and valuing local knowledge must be done by 'unpatterning', by shifting culturally set expectations about 'legitimate' forms of knowledge. Again, this seems to deny the agency and capabilities of locals to fend for themselves—Hussein seemed to be arguing that it is necessary for organizations such as his own to exist in order to translate from indigenous communities to funders. At the same time, Hussein also reiterated the role of Kivulini staff in 'bringing awareness', particularly environmental awareness, to local groups, who 'can't do it alone'. When Kivulini brought information during trips to communities in northern Kenya, it would 'change perceptions', and that would often change action, such as the behaviour of giraffe poachers who come to learn of the potential income from conserving wildlife.

Kivulini's role is to ask 'why?' and to '*lead* communities to knowledge'. Hussein argued that the key is to understand not *who* is cutting the tree but rather what led to that action and what will happen as a result, and to then act on this knowledge. In short, by enabling a common discourse and understanding between the local and the global, Kivulini sees itself as facilitating 'a meeting point of knowledge transfers', from both above and below. A key site for understanding this melting and its effects is one of the local NGOs in the north of the country that Kivulini has partnered with: the Waso Trustland Project.

ii. Waso Trustland Project Motivations: Rights, Access, and Ethnic Conflict

Waso Trustland exemplified the ways that nodes in civil society knowledge networks were able to hold on to their core ideological commitments, even when these did not square neatly with the ideational content of the network as a whole. For Waso Trustland, this ideological commitment centred on its relationship to the Kenyan state. This relationship has long been both adversarial and demanding. WTL's founder and head, Hassan, had a history as a human rights activist, and had indeed been jailed on charges of 'incitement' during a protest. This history had lent him a critical perspective on the role of the state in social projects, including conservation. He stated that WTL should not rely on the government, and often expressed anger at the way that the Kenyan government was handling the ongoing severe drought in the north of Kenya in 2011, claiming that the 'ministers were missing in action' and 'ignoring the issue'. WTL also criticized the claimed mismanagement and corruption in the local council's management of the district's game reserves. Hassan argued that if the community had direct control of the reserves, the benefits would be better managed and equitably distributed. WTL did not hesitated to take government ministries to court over perceived corruption or mismanagement.

At the same time, the staff at WTL did acknowledge the role and usefulness, both potential and realized, of state actors, particularly when it came to conservation and environmental issues. In particular, one of the key mechanisms enabling the existence of the forest conservation movement in Beliqo is the 2005 Kenya Forests Act, which grants legal community control of local forests through the creation of community forest associations—and WTL acknowledged that this was a government policy that legitimized and gave structure to local movements. Hassan was also willing to cede that there were some government agencies that were doing good work—one of these was the Ministry of State for Development of Northern Kenya and Other Arid Lands (Arid Lands for short), which Hassan referred to as 'a small office, but it has done a lot'. In short, although WTL's relationship with the state seemed both fraught and adversarial, the organization acknowledged the power and influence of state actors, from the local level to the national.

A particularly telling anecdote was the evolution of the relationship between Hassan and Councillor Golicha, the elected county councillor for the Beliqo area. WTL campaigned hard against the establishment of the community nature conservancy that Golicha had supported, accusing Golicha of being a puppet, fooled, or out for personal gain, and Hassan spoke of the councillor with great bitterness. Golicha had never visited the WTL office, and Hassan claimed that he avoided WTL staff in order to avoid confrontation. At the same time, Hassan acknowledged that he would prefer to have the councillor working with WTL, and that though they differed on the conservancy question, they might in fact be of similar views and be able to work together on different issues. During my own time at the WTL office, I set up an interview with the councillor, and he ended up coming to the WTL office (for the first time). Hassan joined us at the end of the interview and began a conversation about my research and presence in the organization. By the end of the conversation, Councillor Golicha and Hassan were shaking hands, smiling and asking me to take photographs of the two of them together. Hassan affirmed that they should be working together and that they shared the same concerns. After the councillor left, Hassan turned to me and thanked me for being the mechanism via which the rift between the councillor and WTL was healed, and continued to mention the incident for several weeks afterwards. This is a demonstration not simply of the role of my own participation in the research, however inadvertent, but also that despite its adversarial position, WTL saw the advantages of cooperation with local state actors.

WTL had expanded its attention from land-rights advocacy to resource rights, ecological activism, and grassroots conservation efforts. Yet the way that WTL talked about environmentalism was still centred on the language of rights and access. In explaining that WTL was willing to work with any pastoralist group in the north, WTL's administrator Liban declared that 'the environment doesn't have *boundaries*'. In rhetoric such as this, it was clear that WTL was concerned with boundaries and land tenure—Liban went on to explain that many of the issues and conflicts that WTL dealt with were a result of differences in land tenure between different districts and ethnic groups. In neighbouring Meru district, land was privately owned, and both Hassan and Liban brought up the Meru ethnic group repeatedly as perpetrators hoping to log and sell off the riverine forest around Beliqo village. Thus ideas and rhetoric around ownership and rights to access formed the backbone of WTL's approach to environmentalism (Agrawal 2005b).

Indeed, the ecologically focused conversations I had at WTL were almost always related either to conflict over or access to natural resources such as land or water. WTL's involvement with conservation around Beliqo village originated in its concern with water rights and the use and misuse of the Waso River. WTL became involved in the emerging conflict between the farmers of central Kenya, who were diverting the water upriver for agriculture, and the pastoralists downstream in northern Kenya, who rely on the river to water their livestock. From this concern with the misuse of water, WTL became aware of similar concerns surrounding the riverine forest in the vicinity of Beliqo village. And as Hassan described it, much conflict in the region comes from tensions over land access, and natural resource use also was a major source of conflict. In recounting the way that WTL became interested in the conservation of the Ewaso Niro River and the forest around it, conflict was a prominent theme—not only conflict between the farmers upstream and the pastoralists downstream but also competition with other river users and with ethnic outsiders who were accused of trying to destroy the forest around the river for personal gain. Like Hassa and Liban, the chairman of WTL's board blamed the Meru ethnic group as the source of ecological problems in Beliqo, describing them as 'outsiders with power saws' who cannot be held accountable to Borana law. In his words, formal state mechanisms to stop these outsiders were not working 'due to corruption' and because the government was 'never serious about the environment'.

WTL's view of the connections between state neglect, ethnic conflict, and ecological ownership became clear in a discussion between Hassan, Liban, and Maulit, a WTL legal intern provided by the Kenya Land Alliance, one of Waso Trustland's partner NGOs. They discussed Maulit's discovery of ecological degradation caused by deforestation and the diversion of rivers and springs for farming in a neighbouring district. In this conversation all three were incensed with the state's apathy and neglect and planned to lobby various local government offices. They also linked the drying up of the river with deforestation, and blamed Meru farmers for inciting tree cutting, diverting the river, and encouraging herders in the area to start doing the same, thus endangering the ecology of the region and the future of the herders who need these water sources for their livestock. This conversation highlighted a number of themes: WTL's tense relationship with the state, which is both an important actor and a negative, corrupt, and neglectful one; the ethnic tensions that emerge out of different modes of resource use; the tension over who has legitimate access to these resources; and the central importance of herding for the pastoralist community.

Thus in WTL's lexicon, resources rights and access were intertwined with inter-ethnic conflict, and the ecological is linked with political and economic issues, particularly land rights and state corruption. Throughout my time with WTL this remained the organization's focus, even when engaged with the biocultural diversity rhetoric of the global node and the conservation work on the ground with CFA. Yet for WTL, conservation is not mission drift: as will be outlined in more detail below, WTL is able to forge a viable connection between their emphasis on land rights, government accountability, and conflict on the one hand, and a broader focus on biocultural diversity and conservation on the other.

iii. Waso Trustland and the Creation of Knowledge Networks: Connecting to Global Concerns

WTL played a crucial role in ensuring that the individual aims of each node in this case-study network were 'reformatted' to fit within the discourse of the network as a whole. WTL was adept at doing this, particularly in addressing its own interest in land rights and CFA's interest in livelihood by creating a link between the two and conservation activities. WTL forged this link not only through its rhetoric but also by both spreading information—'sensitization', in the words of Hassa—and by gathering information from the village residents. WTL thus become a mediator between its own interests, local village concerns, and the broader discourses of conservation and local knowledge.

Although Hassan and Liban were primarily interested in land rights, they were clear about wanting to engage with the environment and with conservation. They saw this both as a way to pre-empt what they perceived to be 'land-grabs' by outsiders under the guise of wildlife conservation and as a way to ensure present and future resource rights. From a concern with land rights, they explained, it is a short leap to a concern with what's *on* and *in* the land—in other words, resource rights. In the words of Hassan, one 'can't eat the land'. A focus on land was not enough; one had to also focus on resources and the environment was 'another resource', one that was 'very fragile in Isiolo'. They linked this view with community involvement and the spread of information. They spoke of wanting to 'sensitize' and 'inform' communities about the conservation of the environment, and of vegetation in particular, but at the same time *not* privilege wildlife or the natural world over human life and livelihood. Thus, though WTL had expanded its work into the realm of conservation, its focus had remained on humans. They pointed out that humans and livestock have long co-existed successfully with wildlife, and Hassan stated that it is 'traditional knowledge' that enabled such co-existence, that

'Borana always had indigenous knowledge to co-exist with nature' and have been 'doing it from time immemorial'. This is a perfect echo of biocultural diversity discourse.

Indeed, in a tell-tale reference during the same conversation, the two of them spoke of 'Western language' as 'misplacing' people and livestock in conservation efforts. Hassan repeatedly voiced frustrations with these efforts, passionately stating that the indigenous people of Isiolo district have repeatedly given land to wildlife but have received 'minimal benefit' and that the land in question is 'our property, our rights'. What pastoralists needed was 'information [and] knowledge on how to conserve all resources'. This undermines The Christensen Fund's views, discussed more in Chapter 5, that the key needs of pastoralists were not material, but also undermines Inglehart's (1981, 1995) argument that ecological awareness can only come once material needs have been satisfied. Waso Trustland *was* materially focused, but does not see this as a contradiction with conservation. For Hassan material benefits and land rights became fused with ecology and indigenous knowledge, allowing WTL to create a network that spanned both TCF and CFA, uniting their goals into a broad discourse that creates the links needed for the network to function as a whole.

Although Liban and Hassan utilized the words 'conservation' and 'biodiversity', they see the end goal of conservation as 'benefiting the community' in an immediate, material sense, and this contrasts with the broader emphasis of global environmental movements upon long-term benefits of maintaining biodiversity or mitigating climate change. These more immediate benefits included the possibility of ecological and cultural tourism that would 'bring in resources', as well as the ability to continue and profit from pastoralist methods of livestock rearing. Hassan mentioned that what they needed was 'information on how it is possible to have both livestock and wildlife and tourism *together*'. Thus WTL's discursive focus on 'conservation' was both narrower and broader than that of the biocultural diversity movement: narrower in terms of the location and time scale of expected benefits and broader in the sense that they spoke of conserving not only the environment and 'culture' but also any other 'resources that benefit communities'.

WTL's rhetoric was able to link the ecological to its foundational concerns with land rights and community ownership. As Hassan stated more than once, 'what belongs to everybody, belongs to nobody'—a statement seemingly in tension with the communal land tenure of northern Kenya that WTL strived so hard to protect. Yet Hassan supported community ownership and responsibility for communal land. Indeed, the formation of CFA in Beliqo could be understood as the formalization of this goal of shifting environmental awareness and values to include a sense of community ownership and responsibility. This echoes the literature that has arisen in response to Hardin's (1968) assertion of the inevitable tragedy of the commons. WTL's and CFA's assertions of community ownership echoes the arguments of scholars such as Ostrom (1990), who suggests that the user-managed commons need not end in a tragedy, and recognizes community self-determination as an essential part of effective governance of the commons. In Ostrom's 2002 edited book, Berkes and Young both reaffirm the argument that connections and relationships between different scales of institutions (often civil society institutions) are essential to contemporary governance of the commons (Berkes 2002; Young 2002). This was precisely the process that Waso Trustland was deeply engaged with through their connection both to Kivulini and The Christensen Fund as well as grassroots village groups.

The Waso Trustland Project was primarily funded by The Christensen Fund, and to receive funding WTL had to both facilitate projects that fit within the particular vision and understanding of TCF, and utilize discourse and rhetoric within its grant applications that showed enough familiarity and overlap with TCF's mission. The way that WTL worded their initial grant application to TCF demonstrates their awareness of the need to speak to biocultural diversity, TCF's core interest at the time. The grant application referred to global environmental goals, standards, and mechanisms, including the Convention of Biological Diversity, the Forest Principals of the Earth Summit, Millennium Development Goal 7, and ILO Convention 169. It also spoke of 'endangered indigenous tree species highly valued . . . at international levels'. Indeed, the proposal stated that 'the project intends to address the issue of universal changes of climatic patterns', demonstrating a calculated decision to link the project with the global climate change movement. All of these quotes show a developed awareness, perhaps surprising of a small land-rights focused NGO, of international legal instruments and standards relating to environmentalism.

Not only did the grant application purposely tie the proposal to the rhetoric of the global environmental concerns, it also tailored the project to fit into the more niche concern of biocultural diversity. In the grant application, WTL wrote about the 'traditional community system of managing and regulating resource use'. Several of the activities outlined for the project linked traditional cultural practices with conservation, including collecting oral histories of the ecosystem, as well as identifying 'culturally important' and 'culturally useful' plants. Indeed, the application emphasizes that many of the plants in the forest have medicinal and ceremonial uses, and states that the project seeks to 'incorporate the vast knowledge of the indigenous people', in a direct echo of the indigenous knowledge rhetoric of Kivulini and TCF.

The application was edited by and written with the advice of Hussein at Kivulini, who helped hone the application to reflect the focus and even the language of TCF and the biocultural diversity movement. Hassan highlighted the connection between WTL and Hussein, explaining that Hussein is well known in the region, not as the head of Kivulini but rather as an individual active in civil society, and that Hussein acts 'as the contact person' for TCF in Kenya. The grant approval letter sent to Waso Trustland from TCF (but used generically for all grant approvals) also reinforces the way that WTL fits into TCF's place in the biodiversity movement, referencing an end goal of an 'awareness of the importance of biological and cultural diversity in your . . . community'. Strangely, when The Christensen Fund described WTL's grant in their approval letter, the only reference to the project called it 'community education about Ewaso Nyiro conservation in northern Kenya', and failed to mention the conservation aspect which lay at the crux of the project. Indeed, when I asked Hassan what the main focus of TCF was, he replied not with environmentalism or biodiversity but rather 'culture'—demonstrating an awareness of the unique dimension of the biocultural diversity discourse within the broader environmental movement.

The relationship between Hassan and some of the staff at The Christensen Fund was close—in particular with Wolde, then the Rift Valley programme officer for TCF. I observed Hassan calling Wolde in the UK to ask a quick question regarding a grant application for another source of funding, and Hassan spoke of him as a resource and a support for WTL. The link between WTL and TCF—and through TCF, the broader biocultural diversity movement—was also forged via a visit from TCF's staff members, including Ken (the then-executive director), who had visited WTL and the project in Beliqo. This visit came up repeatedly in conversation at WTL. Hassan pointed out that

> TCF's contribution is that they take the time to visit us, they even visited the [Ewaso Niro] river. Unlike other donors they take [local NGO] partners as real partners. They give suggestions, hold discussion and debates.

Indeed, Hassan went so far as to say that TCF were 'the right people for us' because they 'come down to our villages' in order to 'see the conditions of our people'. Hassan noted that this behaviour was unlike that of other international and national organizations that have funded WTL, which had included the Ford Foundation (which had given one-off funding for community education), the FAO's indigenous fund for agricultural development, UNDP, and a number of national NGOs. The visit both validated and gave a sense of equality and inclusion to WTL. This highlights the relationship between TCF's discourse and practice of privileging community action, participatory development, and indigenous knowledge. WTL understood TCF's visit to be a reflection of their privileging of local action and knowledge, and as such the visit legitimized TCF's biocultural diversity perspective and focus in WTL's eyes.

iv. Inside the Anti-Politics Machine at WTL

This legitimization was not automatic. Hassan made it clear that biocultural diversity, or even broader conservation and environmental concerns, were not what WTL originally sought to engage with. This was reflected in the back-and-forth surrounding the protection of the Ewaso Niro River when WTL was originally seeking funding from TCF. WTL wanted TCF to assist with advocacy and awareness about river use and the diversion of river water by big farms upstream, in an attempt to 'get people to stand and fight for their rights from the government'. Indeed, Hassan noted with regret that both Kivulini and TCF initially believed that the river must be dealt with by the government, not by civil society, and that the issue of resource rights was too wide to be dealt with by a regional NGO. But Hassan kept on insisting, arguing that the river was so central to the livelihood of the Borana people that it could not be ignored, that 'there must be people on the ground talking about this'. Hassan and TCF finally agreed that what would be appropriate for the use of TCF funds and WTL interests would be to work on protecting the forest on the banks of the river rather than the river itself, changing the focus not only from the river to the forest but from advocacy to conservation. This demonstrates the difference between WTL's and TCF's understanding of the role of civil society. Like AKF, TCF seemed to view the purpose of on-the-ground civil society organizations to be project *implementers*, while WTL understood itself to be primarily interested in advocacy and activism.

As a result, TCF made WTL's agenda far less about contentious politics: from an organization positioned *against* and in criticism of the state, TCF convinced WTL to engage with natural resource management in a way that was far less politically contentious, and indeed to work with the provisions of the state (including the 2005 Kenya Forests Act). Much like Ferguson argues in *The Anti-Politics Machine* (1994), global development institutions thus become ideologically and politically moderating. Yet when switching focus to ecological concerns, Hassan held on to his activist approach, and remained engaged with (as well as critical of) the state. The north of Kenya was experiencing a particularly heavy drought during my fieldwork there in 2011, and Hassan agitated for a government response. During my time at the WTL office, Hassan called up a TV station and argued passionately about the lack of appropriate state action. He also told me that 'everyone *must stand and fight* [climate change], climate must be protected at any expense'. Even with a change in focus from land rights to environmental concerns, Hassan did not become entirely depoliticized, and remained focused on access to resources for the north of Kenya. Thus, in Waso Trustland's case, TCF is unable to fully succeed in 'rendering contentious issues technical' (Li 2007: 10).

Waso Trustland's engagement with TCF was thus not purely what MacDonald (1995: 202) calls 'instrumental participation'. MacDonald divides NGOs into 'mainstream', 'progressive', and 'contradictory' (203) largely by how much influence foreign agencies and funders have on them (or how much autonomy they have). Yet in this case study the reality was far messier. TCF held influence over WTL, but while WTL might have been less engaged in contentious politics, it remained a politically engaged organization, and Hassan remained an activist. The back-and-forth between TCF and WTL demonstrated that the links between the global and the regional/local are not monolithic or unidirectional. Hassan planned to continue recommending to TCF that they expand their focus (and funding) to advocacy, and not just cultural and environmental projects. Although this is unlikely to happen, Hassan's description of why TCF agreed to fund a project that still engaged with resource rights is telling: Hassan described it as a product of TCF respect for the organization. In Hassan's words, 'the [Christensen Fund] recognized our efforts, [and has] seen for themselves our problems'. Thus personal (and organizational) relationships become vital in the way that projects are negotiated and values become formed.

This back-and-forth is also reflected in Hassan's simultaneous engagement with Western knowledge (often from the scientific epistemic community around climate change) and local ideas and values. The 2011 drought became a way for me to engage with my interviewees on their view of climate change and ecological degradation. Hassan not only linked climate change with the recurrent drought in the region, stating that 'climate change really affects us—rains used to come twice [a year], now only once', but he also readily equated the heavy drought with ecological damage in the area, stating that 'the drought is caused by destruction of fragile environment'. He equated this knowledge with a broader, scientific knowledge that was missing among local communities, stating that 'locals say [the drought] is natural . . . but science doesn't believe in natural'. Yet while he included himself with this scientific knowledge or scientific community, he fused regional beliefs and scientific consensus. Hassan mentioned that 'the trees bring rain' (an idea widespread in the region and discussed more in Chapter 3) and that 'climate depends on the trees', and that in the face of the destruction of tress, the land would become 'arid' and 'climate changes for the worse'.

Yet although Hassan attributed knowledge of climate change and its link to the drought to a scientific community outside of local knowledge, he also blamed the outside world for it, and privileged local knowledge in responding to and preventing ecological issues. Hassan stated that:

> Some change from industrial countries destroyed the climate. We were caught unawares. There is no way . . . we can stop talking about the environment. That's why pastoralists don't destroy trees: they know trees are important for water and a cool climate. To know is just the basics: we have to share . . . [this knowledge]. Environment is big knowledge, so we create a strategy because local knowledge is limited.

This quote holds a number of contradictions—while Hassan linked knowledge of climate change with scientific knowledge, and acknowledged the limits of local knowledge, he highlighted in the very same interview the ecological knowledge of indigenous communities in Kenya's north. Hassan was quick to credit the Beliqo community with knowledge of the river and forest, linking this knowledge with the use of natural resources, a use that in his view give locals 'true perspective'. Yet the role for WTL, as for Kivulini, was 'sensitizing people, make people aware of climate change'. In many ways Hassan reflects the internal contradictions of The Christensen Fund, and more broadly the writings around indigenous knowledge or colonial knowledge. This is the contradiction between the privileging of local knowledge and the occasional utility or even necessity of global or Western knowledge (Beinart 2000; Beinart et al. 2009), and in our conversations Hassan repeatedly attempted to construct a synergy between the two.

v. WTL and the Communities of Isiolo District: Transmuting Knowledge Categories

Waso Trustland was integrated into the local community, both in Isiolo town and beyond. A steady stream of visitors came through the WTL office every day, for the most part turbaned Borana elders, their beards orange with henna, who sat in Hassan's office, arguing and discussing politics and pieces of news or old unresolved issues. Sometimes young men would come; very occasionally women. They spoke with Hassan about local events, perceived injustices, and political gossip. WTL depends on a network of willing visitors and informers to keep abreast with the issues in the district, and is able to do so because Hassan has a dual identity as both a Borana insider, an elder, and as the head of an NGO connected to the world of international and national development organizations. While WTL's rhetoric of indigenous knowledge seems to be an echo of a broader global concept of the same, WTL actively relies on actual on-the-ground knowledge, in contrast to MSDSP, which lacks this kind of informal access to local communities. In the words of Hassan (and in an echo of Hussein), WTL staff and communities 'discussed' issues first and only then 'tried to draw a way forward'. Of course, this does not mean that WTL did not select for or seek out certain types of information, privileging some forms of knowledge over others, particularly as informed by both their own aims and the aims of the agencies that fund them. Yet in practice WTL did rely on information brought by community members, and in fact went out 'into the field' (to quote Hassan)—that is, into village communities in the district—to 'sit with the communities', gather information, and inform constituents about the issues WTL works on.

Hassan discussed his knowledge relationship with the communities around Isiolo as bidirectional: its purpose was both gaining information and in spreading information and knowledge, or 'sensitizing' the people. Even Hassan's afternoon visits to a local social club in Isiolo were playfully presented in that light—he would speak to me of going to play chess in order to 'sensitize [the] old men'. This idea of the role of civil society being to sensitize or to bring knowledge was brought up several times by Hassan, who lamented the fact that people in the villages were 'disconnected' and 'ignorant', and directly portrayed civil society organizations as the only link to 'information regarding rights, water, education [and] provisions'. This attitude was in striking contradiction to the fetishization of local knowledge at TCF (discussed more in Chapter 5) and even at Kivulini. Hassan and Liban spoke overtly about WTL's role in influencing local understanding and action. Hassan said that he told local communities where WTL worked that 'we built your minds so that you can build the project for yourself'. 'Building the mind' involved not only community education around issues such as conservation but also structural knowledge, knowledge about the way in which these issues can be engaged with on the community level. Hassan envisioned both local civil society organizations and broader networks of regional and national NGOs as 'mouthpieces' and 'points of sensitization' for local communities: both 'having the courage' to highlight injustices and voice community demands to leaders and to create knowledge and 'understanding' in local communities.

As such, WTL was not simply a partner of national-level NGOs such as Kivulini but was also part of broader networks which connect it with other small NGOs with similar regional and thematic focus, such as the Kenya Land Alliance. Hassan spoke of forming 'national networks' around issues of land rights and around conservation. In Hassan's view, if WTL was to be a 'mouthpiece' for the community, then they had to have 'members and partners', including individuals, communities, and organizations, forming a broad network throughout the north. Hassan described this network as stretching both up to the international level (necessarily so in the search for funding) and down to the grassroots (necessarily so in the search for issues, problem areas, and the creation of projects). He argued that it is only through this kind of network—and the information and the resources it provides—that 'injustices' can be highlighted and advocated against. Yet Hassan's interactions with other organizations highlight that different NGOs consider the grassroots to lie at different levels—for instance, the policy-focused Kenya Land Alliance would send interns to WTL because they considered WTL to be grassroots, while WTL staff would go out into the villages of the district to support what they deemed to be the real grassroots activism. This is a key facet of the way civil society knowledge networks function: through an amorphous, ever-shifting construction of geographic categories, and with them, construction of categories of knowledge.

For Waso Trustland, a large part of forming these networks was not only forging connections to other organizations but indeed encouraging the formation of grassroots CBOs in the villages. Although many of the researchers and international non-governmental organization workers I spoke with in Nairobi regarded village-level CBOs with cynicism, viewing them as mechanisms for personal gain or job creation that were often ineffective in terms of community-based action, Hassan expressed great belief in the power and usefulness of such local civil society organizations. Indeed, he directly spoke of WTL utilizing CBOs as mechanisms through which knowledge could be both spread and collected. CBOs in Hassan's view were the 'entry points for sensitization' of local people, teaching community members to 'stand up for their rights' as well as be 'local mouthpieces' who have to be empowered to 'have the courage to ask government leaders regarding social issues'. However, Hassan did echo some of the scepticism towards CBOs as well, explaining that many do not work property or have the knowledge to ever get funding. In other words, in Hassan's view the ineffectiveness of CBO is linked not to cynicism or mismanagement but rather to a lack of knowledge.

When asked why so many CBOs existed in Kenya in general (and in Beliqo in particular), Hassan explained that 'when marginalization is so heavy it is necessary to have a legitimate voice for a community', and creating a formal organizational structure legitimizes such voices. As such, 'CBOs are the most common in marginalized areas' and are the structures 'that people run to'—though at the same time many registered CBOs are 'dormant' because they have no funding. At the same time, Hassan highlighted the knowledge-based role of CBOs in relation to environmental concerns. In his view, 'when there's poverty, concern for the environment goes'. Since 'local knowledge is limited', it is through partnerships between civil society institutions like WTL together with grassroots CBOs that 'priorities' can be decided upon and then 'strategies' for working on these priorities can be worked out. These priorities are not necessarily directly ecologically focused—for instance, in Hassan's view, 'if the infrastructure was there [such as roads, gas pipes, or electricity grids], trees wouldn't be cut [by the community] for fuel'.

There is a tension within WTL's narrative of how the organization became involved with forest conservation around Beliqo. On the one hand, Hassan credited his own history as a resource rights activist for his interest in the right to use of the Ewaso Niro River, along with TCF for shifting his ideas from the river itself to what was happening to the forest on its banks (and the ecosystem more broadly). On the other, both Hassan and Liban claimed that it was the information provided by the people of Beliqo that spurred WTL's interest and concern in the river and forest: the 'the community gave [WTL] knowledge about the river'. Long before the project began, WTL had mechanisms in place to deliberately transfer information both ways—both from WTL to the grassroots, and from the grassroots to WTL. These structures were built into the way WTL operated. Hassan describes the process:

> We go into the communities to discuss new land laws and policies. In the last year we went several times, five or six times depending on funds . . . For community workshops we call people from different villages . . . WTL talks about current issues, and invites people to ask questions, to contribute, do group work. [We ask:] What can we do? Who can assist us? Then we follow up and establish a committee to follow up. That's how the Beliqo project got started.

This is a symbiotic relationship, where information is shared and knowledge, very deliberately, flows both ways. Without such a structure, WTL simply could not operate—nor would it be useful to organizations such as Kivulini and TCF, who so heavily rely of WTL as a way to connect to the grassroots.

The description that Hassan and Liban gave of the role of the Beliqo community in sparking the forest conservation project is varied and at times even contradictory, but perfectly illustrates this symbiotic knowledge relationship. Another element of the story is that WTL took note of erupting inter-ethnic conflict in the region:

> We started off dealing with land, but you can't eat land. We saw conflict coming about due to lack of water, saw the river drying up, so we investigated. We see misuse [of the river] . . . water is the key problem, and eventually we heard about destruction of trees. People came and informed us.

In this version, it is WTL's investigation (rather than community concerns or TCF prompting) that first sparked the Beliqo project, but it also rides on people volunteering information about the destruction of trees. When WTL saw how important the issue was to locals, it helped structure CFA to 'put together all the stakeholders' who were 'concerned with [river and forest] resources in some way'. What these versions of the birth of CFA and the conservation project share is the way that WTL relied on locals for information and project formation. Although TCF seems to have pushed WTL into a certain direction or perspective, it is local knowledge and concerns (together with global funds and broader ideologies in combination with national structures) that served as the impetus for the creation of CFA.

Hassan and Liban's emphasis on the role of local knowledge in their operations echoes TCF's focus on indigenous knowledge and perspectives. Hassan termed this 'the true perspective of Waso [Trustland Project]'—learning the concerns and problems of remote northern communities and passing such knowledge to organizations such as TCF that could enable action. This not only echoes TCF and Kivulini's concerns with local-level ideas and interests but also builds WTL's authenticity and legitimacy with donors. Yet the local ideas the WTL acted on inevitably seemed to fit Hassan's interest in campaigning for land and resource rights. Despite my questions and promptings, Hassan and Liban never brought up specific indigenous ideas around the river or pasture or trees (other than that trees bring rain) of the sort highlighted and valued by TCF and academic writing on biocultural diversity. Hassan never mentioned the possible medicinal, religious, or symbolic significance of ecological resources—unlike Hussein, there was no talk of sacred sites, or the importance of the honeyguide bird. As can be seen throughout this chapter, Hassan's ideas continued to revolve around access, ownership, usage rights, and livelihoods, even after referencing biocultural ideas and concepts in his grant application to TCF.

II. Typologies of Knowledge: Designating Authority, Searching for Authenticity

A key role of the knowledge intermediaries such as AKF Kg and MSDSP, or Kivulini and Waso Trustland, was the way that they created and designated two typologies of knowledge: expert and local knowledge. Expertise points to a position of authority and power within the network: not only the power to set the terms of engagement with global movements and funders but also the power to transform ideas and knowledge into action. The two networks share some similarities in the way expertise was designated and created: *international* expertise, or more particularly expertise founded on education or experience in the West, denoted power and authority. Yet the two case studies also point to variation: in Kenya, expertise could also be created on the basis of local respect or traditional authority, while in the Kyrgyz Republic the very structure of the network limited the boundaries of expertise, both linguistically (to the English language) and geographically (to Europe and North America). At the same time, the organizations and individuals in both cases prized not only the authority of expert knowledge but also what they saw as the authenticity of local or indigenous knowledge—even if, as in the Kyrgyz case, little of it was actually accessed by the networks. Both sets of intermediaries delineated these two knowledge typologies for their own legitimacy, and for the legitimacy of their global partners. At the same time, the designation of expertise and authority within the two networks illustrates how knowledge, whether knowledge from the global, the local, or knowledge created and shared by intermediary organizations themselves, is transformed and formalized into plans for action. Who participates in this process points to the way that power was distributed within these intermediary organizations. Indeed, the ways in which expertise could be gained and obtained also illustrates how intermediaries worked to keep the networks functioning as a coherent whole.

a. The Kyrgyz Republic: Designating Expertise, Valorizing the Local

This chapter has already discussed the expat culture at AKF's Bishkek office, arguing that expatriates working at AKF Kg held the positions of power and epistemic influence in the organization. Such influence was bound up not simply in the organizational structure of the network but also in the ways that expertise was understood and designated in the network. Kyrgyz staff at MSDSP explicitly referenced expat expertise, in particular when describing the role of Laurie in the climate change adaptation project. Pirjan, Aizada, and Talant on multiple occasions mentioned 'the international consultant' or 'reports prepared by an international consultant' or some fact 'according to the international consultant'—although it was clear that I knew Laurie by name and her role in the programme. The word 'international' was wielded to ascribe authority to the knowledge produced by this figure (and Laurie's role was largely producing knowledge—reports, training manuals, syntheses of village assessments). 'International' here was largely a stand-in for the global North—yet the nomadism of the expats in AKF Kg lent further authority to their 'expert' knowledge, as well as the sheen of cross-cultural internationalism. When I would ask Kyrgyz staff members at MSDSP and at AKF Kg whether they had any decision-making power in the selection and design of new programmes, they largely ceded it to Jack (together with Nicolle, Karl, and in the case of the climate change adaptation project, Laurie). However, they did insist that the programmes had to conform to the strategic plan of the organization, and that they had a role in drafting the strategic plan at the annual retreat of the two organizations. However, these meetings were attended by Western staff from AKF Geneva, and the new strategic plan had to be approved by the AFK Geneva office. Thus even when key decision-making *was* nominally given to local staff, it was still controlled quite directly by the global node of the Kyrgyz network.

The weight and authority given to 'experts' from abroad (i.e., the West) were echoed in the background and educations of the local staff members that *were* allowed to take on powerful roles in the Kyrgyz Republic's intermediate organizations. Almost all the staff members of AKF Kg and at MSDSP's head office in Osh were fluent in English, not a common thing even amongst the Kyrgyz Republic's highly educated. Nicolle once complained to me that staff hired in Bishkek and Osh are selected on their language abilities (many actually had English Language as their university degree) as opposed to their knowledge or skills in development—demonstrating that these organizations prize the ability of their staff to connect with expat authorities as well as global partners (many staff members are sent abroad for trainings, which are inevitably held in English). Pirjan was one of the few staff members who did *not* speak English, whose experience and abilities over-rode this requirement when he was being hired. Pirjan mentioned to me on several occasions that he felt disadvantaged by this fact: it was difficult for him to communicate with Laurie and to attend joint AKF–MSDSP meetings, and in fact the job advertisement both for his job and for the coordinator of the third iteration of the climate change adaptation (a job he applied for and did not get) explicitly stated that English fluency was required.

Indeed, positions with decision-making power at the AKF's Bishkek office and MSDSP's Osh office that *were* held by locals are often given to locals with extensive education or experience in Europe or North America. Rahat, the new coordinator for the third iteration of the climate change adaptation project, had a Master's degree from Manchester. Laila, the reporting manager for MSDSP—which is the one position at MSDSP besides that of Talant, the director, that involved communicating with donor organizations outside of the Kyrgyz Republic—did her Master's in Washington, DC and worked there for several years. Mavluda, the communications manager at AKF, lived for several years in New York. All three of these staff members are key in the way the actions and ideas of the intermediaries are presented to outsiders (Mavluda and Laila) or in the way programming is transformed into action (Rahat).

There were some notable exceptions to the power held by Western-based knowledge in the organizations. The kick-off meeting for the third iteration of the climate change adaptation project was attended by over a dozen staff members, including several who could not speak English and several expats, including Laurie, who could not speak Russian. Although the meeting started in English, Laurie insisted that it switch to Russian so that all the local staff could understand and participate in the discussions, and the discussion itself was a lively one, with proposals from MSDSP staff that actually changed some of the details in the way the programme was implemented. However, I was later told by multiple staff members that this was the exception rather than the norm, and that usually such meetings were dull and achieved little. Perhaps the meeting differed from the norm because I was there, or perhaps because it was the first time Laurie insisted that it be conducted in Russian. Yet even in this open meeting the various suggestions put forward by local staff went through a filtering process when they were translated by Talant to Laurie (who then actually chose which ones to implement), as Talant privileged some suggestions over others in his translation and funnelled them into his own vision of how the programme should look. So despite (or even within) such exceptions, knowledge of English or experience in the West ultimately granted power and control over the process that transforms ideas into practice.

Even amongst Kyrgyz staff members that do not have a background or experience in the West, AKF/MSDSP creates expertise by sending them to trainings and workshops held by AKF global staff from Geneva, or by other transnational organizations (such as the climate change training held by GIZ that Pirjan attended) or even sending them all the way to Geneva for trainings in the AKF head office. For instance, Leonora, the human resources manager at MSDSP, went to Geneva for training during my time at MSDSP. This chapter has already made the case that such trainings abroad were another kind of glue, joining the disparate organizational nodes into one network, as well as an attempt by the global to deepen control over what goes on at the intermediary (and thus the local) nodes and to impress Kyrgyz staff with the wealth of Geneva and AKF's office there. They also created 'local' expertise, which echoes the ideas and knowledge of the Western-based, global organizations in the network.

Yet the intermediaries in the Kyrgyz Republic were also deeply interested in participatory, locally generated knowledge, as echoed in the rhetoric of participation that existed throughout the network. Indeed, it goes beyond just the intermediary organizations discussed here—this rhetoric permeates the global nodes and the way the programme was run at the local level. AKF Kg and MSDSP staff repeatedly made references to the term participation. Mavluda mentioned the 'active participation of grassroots knowledge' in the educational films AKF Kg created. Alibek spoke of running 'participatory information sessions' during evaluations of the climate change adaptation project. Jyldyz, the regional manager of the Osh MSDSP office, stressed MSDSP's use of participatory mapping instruments. This rhetoric seems in place largely to conform to the interest in participatory approaches voiced by AKF in Geneva, as well as other donors. For instance, the climate change adaptation project's proposal for the Prince Sadruddin Fund for Environment stated that:

> Since women's and men's *priorities for climate change adaptation* may differ, project activities will be inclusive so adaptation measures are relevant to the full community. MSDSP KG will take specific steps to ensure that women and men *participate, contribute*, and benefit. For example, women will compose 30% or more of participants in all assessment, planning, and implementation activities.

The participatory reality of the programme was far more subtle than what is promised in the proposal. Yet the proposal was emblematic of the way that the rhetoric of participation is diffused throughout the programmes and staff of AKF Kg and MSDSP and its field branches. In this case, the proposal not only stressed local priorities, participation, and contributions but also used the rhetoric of gendered participation, which also demonstrated AKF Kg's awareness of the concerns with gender in development amongst international funders. Participation cropped up repeatedly in conversations about the climate change adaptation project: Talant insisted that the 'main [climate change adaptation] project approach is participatory' and its success rode on the interest of local people, and Laurie emphasized the importance of the participation of marginalized groups in the climate change adaptation project.

Such participatory rhetoric seems in tension with the privileging of foreign expert knowledge discussed above. Yet the two serve to balance each other—expert knowledge gives the intermediary nodes authority, while focusing on participation brings authenticity, enabling MSDSP to claim to be responding and integrating the ideas and genuine needs of the people it serves. MSDSP can respond to the critique that NGOs are unrepresentative by pointing to its participatory ideals. It also placates the participatory and local focus of the global institutions that fund AKF Kg and MSDSP's work, discussed further in Chapter 5. Participation thus becomes an ideal to aspire to and a rhetoric to unite behind. At the same time, the emphasis on local reality gave MSDSP—and through them, the Aga Khan Foundation—a claim to authentic knowledge and experience.

b. Kenya: Universities and Knowledge Commons Setting the Network Agenda

In the case of Kenya, expert and local knowledge was also simultaneously delineated and privileged. In this case-study network, spaces of academic and professional interaction—in particular conferences and universities—played a key role in this process. Such spaces function as knowledge commons—spaces where knowledge is pooled and shared (Joranson 2008) in this civil society network. Such spaces both connected nodes—particularly global nodes such as The Christensen Fund with NGO intermediaries such as Kivulini and Waso Trustland—but also privilege and spread particular types of knowledge. These spaces facilitated not only the exchange of ideas and knowledge and the creation of values but also the creation of *personal* relationships between the leading figures at each of the nodes of the network. These in turn played a key role in the way that institutional relationships unfold—and the way that both people and organizations influenced one another.

For instance, universities played a key part in the Kivulini creation narrative, according to Hussein (Kivulini's founder and then-director) and Ken (the then-executive director of The Christensen Fund)—narratives that were also echoed by the staff of Waso Trustland. Hussein and Ken were friends at Oxford in the mid-1980s. After falling out of touch, they reconnected at a conference in Europe, at a time when Ken was working for The Christensen Fund and Hussein was working for the National Museum of Kenya. It was at this conference that Ken urged Hussein to become directly involved with the communities in the north of Kenya. Although this first led Hussein to work for The Christensen Fund in East Africa, Ken urged him to start his own organization to engage directly with communities, and Kivulini was born. Thus it becomes a story of coincidences, rare access, and chance encounters building personal relationships that link together people, places, and institutions in our network. Not only Hussein and Ken but also Wolde and Hassan all mentioned this 'birthing' story, with references to the shared experience at Oxford and reconnection at an international conference. It illustrates the role that such mechanisms play in forging the links in this knowledge network, creating the kind of connections that enable certain actors, such as Ken, to influence the values and actions of others, such as Hussein, and to provide them structural support. Yet the role of formalized spaces for knowledge sharing in creating values, spreading knowledge, and influencing action is perhaps even more clearly illustrated in the case of Hassan and the work and relationships of Waso Trustland Project.

Unlike Kivulini, Waso Trustland Project was founded long before it formed a relationship with The Christensen Fund. But the pivotal moment in Hassan's narrative of how WTL shifted from its focus on land-rights advocacy towards environmental and cultural diversity was the 2005 World Conference on Ecological Restoration held in Zaragoza, Spain. Hussein brought Hassan to this conference to speak as an 'indigenous elder' on the role of indigenous knowledge in environmental restoration. Hassan credited this conference with two vital occurrences: the start of his interest in the environment and the beginning of Waso Trustland's relationship with The Christensen Fund.

This relationship began with an in-person meeting between Hassan and Ken at the conference, facilitated by Hussein. Gira, the chairman of the board of Waso Trustland, described the event as an opportunity to generate the 'interest' from which Waso Trustland's relationship with The Christensen Fund emerged. Thus the conference acted as a space where different levels of knowledge networks meet, and where the relationships on which the network is built are formed, outside of the formal mechanisms of grant applications and funding agreements. The conference was also where a seemingly bidirectional—but unequal—exchange of knowledge took place. Hassan attended the conference with the intention of sharing indigenous knowledge and perspectives, but his own knowledge expanded there; he admitted that attending the conference changed his values and actions, bringing his attention to the environmental priorities and knowledge lauded and privileged by the conference.

Hassan has also attended four of the UN Conferences on Indigenous Peoples in Geneva, and his experience there illustrates the role knowledge commons such as conferences play in spreading and creating shared framing and ideas in civil society knowledge networks. When I questioned Hassan as to *why* a rights-focused organization such as Waso Trustland was interested in indigenous knowledge, Hassan credited these conferences for making him realize the centrality of culture as 'another resource' to protect. Hassan described the first time he attended the conference in Geneva, where during a day of cultural sharing Maasai delegates from Kenya came with 'marvellous' traditional dress and performances. Hassan described how he felt 'embarrassed' that he did not have the same cultural artefacts to share, asking himself, 'What about our Borana culture?' Hassan credited this moment of shame, brought about by the exposure afforded by an international conference, with awakening his awareness of the significance of culture in the global realm, strengthened in turn by The Christensen Fund's emphasis on biocultural diversity.

Particularly startling in this story is the fact that Hassan travelled to Switzerland in order to realize the value (globally) ascribed to cultural expression. Thus international conferences act not only as an avenue for exposure to knowledge—such as seeing Maasai culture presented—but also to the value and uses ascribed to such knowledge by global (or global North) organizations. Conferences are in themselves an aspect of the global node of the network, helping to forge the interpersonal connections that then create the institutional relationships upon which the network is based while also privileging certain types of knowledge and discourse that then become an integral part of the overarching discourse of the network.

Relationships and the spaces—such as conferences and universities—where personal and institutional relationships are built and knowledge is shared are crucial in building civil society knowledge networks. These spaces are not just mediated by powerful global North institutions (such as the University of Oxford or the UN). Personal relationships between 'middlemen' such as Kivulini and Waso Trustland and the people of Beliqo are also crucial—not only does Hassan make a point of visiting Beliqo frequently to implement and aid the Community Forest Association there, but he also hosts an annual 'partner's meeting' of the grassroots communities and organizations Waso Trustland works with, and pays for the expenses of these partners to attend the meeting. The echoes the way The Christensen Fund pays for the expenses of 'middlemen' NGOs such as WTL to attend conferences and meetings in the West. At the same time, personal relationships and histories also played a major part—it was no coincidence that Kivulini's director Hussein was originally from Beliqo, and was well known and remembered there. Indeed, personality politics played a major role in the functioning of such a network—both Hussein and Hassan are 'big men' well known in Beliqo for personal characteristics as much as their role in creating the Community Forest Association.

The variety of such spaces and relationships also point to the variety and fluidity of different types of knowledge implemented in the networks, and the way that such knowledge was perceived and utilized by the nodes. As argued in the Kyrgyz case, some types of knowledge were seen as more crucial than others because they were designated either as 'expert', 'authoritative' knowledge or 'privileged', 'authentic' knowledge. This is a subtle distinction, and in the case of TCF and the Kenyan organizations, often a fluid one. In Beliqo, Hassan of Waso Trustland was a source of 'expert' knowledge, bringing not only information about ways to protect and conserve the local forest but also knowledge of state and global legal mechanisms and financial resources to do so. It was Hassan who suggested forming a Community Forest Association in the village and who continues to guide it and find it resources. Indeed, even before the forest conservation project, Hassan travelled around the villages of the district, holding workshops and spreading information on land and ecological rights.

However, as described earlier, Hassan was first invited to a conference in Europe in the role of an 'indigenous elder', and asked to speak because of his privileged access to local, indigenous knowledge and traditions. There he created authenticity through representations of local or indigenous knowledge. Yet in our conversation about this Hassan seemed to be ambivalent about being presented in this role, and gave the impression that he was more comfortable in the role of activist, bringing the authority of 'expert' knowledge to the local, rather than as indigenous elder bringing the authenticity of local knowledge to the global. His ambivalence points to the fluidity of such categories of knowledge, especially amongst intermediary actors in the networks—Hassan was able to both utilize such categories and shed them, adopting different ones on different occasions for authority or legitimacy with different nodes and different audiences.

Hussein of Kivulini, who first brought Hassan in the capacity of an indigenous elder to the conference in Spain, was himself from the village of Beliqo (and thus could be classified under the indigenous label), and old enough to be considered an elder. Yet he felt he could not (or did not want to) take the role of indigenous elder himself, be it because of his Oxford doctorate degree, his residence in Nairobi, or his job at Kenya's National Museum, and preferred to continue with the role of 'expert' and advisor to Waso Trustland. Thus these categories are not only fluid but also influenced by a myriad of factors, such as personal histories, institutional relationships, context, and the particular nodes to which the knowledge is transmitted.

The fluidity of such categories is precisely where the model of civil society knowledge networks diverges from the idea of epistemic communities, with their presumption of recognized expertise and 'an authoritative claim to policy-relevant knowledge' (Haas 1990, 1992: 3). What is missing in the epistemic community model is a critique of what (and who) constitutes an expert. As the case-study networks demonstrate, 'communities of knowledge' are peopled not only by recognized professionals (a culturally biased and elitist vision of epistemic authority) but also by any agents involved in generating a cohesive transnational discourse around a particular issue (Toke 1999). In our case study, this was Hassan while speaking in Spain, but also Kivulini when helping Waso Trustland shape a new programme. All transmit expert knowledge not only to policymakers outside the network but also to each other, to the knowledge network as a whole, and to those living in Beliqo.

III. In Conclusion: Epistemic Independence, Epistemic Conformity

The structure of the network in Kenya was in many ways different than in the Kyrgyz Republic—which makes the similarities in the ways such networks of development organizations functioned all the more telling. The intermediary organizations in Kenya were far less inter-dependent, and their ties were far less organizational—and instead were ties of discourse and ideas. Nevertheless, despite being knit together by epistemic rather than structural ties, the organizations in Kenya were motivated by disparate aims and goals, ranging from land rights to cultural conservation. The fact that the organizations were able to align behind the discourse of biocultural diversity points not only to the broad flexibility of the idea but also to the ways in which becoming part of a civil society network can shift and turn the ideology and practice of the organizations involved, as is the case with Waso Trustland. Yet WTL held on to its ideals and politics, while still aligning with and adopting concepts from the network as a whole—particularly ideas about the value of both environment and culture.

In a similar fashion, each of the development organizations working on the climate change adaptation project in the Kyrgyz Republic not only played a different part in the network but also understood and connected with the others in different ways, ranging from formalized institutional relationships to personality politics. Each participated in climate change adaptation for a variety of different reasons. If AKF Kg in Bishkek served as an intermediary between the global Aga Khan Network and the broader movement around climate change adaptation by acting both on *fiscally pragmatic* and *representational* aims, then MSDSP adapted AKF Kg's representational formulations to fit its own aims of fulfilling and maintaining its areas of expertise. It was helped in this by the organizational nomadism of locals working in the developing sector in the Kyrgyz Republic, which allowed them to adapt a variety of global discourses and ideas to MSDSP's concrete areas of action and expertise. Yet their relationship to each other and the programme as a whole created a network that broadly shared an understanding of climate change adaptation, as well as of the kinds of programmes that enable the transformation of knowledge into action, enabling the network to function as a whole. Each of these organizations had disparate goals and aims that were dictated by their organizational histories, entrenched ideas, and positions in the network, and these goals and aims followed the internal logic of these histories and organizational cultures. Yet despite having a variety of different aims and goals, they connected into one network that both created and transmitted ideas and transformed them into action.

The patterns that emerge from the interactions and relationships between these organizations and individuals show that these intermediaries were more than mediators—they themselves shaped the processes by which ideas and knowledge were created and spread in the networks. While the structures and power disparities in these networks mattered, and affected which ideas are privileged over others, at the same time the individual actors *in* institutions also mattered. Laurie, Pirjan, and Talant; Hussein and Hassan—these individuals also influenced the processes by which certain ideas were privileged, transformed, or ignored. Yet at the same time, institutional processes and events ranging from monitoring surveys to trainings and conferences also shaped the ways in which knowledge and ideas were created, how they were transmitted, and *who* they were transmitted to. External, non-civil society also played a role—both networks cultivated a particular understanding of (and thus relationship with) the state.

One of the most telling ways this affected knowledge production was the way typologies of knowledge were created amongst the intermediary organizations and individuals in these two networks in order to grant legitimacy to ideas and the ways in which they were implemented. While expert, usually foreign- and Western-based knowledge of consultants and development nomads denotes epistemic *authority*, this alone was not enough. The organizations in these networks also went out of their way to delineate local or indigenous knowledge. This not only connected them to the interest of both global nodes in participatory approaches and grassroots knowledge but also served to give the work and ideas of these organizations *authenticity* as reflecting local needs and interests. Yet these labels were fluid—Hassan could move from being a development expert in the villages of northern Kenya to an indigenous elder at a conference in Spain. In the same way, MSDSP or WTL might be considered 'local' organizations by the global organizations that fund them, but they themselves see the village communities to whom they pass on both funds and ideas as the true grassroots.

5

Global Movements and International Foundations

Creating Transnational Knowledge

> Global movements and discourses are the key—they are far more powerful than foundations. (Ken, executive director, The Christensen Fund)
>
> After the Soviet Union [fell apart], information became especially valuable [in Central Asia]. Access to information was hard enough to begin with, and information is power, and this mentality persists. (David, head of the Prince Sadruddin Aga Khan Fund for the Environment, Aga Khan Foundation, Geneva)

While the overarching argument of this work proposes that all the nodes in civil society knowledge networks produce and shape ideas, the global nodes have the most overt epistemic power—at least at first glance. Global development institutions such as charitable foundations or international, Western-based NGOs are the primary source of resources in these networks. As such, they are actors with the explicit power to set the development agenda of networks of development institutions they engage with. The aim of this chapter is to explore the ways in which this development agenda emerges out of the movements and epistemic communities that global development organizations both engage with and help create. However, this chapter will argue that this agenda or 'knowledge commons' also emerges out of a wider community comprising academia, intergovernmental organizations, international consultants, conferences, and other 'advisory' organizations. Such a variety of links ties the epistemic content of global development institutions to a far broader range of actors and mechanisms for knowledge creation than the network itself.

This chapter examines global movements as well as the international development organizations that create, propagate, and implement their ideas and interests. As described in Chapter 2, both The Christensen Fund and the

Civil Society Knowledge Networks. E. Fouksman, Oxford University Press. © Elizaveta Fouksman (2026).
DOI: 10.1093/9780198943723.003.0005

Aga Khan Foundation participated in and adopted ideas from environmental movements, though they had contrasting approaches and philosophies. The Christensen Fund both supported the cluster of movements that Martínez-Alier calls 'The Environmentalism of the Poor' and had some affiliations with what he terms 'The Cult of Wilderness'. In contrast, the Aga Khan Foundation's environmental and natural resource management programming sat squarely in what Martínez-Alier terms 'The Gospel of Geo-Efficiency'. This chapter uses these affiliations to examine the relationship between global movements and the institutions that support and shape them, using The Christensen Fund as an example of the way global civil society institutions can foster and create global movements (in this case, biocultural diversity) and the Aga Khan Foundation as an example of the way that such institutions can 'plug into' and adopt established global movements (in particular, climate change adaptation).

While the focus of this work is on ideas around the relationship between natural resource use and development, it is impossible to ignore the many other global development discourses and practices these two foundations adopt and propagate: these ideas include participation, gender equity, civic engagement, indigenous knowledge, and good governance. Indeed, this chapter examines how global foundations present themselves and how they are understood by others by looking closely at the development rhetoric that they adopt and insist upon: impact, accountability, sustainability, and participation. Much of this rhetoric is linked to the ways in which these foundations understand, speak about, and forge relationships with the local as well as with the intermediary organizations they fund.

Both the Aga Khan Foundation and The Christensen Fund are embedded in a mesh of other global development actors. I argue that such transnational development institutions forge global epistemic communities not only by using funding to create connections to and from other global institutions (as demonstrated by the Aga Khan Foundation) but also by cultivating relationships with academia and with intergovernmental institutions, particularly through the use of conferences, workshops, and university networks. At the same time, both foundations attempt to build authenticity and legitimacy by trying to forge connections to the grassroots—or at least to NGO intermediaries—through field visits, workshops, trainings, and (in the case of TCF) festivals. Intimately tied to the idea of legitimacy and authenticity is power. Indeed, power is a recurring theme throughout this chapter, which argues that while the global nodes of each of the case-study networks exercised overt power over the epistemic content, discourse, and actions of the network as a whole, they were also dependent on the other nodes for knowledge and through it, legitimacy. This legitimacy was necessary both for relationship-building with other organizations in the development sphere and for 'personal physiological motivations' such as self-respect, internal consistency, and purpose (Cleaver 2001: 48). As such, TCF and AKF acted both as epistemic gatekeepers, picking and choosing some norms and ideas over others, and as idea promoters, trying to promote their vision of development to other global actors and institutions. Yet in their dependency on the local for epistemic authenticity, they were less all-powerful then might initially appear. They might have had the resources, but they also had to constantly justify, both to themselves and others, whether they are allocating them legitimately and in a way that reflects local concerns.

I. Global Development Institutions and Global Movements: Creation or Adoption

a. The Christensen Fund

i. Creating and Connecting the Biocultural Diversity Movement

The Christensen Fund makes for a particularly useful study of the way global development institutions create and take part in transnational movements and epistemic communities because of its overt interest in building a transitional movement around biocultural diversity. While the Fund has now moved away from biocultural diversity towards more straightforward engagement with supporting indigenous peoples' movements, at the time of this research in the 2010s, it had an explicit 'Global Program', which funded 'international efforts to build global understanding of [biocultural diversity] issues,' and whose goal was to 'catalyze a shift in the understanding of the interdependence of biological and cultural diversity, and the importance of local stewards and Indigenous Peoples in the maintenance of this diversity' (The Christensen Fund 2014b). The aim of TCF on the global stage was to spread ideas and shift understandings in order to promote the concepts of biocultural diversity into the global mainstream development and environmental discourse. This included both 'legal and policy frameworks' that promote biocultural diversity and 'raising public awareness' (The Christensen Fund 2010). Ken, the executive director of TCF, emphasized that global movements and discourse were key for enacting change—and were far 'more powerful than foundations'. An important part of the Fund's work is giving biocultural diversity 'special attention in terms of knowledge building'. In our conversations, Ken argued that discourse must come before action, that biocultural ideas first had to be developed and then broadened and applied. In other words, TCF acknowledged that biocultural diversity was not only the main aim of the projects they support, but also a paradigm that they hope to spread.

Indeed, Ken described TCF both as one of the first and few foundations to push the ideas of biocultural diversity in global forums such as the UN and academic communities, but also as having largely succeeded in doing so. He emphasized the impact of TCF in forging and giving voice to biocultural ideas—in his words, the absence of other funding has meant that TCF has a huge imprint as the main funder and organization behind biocultural diversity. Yet the staff at TCF were careful to portray biocultural diversity as an established and accepted global paradigm beyond The Christensen Fund: Ken told me that 'there are many biocultural diversity movements', all with their own different dynamics and languages, and TCF was not interested in managing this or 'in "branding" biocultural diversity *as* TCF'. Both Ken and Wolde, the programme officer for TCF's Rift Valley programme, described to me the growing acceptance of biocultural diversity amongst global development institutions and the 'global acknowledgement of local knowledge importance in environmental concerns' in both policy and scientific circles. Wolde mentioned the FAO, UNESCO, the University of Oxford, the Ford Foundation, and the International Union for Conservation of Nature as some of the organizations that were giving biocultural diversity 'more currency'. Indeed, an important part of the way that TCF functioned as a *global* node was that it understood itself as part of a global movement concerned with biocultural diversity that includes organizations such as UNESCO, FAO, the Global Diversity Fund, and the Ford Foundation.

Both idea creation and spread were explicitly highlighted in TCF's rhetoric—their 'Mission Explication' document stated:

> We seek not only to *co-create knowledge but to get it out from our organization into wider society*, deploying media and engaging in the professional associations and *networks of philanthropy*, and of the indigenous, environmental and arts communities.
>
> **(*Understanding Christensen's Mission*, 2010, my emphasis)**

Networks and knowledge creation are overtly acknowledged in this statement. Within these wider global networks, TCF played the role of what a number of international relations and international law theorists term 'norm entrepreneur' (Finnemore & Sikkink 1998; Carpenter 2007a, 2007b; Carpenter 2010), 'meaning managers' or 'meaning architects' (Lessig 1995), and 'transnational moral entrepreneurs' (Nadelmann 1990; Price 2003). These are agents that first construct problems into issues that warrant international attention and then promote the acceptance of new transnational normative and moral standards and frameworks to address these issues. Yet if a norm is 'a standard of appropriate behaviour for actors with a given identity' (Finnemore & Sikkink 1998: 891), then what is left unexplored by this literature is the crucial constitutive part of creating a new norm—defining and promoting its ideational content. Thus such transnational meaning architects must promote not simply new moral and normative standards but a new set of knowledge and ideas that form the base for new policy or behaviours. This is exactly what The Christensen Fund aspired to do through its Global Program: promoting the idea of biocultural diversity and thus acting as an *idea* entrepreneur on the global stage.

However, TCF was able to create these successful global connections and utilize such networks in part by allowing the concept of biocultural diversity to be interpreted loosely and openly by the other institutions and movements that TCF connected with—and by adopting the language, rhetoric, and concerns of other global movements, and linking TCF's work with these concerns. These 'adopted' concerns ranged from climate change to indigenous knowledge, from conservation to resource rights. In TCF's claim to be solving bigger problems than biocultural diversity—or to be using biocultural diversity to solve other issues—TCF programming was in fact similar to the broad range of programmes adopted and adapted by the Aga Khan Foundation (discussed in more detail below). In this way, The Christensen Fund was not only a meaning architect or idea entrepreneur but also acted as a gatekeeper around what fits under the biocultural diversity umbrella. While the Fund promoted biocultural diversity to other transnational actors, it decided what organizations, individuals, and actions would receive TCF's support—and thus would be considered part of the set of ideas folded into biocultural diversity.

If TCF acted as gatekeeper, theirs was a swinging gate, opening for a wide variety of actors and interests. For instance, Ken tied TCF's work with climate change concerns by pointing out that the link between climate change and biocultural diversity was becoming increasingly acknowledged in the public policy arena. Besides climate change, both Ken and Wolde frequently linked TCF's work with broader indigenous movements. Ken linked TCF's work to 'an indigenous developmental vision', which integrated rights, environmental concerns, and culture, and was becoming both increasingly globally widespread and has penetrated down to local communities thanks to the movement of ideas and experiences. Indeed, Ken portrayed TCF's work in northern Kenya and Ethiopia as largely bringing this 'indigeneity' movement to the communities there, to displace the old modernization approach to development. To Ken, modernization was a 'contradictory way of engaging in the world' to the indigenous identity movements or a rights-based approach to development. In Ken's vision, this shift away from modernization had already happened for the Maasai-speaking peoples in Kenya's south, whose indigenous organizations have become a 'part of a global indigenous identity' that was highly engaged with 'the outside world' and with 'postmodern development discourse'. This shift was still missing in Ethiopia and Kenya's north—hence the space for TCF and its emphasis on the creation of indigenous identity.

For TCF, 'the range of options and relationships between people and nature' was vital for global wellbeing in the face of increasing ecological, economic, and political uncertainty. TCF's mission statement argued that focusing on both environmental and cultural diversity as well as the intersection of the two is a way to engage with broader global challenges. These challenges include 'change (even breakdown) in the dominant system', 'uncertainty', and instability (particularly that brought by climate change). TCF made the case that 'ways of life and landscapes' would become a valuable resource in this unstable future (TCF 2010), where 'resilience' (biological, ecological, and cultural) is needed to adapt to such uncertainty. Indeed, Wolde linked biocultural diversity to the contribution of indigenous knowledge to the world, which includes not only knowledge of biological diversity but even of alternative social and political systems. He argued that diversity is a positive force and a source of creativity, drawing the comparison to the diversity and the creativity of the San Francisco Bay Area, where TCF had its headquarters. Wolde clearly found the analogy valuable, although the reference to the Bay Area invoked a rather different, cosmopolitan, and metropolitan-based diversity that was not in the same way rooted in the indigenous local knowledge. Thus for TCF, biocultural diversity was both inherently valuable and a way to engage with broader global issues. This broader engagement in turn enabled TCF to link to other funders and intergovernmental organizations that might not be directly invested in biocultural diversity—and be more persuasive as an idea entrepreneur.

Indeed, capacity and network building were also explicit goals of the Fund, with three different justifications and aims for such networking. All three demonstrate a sophisticated understanding of power within global movements and networks. The first was tapping into new financial and physical resources beyond TCF's scope: in TCF's words, 'success requires the connected efforts of numerous institutions, including other funders far beyond

Christensen . . . [which] is so small that we are sure to fail unless we can influence the wider field of philanthropy and other resource-rich institutions'. TCF became David versus Goliath in this vision, projecting a radical new vision despite its small size. But this was also a realist, utility-maximizing position, acknowledging the power and influence of resources. Ken saw TCF as largely succeeding in this—according to him, because of their efforts biocultural diversity was by the mid-2010s attached to big funding and a framework that was mobilizing money between the UN, universities, development agencies, and local 'radical groups'. (In hindsight, such optimism now seems a bit premature.) The second aim of such networking is creating new and syncretic knowledge by bringing 'together different kinds of science and experience across and beyond the particularities of different communities and places' (TCF 2010). This is linked to the openness and flexibility of the biocultural diversity mission, which, as argued above, enables and encourages biocultural diversity to become part of other global movements and paradigms. The third aim of TCF's explicit network building dealt overtly with power dynamics, as TCF argued that building global partnerships and networks allows 'the historically marginalized' to 'find new sympathetic partners in powerful institutions'. TCF was part of a variety of larger umbrella philanthropic organizations, and, as will be discussed more below, actively used international venues such as conferences to forge such partnerships, particularly with UN institutions and other intergovernmental bodies.

However, there was an internal contradiction within TCF's rhetoric. While the organization explicitly engaged with building and taking part in wide-ranging global movements and development efforts, TCF also portrayed itself as a radical outsider to the development mainstream. This was particularly evident in my interviews with TCF staff. Ken described TCF's work as 'questioning dominant Western narratives of wellbeing and development'. In his words, not only was TCF outside such mainstream narratives but they were also on the cutting edge or amongst the avant-garde of development actors, since TCF rejected 'one factor development' and embraces 'complexity', 'diversity', 'multi-factor systems', and 'systems thinking' in development. This was echoed with even more vehemence by Wolde, who contrasted the pastoral livelihoods and cultures that TCF supports with market capitalism. 'Their sustainability frightens the market', he said, and in his view it was the advent of market capitalism that led to food aid and dependency on global food markets.

Indeed, Wolde lambasted not only market capitalism but also mainstream development practice. In his words, 'NGOs brought the language of begging' to pastoralist communities. Wolde contrasted both market capitalism and such NGOs with The Christensen Fund, which he argued understood and worked with not only indigenous food markets but also the true, deeper needs of indigenous communities. This was a drastically different perspective from the Aga Khan Foundation, which, as will be explored below, very much saw itself as part of mainstream development and market capitalism approaches. Wolde illustrated his point through the example of a TCF visit to a community in northern Kenya. The community told TCF that what they really wanted was support for a trip to ethnically and culturally linked communities in southern Ethiopia. Wolde pointed out that this was not a physical need, but rather a spiritual and cultural need, linked to traditions, rituals, and the arts. In short, Wolde made the argument that indigenous communities had what Inglehart (1981) would term post-material needs, and that these are in fact more significant than the material needs addressed by mainstream development agents. This not only reiterates the radical outsider position of The Christensen Fund but also points to the issue of legitimacy and authenticity which recurs within TCF's rhetoric. TCF must build legitimacy not only in the eyes of other organizations, especially those addressing connecting issues such as climate change and indigeneity, but also internal legitimacy by being consistent with its self-perception as a radical outsider to mainstream development, forging a novel path to address the 'true' needs of its grantees.

ii. International Conferences: Mechanisms for Global–Local Connections

Part of The Christensen Fund's role as an idea entrepreneur was nudging other organizations and activists towards ideas around biocultural diversity, conservation, and indigenous culture. Wolde highlighted that TCF not only played a significant role in formulating and promulgating the global discourse of biocultural diversity but also actively involved the grassroots in such global engagement. TCF did so by flying indigenous elders between different countries and conferences where they can interact with such global movements—and affirm their knowledge by seeing how it is valued at such conferences. Indeed, Ken estimated that between a third and a quarter of TCF's grant-making was spent on 'global' initiatives. Ken argued that TCF has 'enabled thousands of grassroots leaders to move around the world' by funding and arranging for them to attend global—though often Northern-based or funded—conferences. Indeed, while I was in Kenya, Hussein, the director of Kivulini, travelled to Mongolia for a world food festival and to Washington, DC for a communication workshop, both in the space of a few months, and both arranged and funded by TCF. Ken openly admitted that the conferences and events TCF was concerned with were not necessarily focused on biocultural diversity, reemphasizing the above-mentioned openness and flexibility.

Despite critical or even anti-global rhetoric regarding 'globalization's erosion of diversity' (The Christensen Fund 2010), TCF simultaneously pragmatically forged partnerships between the global and Western and the local and indigenous. These advantages went beyond re-evaluation or affirmation of the worth of local cultural diversity. TCF was also concerned with the exchange of knowledge between the local and the global. Ken spoke of the ways in which attending conferences could give local activists 'language and conceptual tools' to engage with issues they are concerned with within the broader rhetoric of diversity, and Yeshi, a grant associate at TCF, spoke of international forums as showing communities 'what's possible'. Thus TCF used global forums such as conferences as venues where the local activists they fund and bring can pick up language, concepts, and ideas to enable them to rework and present their concerns in ways that would be valued—and funded—by global movements.

Of course, for TCF, exchange needed to go two ways—they saw the communities they worked with as having much to share at global conferences and with Western actors that would 'support learning and flow of ideas between different places or contribute towards the development of global knowledge and practice' (The Christensen Fund 2010). Syncretism was the ultimate goal of this exchange. As stated by TFC's Mission Explication document:

> . . . this involves creatively integrating the 'old' and the 'new' to find what works best, and deploying international instruments like World Heritage Sites and local initiatives like music festivals and locally conserved areas for wildlife and crop genetic diversity.

However, despite such syncretic aims for this knowledge exchange, TCF did acknowledge the power of global movements and Western institutions, not only in granting resources and voice but also in conferring legitimacy. Ken described the bridging of 'radical new ideas and the establishment' as a major contribution of TCF's involvement with global conferences, and that 'connection with global movements is crucial to . . . [the] sophistication of local movements'. Yet Ken was careful to delineate what TCF does and does not do, and attempted to distinguish TFC from the hegemonic tendencies of most of just Western-based 'global' movements. When speaking about bringing local actors to international conferences and events, Ken emphasized that TCF works to create meetings and promote speakers but does *not* directly promote their own ideas or initiate resolutions, though it might play a big role in getting resolution passed and enabling local actors to be heard. Although this fit neatly into the Fund's radical self-vision, these claims were in tension with TCF's role in promoting biocultural diversity as a global movement. Thus The Christensen Fund tried to navigate the fine line between control and facilitation, safeguarding their own legitimacy by emphasizing that they did not control or manipulate local actors, only empowered them.

However, the control that TCF did have in these meetings and conferences was in fact substantive, even by Ken's own admission, particularly when it came to selecting who and what gets voice at such meetings. For instance, TCF played an active role in helping groups of their grantees prepare for the UN's 2014 World Conference on Indigenous Peoples and funded travel for these groups to preparatory meetings to create agendas for the conference. Inevitably this affected the voices heard and the agenda. TCF played an even larger role at the World Parks Congress, particularly at the 2003 Congress in Durban, where TCF supported and funded the issue of indigenous control and protection of land. TCF not only selected who amongst the communities they support comes to these meetings but, in Ken's words, tried to 'curate the outcomes at the meetings'. In order to get indigenous or grassroots voices heard, TCF staff had to do more than fund attendees—they also researched and kept in touch with the sequence of global meetings, arranged the practicalities of presentations, facilitated informal introductions, and, in Ken's terms, 'broker[ed]' those interactions. In other words, 'giving voice' was not a neutral process.

For Ken, a success story was when the 2013 World Parks Congress focused on indigenous knowledge and land rights without any input from TCF. Yet even after achieving what it saw as success, the Fund still remained involved in bringing both old hands and new voices to the table. Conferences and meetings were mechanisms through which TCF facilitated the flow of people—largely from the global South to the North—and thus the flow and mingling of ideas, values, and worldviews, and the creation of legitimacy for the actors they support. Through this process TCF gave currency and voice to certain ideas, groups, and individuals. Thus the roles that The Christensen Fund adopted ranged from norm entrepreneur (in relationship to other transnational organizations) to gate-opener (when it came to providing a platform for grassroots groups and activists at various global venues), to gatekeeper (when deciding which issues and agents fit within their mandate).

iii. Building South–South Links: Festivals and Exchanges

As much as Ken emphasized TCF's role in building global and local links, he also stressed the importance of South–South connections. Ken saw this as another strategy for empowerment and legitimization of local groups: in his words, 'horizontal connections' were essential 'to overcome powerlessness in face of world players'—for instance, to fight off exploitation from resource extractive industries. TCF's role was to expand the means for such networks and connections to form by maximizing the knowledge, awareness, and information available to local actors—including of their analogues elsewhere. The *mechanisms* through which TCF was able to do so were intentionally experiential. Such knowledge was shared through arranging exchanges between different communities working on similar issues—or communities sharing historic and cultural links, such as northern Kenya and southern Ethiopia. It was also shared through music and cultural festivals—largely aimed at locals rather than tourists, though with a cross-festival exchange component—that TCF supported in several of the regions where the Fund works.

Ken spoke far more extensively and enthusiastically about festivals than conferences, perhaps in part because festivals fit more neatly into TCF's self-perception and self-promotion as being above all engaged with indigenous concerns and connections—and because these festivals also claimed to promote local and traditional cultures. For Ken, such festivals were 'axiomatic of what TCF supports'. Like the conferences discussed above, these festivals were meant to generate interactions, transform values through conversations, and in so doing increase an 'openness to transformation' while nurturing 'lateral open-ended creativeness'. Yet while nurturing creativity, syncretism and imagination, festivals were also connected to TCF's conservationist or revivalist bent: they were meant to revive indigenous languages, economies, and re-valuing of local flora and fauna.

This can be seen in the examples of the Blooming Apricot Festival in southern Kyrgyzstan and the Kyrgyz Horse Festival. TCF was intimately involved in starting and funding the former, and while the latter started without TCF involvement, TCF funded and supported its expansion and growth. According to Ken, the Apricot Festival led to a turnaround in apricot production in the region, and the Horse Festivals brought back the almost extinct Kyrgyz horse and helped create a system for its breeding and preservation. This happened through self-organized local initiatives that grew out of the festivals—not through direct TCF interventions or funding of these conservation initiatives. For Ken, this was the perfect example of the 'new energies and visions' that emerge through festivals to bring people together to solve communal problems. He also linked the results to the sustainability of local ownership—in his words, a local interest in breeding the Kyrgyz horse was far more sustainable 'than TCF itself buying and breeding horses'. This runs parallel to some of AKF's rhetoric around ownership and sustainability, analysed in more detail below, which they too saw as the path to successful long-term impact.

Such visions of local empowerment and ownership are closely linked with two effects of festivals: presence within public space and connection with local government and the state. Ken stressed that festivals got attention and thus voice in the public arena, and that publicity and attention from the press and airtime on television enabled festivals and local cultures and concerns to 'symbolically occupy public space'. This in turns led to greater confidence and legitimacy. Ken argued that it also led to positive attention from the state, particularly local government. The Blooming Apricot Festival convinced the local government to support apricot production and marketing. According to Ken, the same happened at an Australian aboriginal cultural festival TCF supported, to which they 'deliberately invited Australian elite' and were able to have 'a big impact'. Thus beyond bringing people together and reviving or conserving culture, languages, and biodiversity, the festivals legitimized local groups, gave them public voice, and linked them to partnership with local governments and markets—perhaps the very market partnerships Wolde criticized in his radical vision of TCF and the people it works with.

Festivals emphasized TCF's radically pro-local stance, even towards global events. Ken compared TCF's work with the Aga Khan Foundation's, which also invests in culture, for instance in Central Asian music, but in Ken's view focuses on bringing this music to the world stage—in contrast to TCF, which focuses on 'internal' (i.e., South–South or even in-country) exchange. However, Ken also told me that TCF works with the Aga Khan Foundation on festivals and music in the region, underscoring the pragmatic flexibility of the Fund. I attended one of the festivals—the 2012 Festival of a Thousand Stars in Arba Minch, in the south of Ethiopia. This festival epitomized the anti-international, pro-local stance voiced by Ken. There were very few tourists there—a few Israelis, some of whom had been hired to do the sound for the festival,[1] a small handful of tourists, and a delegation from The Christensen Fund. The festival had little publicity, almost none internationally, and most of the audience seemed to be local people. Indeed, it would have been almost impossible for a foreigner to find out about the festival, as there was no festival website or press release. Attendance was free,

[1] The fact that Israelis were doing the sound was a discord with the local nature of the affair—surely there were Ethiopians who could have done the sound?—and perhaps demonstrates that the festival was less of a homespun project than TCF would like to think.

and the production of the festival itself felt unpolished but exuberant in the enthusiasm of the performers and the audience, many of whom—especially children—danced to the music. The performers were troupes from southern Ethiopia and a few from northern Kenya. Indeed, I had already met one of the north Kenyan groups. Waso Trustland had introduced them to me during my fieldwork in Kenya as a woman's group rather than a cultural troupe, which demonstrates the malleability of such development institution-focused labels. All the troupes preformed in traditional dress with their own (traditional) instruments—there was no obvious attempt to appeal to a global audience or develop a fusion of genres or styles. However, the one newspaper article in the Western press about the 2013 festival hinted that the festival's local organizers hope that it will begin to draw tourists—hopes that seem divergent from TCF's approach (Fortin 2013).

The Christensen Fund thus had a strong and unifying agenda. Yet it is the malleability and varieties of its ideological commitments and levels of pragmatism that enabled many of the interactions between the different organizations, communities, and individuals in this civil society knowledge network. In the case of The Christensen Fund, these interactions were deeply linked to questions of power, norm-creation, and gatekeeping. This is similar to many of the dynamics of the global Aga Khan Foundation.

b. Aga Khan Foundation

i. Climate Change Adaptation

Unlike The Christensen Fund, the Aga Khan Foundation did not have an overt aim of pushing forward a global movement. They were adopters of environmental discourses, not creators—and reluctant adopters at that. The Aga Khan Foundation presented two inter-connected narratives about the way that climate change adaptation became an agenda for the foundation. The first was a pragmatic, resource-orientated, at times cynical one presented by David, head of the Prince Sadruddin Aga Khan Fund for the Environment (PSAKFE) at the time of research. David played a key role in both conceptualizing and guiding AKF's environment-related programmes in the 2010s, including the climate change adaptation programme in the Kyrgyz Republic. David's initial response when asked why and how AKF became interested in climate change adaptation was straightforward:

> Climate change is where the donor money has gone for both [natural resource management and disaster risk reduction]. Most things in both the environment and development world are donor driven, nothing more.

This quote demonstrates the resource-orientated stance of AFK, motivated by the fact that it is increasingly relying on external funding—although it still presented itself as an implementing foundation with an endowment dedicated to funding its own. Despite the foundation's endowment and internal grant-making, AKF was eager to have its programmes supported by external donors as well, which meant they had to align with donor interests. David emphasized the donor shift to climate change adaptation in our conversation, saying that AKF's interest started as a way to capture donor money, much 'like the "gender lens"', and that he wanted to develop AKF's work around it further 'because that's where the funding is coming from'.

Mark, the Geneva head of AKF's natural resource management (NRM) programme at the time of the research, echoed David, albeit in a less blunt and pragmatically focused fashion. Mark repeatedly told me that AFK's natural resource management programme aimed to raise rural income and standards of living—and that environmental and sustainability concerns were second to achieving economic aims. Although he was quick to acknowledge that ecological costs and concerns were an integral (though not primary) part of this aim and that climate change did affect the future livelihoods of the communities AKF works with, Mark insisted that it is not a focus of AKF as a whole. However, in Mark's words, climate change adaptation was 'a new *lens* in which there is a lot of donor money' and AKF hoped to leverage more 'big funders' such as the World Bank into its climate change adaptation programming. Such pragmatic, rather than idealistic, interests make the Aga Khan Foundation particularly attuned to global movements and changing agendas in the development sphere. Thus AKF was forced to be aware of the interests and norms of the broader development community, while The Christensen Fund in contrast used its own funds to further new interests and approaches. AKF was neither a gatekeeper nor an idea entrepreneur—rather, the foundation was one of the adopters that transformed new or marginal ideas and issues into widely accepted norms and knowledge, in a process that Finnemore and Sikkink (1998) call 'norm cascade'.

Yet despite protests to the contrary, AKF did have its own agenda within the environmental realm: natural resource management and disaster risk reduction. AKF might have had a fund that was broadly 'for the environment', but it was clear through its programming that it was part of Martínez-Alier's 'Gospel of Eco-Efficiency'(Martínez-Alier 2002), with its focus on technological and economic solutions and a view of nature as recourses to be efficiently managed. Both David and Mark repeatedly mentioned that AKF planned to mainstream climate change adaptation into its existing natural resource management and disaster risk reduction programmes (the latter is where it currently sits) rather than continuing it as a separate programme. This meant that, as David said, activities on the ground would not change; they would just have a more 'intentional' climate change adaptation lens. The decision to mainstream climate change allowed AKF to remain committed to their core interests and areas of work—agricultural and infrastructural development. Thus AKF was navigating the intellectual landscapes and epistemic communities on the global level to reposition their programmes as always part of an evolving set of norms and ideas—while still acting on the same fundamental concerns. Indeed, this continues through all levels of the network—as explored in Chapter 4, AKF Kg and MSDSP Kg follow a similar process of simultaneous intellectual rebranding and ideological continuity.

However, it would be a mistake to presume that such repositioning did not alter and shift AKF's ideas and programmes. Both Mark and David made several assertions that belied the pragmatic view that climate change adaptation programming was simply a way to 'dance to the donor tune'. In fact, both David and Mark argued that mainstreaming climate change adaptation into other programmes is the best way to approach the issue, implying that this is what anyone who wants to do adaptation should be doing:

> Climate change and adaptation is not a separate programme, but part of the development work . . . The focus is mainstreaming climate change, not treating it as a separate and distinct programme, since *it really should not be [a separate programme] in any organization* as all the work on this is embedded in other development work.

Despite David's focus on resources, he had a normative idea about how climate change adaptations should be run in all organizations. He sees AKF as contributing to knowledge in the global development community on how to best implement climate change adaptation programming. This was echoed by Mark when he complained to me that there were not enough international organizations interested in mainstreaming climate change adaptation into other projects, that donors were funding a 'confused portfolio of activities' in relationship to climate change, and that they needed a different investment model—one that would fund mainstreaming. Thus Mark too saw AKF's approach to climate change adaptation as normative, as a way of doing things that should be disseminated and adopted in the global development realm. The combination of this normative approach together with a commitment to mainstreaming means that AKF viewed ecological and environmental concerns as a *technical problem* tied intimately to livelihood and long-term economic rural development. Despite David and Mark's assertions that the climate change adaptation programme grew out of the shifting epistemic interests of a global donor community beyond AFK, they also implicitly acknowledged that it became part of the expert approach to finding (and sharing) 'technical solutions' to the problems of the global South (Li 2007).

At the same time, a contrasting narrative around the AKF's interest in climate change adaptation emerged out of the organization's written materials, both public and internal, on its environmental concerns. This narrative insisted that ecological concerns are a vital part of AKF's work, but at the same time went out of its way to justify and promote the mainstreaming approach discussed above. Indeed, in AKF's 2011 overview brochure, 'AKF and AKDN: A Continuum of Development', environmental work is listed as part of its core activities: 'In most areas where it works, the Aga Khan Foundation (AKF) integrates activities in health, education, rural development, environment and civil society' (AKF 2011). Here environment was presented as one of the core five areas AKF works on—but it, along with everything else, is 'integrated'—meaning that there was no pressure to have separated or dedicated environmental programming. This was justified in more detail in AKF's brochure 'Environment and Development' from 2006, where AKF stated its environmental position: 'The challenge of improving environmental conditions lies . . . in the penury of natural resources that often forces people to consume the few assets available to them . . . [this] require[s] integrated, multidisciplinary solutions' (Aga Khan Foundation 2006b: 2). Again, this fits neatly into a broader cluster of environmental movements that look for economic and technological solutions to ecological problems (Martínez-Alier 2002). Environment is linked to poverty, and poverty is a technical problem with solutions that are, once again, '*integrated* into broad area development projects' (Aga Khan Foundation 2006b: 2, my emphasis). In short, while AKF's published material for the public framed environmental concerns as central to the foundation, it reinforced the institutional focus on technocratic solutions to poverty that deal with the environment incidentally, as a by-product, not a focus.

The existence of a small dedicated environmental fund—PSAKFE—within the Aga Khan Foundation ensured some environmental concerns were addressed in AKF programming, particularly through 'Natural Resource Management in fragile zones' (Aga Khan Foundation 2006a: 9). In internal material, PSAKFE advocated for the relevance of climate change for both conservation agriculture and disaster risk reduction. In conversation, Mark, while repeatedly stressing that the natural resource management programme of AKF is ultimately interested in economic development and infrastructure, also returned multiple times to the programme's interest in conservation agriculture. He stressed the importance of not 'follow[ing] broken models' by automatically using mainstream methods of natural resource management. At the same time, he also reiterated the programme's commitment to these same models, saying that it is foolish to turn farmers away from fertilizers, but that one can also use alternative techniques that were both more sustainable *and* more profitable. But this, in his words, needed infrastructural investment and the involvement of larger companies and commodity traders. Even David, despite his insistence that climate change adaptation is 'dancing to the donor tune', later in our conversation told me that AKF must give 'urgency' to climate change.

Thus in both my research and in its published material AKF seemed to be internally conflicted. This conflict and tensions point to the slow process of *epistemic shift*, the gradual adoption and growing interest and commitment to a new set of ideas and concerns. The rhetorical space between AKF's assertions that environmental concerns are vital and its concurrent demurring from this very centrality and insistence that environmental concerns are encouraged by outside donors rather than internal interest is the very site of idea uptake and organizational shift—and I would make the case that the normative assertions discussed above point towards slow organization absorption of the ideas of the global epistemic community around climate change. At the same time, these contradictions illustrate Finnemore and Sikkink's (1998) argument that international organizations choose to adopt new norms and ideas *both* to maximize utility (in other words, to get what they want) and to satisfy a 'logic of appropriateness' (March & Olsen 1998: 949) which follows out of a sense of duty, responsibility, or moral obligation. The way AKF explains its involvement in climate change adaptation shows that both realist and idealist motives are concurrently operating within the organization when it comes to its interest in environmental ideas and programming.

ii. Participation

While the Aga Khan Foundation's relationship with climate change adaptation and broader ecological concerns might have been ambivalent, the organization was fully and unequivocally committed to another set of global norms and ideas: those around participatory development. Participation, local knowledge, and local needs repeatedly came up unprompted during my interviews with staff at AKF's Geneva office. Indeed, both the foundation's public and private discourse emphasized participation. Mark repeatedly referred to AKF's work as 'community based', telling me that AKF focused on what the communities want, respected community perspectives, and shifted its priorities with community priorities. Indeed, Mark characterized AKF's mission as 'working with communities to address *their* needs'—echoing the discourse of community needs-based approaches (Chambers 1983, 1986, 2004). He said the same of the natural resource management programme he oversees—its priority was to respond to people's (economic) needs, and in the case of the climate change adaptation programme, 'community is central—climate change is second'. Mark attributed this emphasis to the Aga Khan himself, who told the staff at AKF to build on community interests and to trust local knowledge and people.

Mark applied this participation rhetoric specifically to the climate change adaptation programme. In Mark's words, community participation in programme management and planning was 'done all along' and AKF did not push fads onto communities or distort community needs. Pushing fads is how one loses community support, and Mark argued that this was the danger with climate change adaptation, and the reason that it must be integrated into 'real concerns'—like pasture and water management. (This of course presumes that such management is what communities prefer to prioritize.) Indeed, Mark showed acute awareness of the weaknesses of development organizations when working with local communities—he spoke of the danger that development projects could distort people's interests and form local groups that fall apart the minute a project ends. The ideal of using pre-existing community-based organizations as a way of ensuring both participation and success was also echoed by David when he stressed that the climate change adaptation programme uses 'empowered village organizations', and that this is the AKF 'model'—along with bottom-up planning, which was a hope if not always a reality. Indeed, participation and success seemed to be synonymous in the rhetoric of AFK Geneva.

As demonstrated by the preceding chapters, this vision of participation was quite different from the way the climate change adaptation programme ran on the ground—though the ideals and the rhetoric of participation existed throughout the network. However, the entire global organization was committed to this idea of participation and participatory development, despite also being committed to finding technical solutions to problems it deemed largely economic, in contrast to TCF's anti-market capitalist and radical stance. Its promotional material stressed that the foundation gives money to 'local organizations interested in testing new solutions, in learning from experience and in being agents of lasting change' (Aga Khan Foudantion

2006b: 3). This was echoed in the foundation's annual report, which states that AKF focuses on 'inclusive, community-based development approaches, in which local organizations identify priorities and implement projects with the Foundation's assistance' (Aga Khan Foundation 2006a: 7).

iii. Global Structures and Connections: Networking, Fundraising, Conferences, and the Academy

The Aga Khan Foundation's global connections were quite different in scope from The Christensen Fund's. In part this was due to the structural difference between the two foundations discussed earlier: in addition to its own endowment, AKF actively looked for external funding. It was far more attuned to what multilateral agencies and big donors were interested in funding and thus to what was already in the epistemic mainstream in the development community. Unlike The Christensen Fund, AFK was less committed to pushing its own global agenda and creating a global epistemic community and international consensus. Yet this very financial dependence meant that AKF created relationships with other global funding agencies, ranging from the World Bank to a number of national development agencies (such as the Canadian International Development Agency) to faith-based international development agencies (such as the Interchurch Organization for Development Cooperation). In this way, AKF formed global networks of its own, contributing to global epistemic consensus. This happened not through a clear agenda but rather through the mechanisms of funding calls and funding proposals. This process was diffuse—as described in earlier chapters, AKF's country branches participated in funding calls and proposal writing, and AKF had fundraising branches in the USA, UK, and Canada to help channel these proposals and form relationships with donors. However, the Geneva office was the key player in integrating AKF into this global community, advising country branches, creating connections, and following up on funding opportunities. In Mark's words, it was the Geneva office's main function to 'stay in touch with global best practices' and to 'engage with international programmes'. It was also the Geneva office's job to spread the epistemic content of these international programmes and practices through trainings for country office staff and by bringing a few staff members from each country to a few international conferences or events every year.

Although AKF did not fund other development organizations outside of the Aga Khan network, they did see themselves as setting norms and creating ideas and communities of practice in international development. As AKF's 2006 Annual Report states:

> The Foundation is committed to sharing lessons from its field experiences through collaboration, public dissemination and policy dialogue. Models that the Foundation has promoted have been adapted and replicated by governments and international donors across a spectrum of environments and economies. (Aga Khan Foundation 2006: 8)

When I asked staff at AKF's Geneva office how this knowledge diffusion happens, the answers focused on the personality of His Highness the Aga Khan (at the time the Aga Khan IV, succeeded in 2025 by his son Aga Khan V). According to Mark, networking and global thinking happened largely through personality politics and the Aga Khan's personal networks—for instance, in fostering relationships with other individuals that have large global foundations, such as Bill Gates or then-Prince Charles. But the foundation was also institutionally engaged with global epistemic communities through technical global workshops and networks, for instance by participating in the Global Innovation for Agriculture Forum and Conservation Agriculture global meetings.

Despite not being interested in propagating a particular perspective or agenda in the same way as The Christensen Fund, AKF is connected to academia and the academy in ways that sound quite similar to TCF. Both Mark and David spoke to me of an academic at Cornell University whose work on conservation agriculture has influenced AKF. Notably, both mentioned that this professor is Ismaili, and thus part of AKF's consciously forged ties to the Ismaili community, which parallels the highly personal networks that TCF forges to the academy. Both David and Mark also emphasized the role of the nascent University of Central Asia in providing knowledge and research for the Aga Khan Foundation, particularly around climate change and adaptation. David saw the University of Central Asia as a source of both 'scientific' and 'community' knowledge, by collecting both hard data (for instance, from weather stations) and community observations, as well as playing a role in spreading this knowledge through programmes in local schools—a teaching role that was seen as part of the climate change adaptation programme's mandate.

Thus academia played a role in providing both information and services to AKF. While UCA could be seen as a special case, since it was set up under the purview of the Aga Kahn in part specifically for this purpose, Mark provided another fascinating (and unprompted) example: Faisal Devji, a historian now at Oxford who wrote critically about the role of the Aga Khan Development Network and its effect on civil society and local politics during the 2012 political crisis in Khorog, Tajikistan (Devji 2012a, 2012b).[2] Mark believed that Devji's criticism of AKF's work and its effect of crowding out local institutions and depoliticizing development actually changed the organization—in his view, AKF responded to the critique and began to strive to be more pluralistic and less politically involved, create arm's-length institutions, and support competing civil society organizations, urban projects, and political dissent. Certain academics are thus part of the global epistemic community that influences the rhetoric and ideological content of the foundations. However, it is important to note that Devji is also Ismaili—he has been called 'the world's most prominent Ismaili intellectual' (Kucera 2013) and at one point headed the Aga Khan-funded Institute of Ismaili Studies, an Ismaili-focused research centre in London. While critical, he was thus in some ways an insider to Aga Khan institutions. And once again, Ismaili networks were a connecting factor despite the foundation's insistence that they were a non-religious, non-sectarian (i.e., non-Ismaili) organization. In short, the Aga Khan Foundation was tied to global epistemic currents not only through its relationship to funders but also through conferences and academic influence. However, much of this depended on personal networks and communities, be it the connections of His Highness the Aga Khan or the inner circle of the Ismaili community.

II. Envisioning the Local: Building Relationships, Forging Authenticity

a. The Christensen Fund

Despite having an explicitly global programming component and acknowledging the importance and the power of forging and nurturing international connections, The Christensen Fund's rhetoric focused on the local level—in Ken's words, 'most of what TCF does is enabling local work'. The Fund's publicity material and its staff both spoke extensively to the relationship between local groups and activists and TCF. Three main themes run through this material: the tension between local autonomy and the Fund's direction and

[2] Tensions have long existed between this ethnically distinct part of Tajikistan (the Pamirs) and the central government (particularly during Tajikistan's civil war in the 1990s). After a high-ranking Tajik military commander was killed near Khorog in July 2012, the government carried out a military operation against the town, making clear that autonomy would not be tolerated. Many citizens took up arms to resist the military operation. The Aga Khan and AKF used their authority in the region to broker a ceasefire and convince city residents to stop fighting (Kucera 2013).

influence; the power relationships that inevitably form around this tension and how they are resolved and understood by TCF; and the legitimacy or authenticity of TCF's work and relationships with organizations and activists in the global South.

i. Directing or Empowering: The Tension between Autonomy and Change

Much like the Aga Khan Foundation, TCF used the broad language of participation and locally led development. Wolde told me that decisions must be made from the bottom, with community involvement and ownership of projects and project resources, and that the emphasis of TCF's work must be on inclusion rather than marginalization. Ken reiterated the point and linked it to the decentralized nature of the Fund, telling me that the programme officer for every region has their own unique strategy for funding distribution, which is 'shaped by context, by what is important to people, and what they'd like to change'. This emphasis on local needs and participation went as far as to efface and minimize the role of TCF itself in its rhetoric. In Ken's words, 'institutions are essential for mobilizing resources, but can make complications and difficulties for movements—movements, individuals and issues should be core [to our work], *not* funding institutions'. Indeed, this is tied to TCF's cultivation of a radical self-vision, particularly in comparison to other international foundations. Ken stated that in trying to be 'responsive to the goals and objectives of the leaders of [local] movements', TCF was 'fairly extreme' in its decentralized approach: not only were its programme officers located 'on the ground'—that is, in regions where they oversee funding[3]—but TCF's programmes 'involve multiple initiatives and grantees evolving in context', as opposed to the much larger initiatives of other foundations which are centralized.

Yet along with TCF's discursive emphasis on local wants and needs, the Fund did still cherry-pick those organizations and individuals that fit into its interests and mission. It did so by delineating and selecting the individuals and movements it worked with through the concept of 'stewards' or 'custodians'. This is the 'brand' of local that TCF wants to work with:

> These are the individuals, institutions and small communities whose role and passion it is to care for, embody, perform and explain knowledge, relationship, lands, species, art forms and indeed all manner of beautiful unusual biocultural things

[3] With Wolde, who lived in Oxford, as a notable exception.

> across the generations . . . Typically being a custodian is a responsibility towards something of collective benefit rather than a right over it.

Through this vision, the Fund managed to be selective in its local partners while maintaining the framing of local autonomy. The way in which TCF found and selected such movements and partners was highly personal, based on existing networks and the knowledge of its staff members, who were often well connected to the regions they work in. Ken told me that TCF worked with the grantees it knows: while the foundation did receive a few cold calls, this was rare, and instead TCF staff members knew most of the possible 'stewards' in the field and cultivated relationships with them, and then encouraged them to apply for grants. In this way, TCF cultivates the local it seeks for.

If such organizations were scarce on the ground, TCF created them. Ken maintained that organizations interested in issues connected to biocultural diversity often did not exist before TCF arrived—indeed, it is notable that the terms 'stewards' or 'custodians' pointed more to individuals than organizations or collectives. In Ken's words, TCF either shaped existing organizations to fit TCF's interest or the existence of such organizations is suggested to activists on the ground, to whom TCF then gives grants. TCF 'play[ed] an intimate role in the formation of organizations', particularly through staff networking and personal connections, and there is a high continuity in its grant-making, most of which goes to the same organizations over many years. For instance, in TCF's East Africa programme in the early 2000s there were not many organizations that TCF could support, and 'the programme officer was initially building and encouraging organizations'. As a result, the organizational landscape for TCF was now 'very different, with many well-developed organizations, networks, plans and confidence'. Once again, this feeds into the narrative of TCF exceptionalism. Ken argued that these personal relationships with grantees enable an intimate relationship that goes beyond money, where, 'unlike most foundations', TCF could help grantees with many different problems, such as board fights.

Despite the rhetoric of local agency, TCF was not afraid to reshape its grantees through selection and personal relationships and involvement in their organizational formation. The staff members at TCF were aware of this power discrepancy, particularly Jeff, director of grant-making until 2014. He spoke of the disruptive power of any development organization, particularly the disruptiveness of money, questioning whether it was possible to use development organizations without losing underlying traditional structures in local societies—for instance, displacing traditional authority, or shifting leadership from elders to youth, which for him could be 'part of an insidious modernization agenda'. However, Jeff argued that there was also a benefit to this disruption; that it could displace local power structures but also empower new structures, for instance women's groups. At the same time, Jeff was the only staff member at any of the organizations in this case study that acknowledged the ability and agency of local groups to co-opt the opportunities afforded by development institutions. This too had a downside—Jeff acknowledged TCF's complicity in supporting the tendency for communities to become 'NGOized' in order to tempt funders. Yet it built on what Ken termed the ability of foundations to 'attract attention and legitimacy to organizations and movements through money' and 'level the playing field between locals and globalizing forces'.

In short, TCF saw itself affecting its grantees not only via selection or organizational creation but also through new knowledge, including knowledge about how to participate and co-opt the world of development institutions. Ken made this explicit: in his words, the relationships TCF nurtures with grassroots groups have a 'communication and learning component' that is meant not to 'overwhelm grantees with a rigid framework' but does explicitly 'tie back to TCF strategy—and hopefully enables more change within the timeframe of the budget of a project'. TCF is thus able to influence local agenda as a project develops. In the case of Waso Trustland Project, Ken acknowledged that the organization was originally 'focused on rights discourse' and that TCF did not support this, and instead supported the organization to shift to 'indigenous counter-narratives' around the intersection of 'conservation, development and culture'. Not only did TCF acknowledge bringing ideas to its grantees about the Fund's own interests and areas of focus, but TCF is also not afraid to get involved in the implementation of the projects it funds, for instance by 'bringing its knowledge to crucial aspects [of the projects], and connections to other regions with similar projects'.

However, this acknowledged influence lies in tension with the emphasis on bottom-up and grassroots imperatives discussed above. Ken stressed that TCF 'barely' introduces imperatives to the grassroots but rather presents knowledge and offers 'new horizons of what can be achieved and ways to achieve this'. Indeed, TCF's mission statement explication depicts the organization as a buttress:

> The Fund is choosing to 'buttress' these [grassroots] efforts, not just fund them—that is, we will back them, bolster them, support them and, in a *gentle solid* way,

> engage in co-creation at times, but not ourselves seeking to direct the process, just as the 'buttress' on the wall of an ancient tower or rampart serves to secure and yet not dominate the crucial wall.

The metaphor engages with this tension between local autonomy and TCF's involvement—the organization rejects 'direct[ing] the process' but acknowledges that its influence and involvement go beyond funding. I asked Ken directly if TCF changes its grantees, and his answer was 'Yes, definitely'. He termed TCF's involvement as 'thick grant-making': 'the programme officer influences projects and organizations through dialogue, [he or she] probes, asks questions, pushes, brings information'. Yet such involvement remains in fine balance with TCF's protests that the Fund does not impinge on local autonomy. Yeshi, the grant associate at TCF who works under Wolde, told me that Wolde might push or encourage communities, but tries not to impose—in her words, he 'just gives voice to what they want to do'. Wolde echoed this when he flatly told me that 'we're not telling them [i.e., the grantees] what to do'—that TCF's goal is to work with the approaches in indigenous cultures to biodiversity, and thus TCF purposely does not implement or operate any projects to this end, so that, in Wolde's words, these are 'not *our* projects'.

Ken expressed this balance by insisting that 'TCF doesn't or barely introduces new ideas to locals of what they want to do'—in his framing, TCF focused on introducing knowledge of 'new horizons of what *can* be achieved and ways to achieve it'. Thus 'communities decide what's important'—though Ken did admit that TCF often formulated this into arguments on an intellectual level, despite its reluctance to speak for indigenous groups. In short, while influence and knowledge might come from TCF, the Fund's rhetoric insists that autonomy and ownership remain with the local. Indeed, not being an operating or implementing foundation (unlike the Aga Khan Foundation) seemed a point of pride with Ken, even on pragmatic grounds. He argued that operating foundations such as AKF operate in a 'closed circle'—they themselves 'decide what's important, how to solve it, try to solve it themselves, and then evaluate'. Ken claimed that this is inefficient, costs a lot more, and bypasses critical feedback. He depicted TCF as the opposite of a closed loop—by focusing on building capacity, it outsources the task of both finding and fixing problems. Thus fundamentally TCF saw itself as promoting grassroots inputs into the biocultural diversity movements—picking up ideas and giving them voice and support. This did not fully counterbalance the power inequalities within the network: the global wielded resources and voice, and from this privileged position it controlled, filtered, and reformulated knowledge flows. Yet in spite of this, knowledge was constituted and flows throughout the network, in both directions. Indeed, TCF originally funded international organizations, but in Ken's words, 'conservation is so politicized, that outsiders couldn't make a change' and locals are needed to do so. Yet while TCF saw its role in 'pass[ing] resources and power to grantees and partners by making grants' (TCF 2010), nodding to the link between power and resources, the organization is somewhat more reluctant to admit the power it holds to fundamentally sway and influence the local.

ii. Forging Connections and Cultivating Legitimacy: Intermediaries and Mission Drift

TCF used two practical mechanisms to create connections with the grassroots stewards it hopes to empower and support. The first was a philosophical pragmatism or openness within the biocultural diversity concept, mirrored by the Aga Khan Foundation's own openness in interpreting climate change adaptation and participation. Just as TCF connected to global movements concerned with issues ranging from climate change to indigenous rights, so they are able to use a flexible and open interpretation of biocultural diversity to forge connections with grassroots activists and organizations with a range of concerns. This openness was used in part to justify the influence discussed above that TCF exerts over its grantees—Wolde told me that while TCF might nudge the thematic focus of its grantees towards issues around biocultural diversity or conservation, TCF's own approach was flexible and open, and not 'a single thread'. And Ken mentioned that not all of TCF's grantees fall neatly within the biocultural diversity category—some might focus on conservation alone. Indeed, Ken described TCF as being somewhere in the middle between openness and specificity: while TCF has strategies it tries to follow in its grant-making, it is simultaneously open and flexible, allowing 'lots of ragged edges and holes' in its strategies.

The way that TCF negotiated this openness is illustrated in Ken's response when I asked him if Waso Trustland's shift to conservation issues from land rights (discussed more in Chapter 4) was a case of materially motivated mission drift. Ken replied that mission drift *did* occur, but at the same time 'community partners' had their own ideas and a holistic approach which included conservation, and that both of these led WTL to consider a broadening of rights discourse, which 'clicked into place' under these circumstances. This echoes Nina Hall's argument around the agency of individuals (in the case of Hall's work, individual bureaucrats in international organizations) in mission expansion by linking current areas of focus to new issues (Hall

2016). Ken also referenced Hussein's role in galvanizing a more 'culturally and environmentally grounded approach' to many of the concerns in the Kenyan north. Indeed, Ken portrayed the shift of Waso Trustland from rights to environmental and cultural concerns as part of a larger development trend in the region: in his words, 'a more culturally and environmentally grounded approach seems to really work . . . [as an] alternative of standard development model that did not' and thus this new approach 'captured intellectual energy'. This simultaneously reemphasized TCF's exceptionalism (as opposed to standard development models) and its involvement in broader trends and movements. At the same time, Ken's response shows that he was aware of TCF's power to set the concerns of such a network as a whole.

Such pragmatic flexibility allows Waso Trustland to remain a land-rights NGO while engaging with TCF and ideas of biocultural diversity. Similarly, as discussed earlier in the book, many residents of Beliqo were concerned less with preserving local traditions and biodiversity and more with the livelihood impact of the forest conservation project that TCF funds there. While this contradicts some of Wolde's claims around the centrality of 'post-material' needs such as cultural exchange, it does not in fact go entirely against the grain of TCF discourse. In describing their East Africa programme, TCF stated that it backs communities' 'efforts to *sustain and adapt their own livelihoods* and environmental management systems to advance their food sovereignty, resilience and sustainability by building upon their cultures and local knowledge'. This fits closely within an 'environmentalism of the poor' framework (Martínez-Alier's 2002), with its concerns with securing livelihood while taking pride in indigenous sustainability and biodiversity. TCF's agro-ecology and pastoral livelihood programmes aimed to 'strengthen', 'diversify', and 'enhance' livelihoods through approaches ranging from agro-ecosystem to eco-tourism, from natural resource management to crafts development (The Christensen Fund, 2014a). Thus TCF managed to tie biocultural concerns with interests as wide-ranging as livelihood and food sovereignty, and in fact presented culture and local knowledge as mechanisms for addressing livelihood concerns. Ken echoed these ideas when he maintained that TCF is concerned with the 'evolution of indigenous economies' and 'cash-based livelihoods that aren't destructive'. Thus the biocultural diversity concept envisioned by TCF was malleable enough to encompass material and livelihood concerns, and even claim them as part of its focus.

Indeed, Ken and Wolde argued that biocultural diversity's conceptual breadth was proof of its relevance and utility, and a defence against assertions that it is romantic conservationism, or even ethnocentric and thus divisive in its aims of identity building. Both Ken and Wolde's rhetoric about indigenous knowledge presented 'the community' in monolithic and rather static terms. Yet Ken insisted that TCF is *not* preservationist—he stated that the romantic idea of indigenous social isolation is unrealistic, and one cannot stop change or cut people off from global processes. This echoes Wolde's claim that 'creating hybrids is the underlying aim' of TCF. Yet while Wolde rejected a romantic, preservationist interpretation of biocultural diversity ideas, he simultaneously insisted on the utility of indigenous knowledge and biological and cultural diversity, arguing that 'traditional lifestyles can offer a lot to the world, for instance animal and plant varieties' and that 'when you rubbish traditions and systems, you lose that too'. In Wolde's view, 'tradition' thus *is* worth preserving, since it 'acts as reserves for us' and also gives 'us' (i.e., the global North) alternative social, political, or legal systems. In short, TCF lay in contradiction, including between encouraging preservation of 'tradition' and encouraging new 'fluidities' and syncretism. Yet it was the very fluidity and openness of the way TCF interpreted its vision of biocultural diversity that allowed it to successfully create connections with a diversity of needs, interests, and actors on the ground.

Beside 'mission' fluidity, another tool that TCF uses to connect with the grassroots was intermediary organizations and individuals who can help forge and sustain such connections for them. Such intermediary organizations were explicitly part of TCF's strategy—the Fund framed them as 'partners' and 'allies', as 'unusual scientists, scholars, artists and advocacy groups', and stated that:

> We value allies because we find that there are an amazing variety of weird and wonderful outsiders out there on the ground making a big difference. And we value allies because they are often *the only way to get resources—financial and other—into the lives of the stewards* themselves. Meanwhile *stewards also have vision and know-how that the wider world needs to hear* also, and again, where appropriate, *allies can assist* this also. (*Understanding Christensen's Mission*, 2010)

The role of such allies in a knowledge network is made explicit here—both to pass resources (including knowledge resources) to the grassroots and to bring the perspectives and ideas of the local to 'the wider world'. Ken was realistic about TCF's ability to reach the communities it wanted to work with and saw the role of intermediary organizations (such as the Kivulini Trust in Nairobi) as a 'facilitator, connector, generator; a factor of the wider movement of ideas' as well as a 'way [for TCF] of getting to small local organizations . . . and deploying global resources'. However, in its published material, TCF claimed that it focuses on 'THEIR alliances' (TCF 2010); that is, on partnerships that locals have chosen. This vision belies the reality of picking out regional activists and co-starting organizations with them (such as Kivulini) described above. Like AKF, TCF's rhetoric of local control did not square with the practical barriers of reaching and working with local communities. As Yeshi noted, TCF tried to avoid 're-granting' (giving funds to intermediary organizations who them pass them on to grassroots projects), but this was difficult in practice as TCF 'needs the capacity [of these intermediaries] to follow up with little organizations'.

However, this is not to say that knowledge and power flowed in one direction. TCF's assertions that intermediaries bring to light grassroots concerns was tied to TCF's quest for legitimacy and authenticity. TCF needed worthy organizations and projects to apply for grants, and needed knowledge about what is happening on the ground. Only with this knowledge—with reports, photographs, and 'results'—does TCF gain authenticity and legitimacy it needs to speak for and to such concerns, to act as an advocate for indigenous perspectives on the global stage, supported by claims of closeness, participation, access, and knowledge of communities' needs and perspectives. As Ebrahim (2003) points out, donors need NGOs for information that legitimizes their existence and their funding decisions.

iii. Authenticity, Legitimacy, and Power: Staff Insiders and TCF Visits

'Partners' and 'allies' are not the only mechanism through which TCF attempted to forge close connections with the grassroots. When I asked Ken about the gap between the foundation and actors on the ground, he went out of his way to depict how TCF attempted to forge closer links with the grassroots by employing staff that themselves could be considered part of the movements and peoples TCF attempts to help. He made the case that programme staff members were 'tangled up in the movements they fund' and thus are ultimately 'insiders' and participants. This included both the staff members (three programme officers and two support staff) based in TCF's programmatic regions outside of the Bay Area and those, including Ken, based in the San Francisco office. Ken seemed to be presenting TCF staff almost in an intermediary role, a position they are able to take up because they claim to belong to the grassroots. These claims seem somewhat tenuous, however, considering that the majority of TCF staff had been educated in Europe or North America and reside there as well—for instance, though Yeshi is from Ethiopia, she has a Master's degree from the Institute of Social Science (ISS) in the Netherlands. Instead, these assertions emphasized TCF's desire to demonstrate its close connection to the grassroots, a connection that would authenticate the foundation's discourse privileging the local as the authentic repository of indigenous knowledge and as the crux of the foundation's work.

In a conversation two years later, Ken reiterated the point, emphasizing the wide diversity of worldviews and perspectives and the 'depth of knowledge' held by TCF staff, for instance of local languages and contexts, songs, and plants. In Ken's words, being a 'staff-rich foundation' meant that TCF was able to 'work on complex issues'. Diversity of staff was thus linked with insider knowledge and enabled the 'human relationships between staff and communities'. While Ken presented this as a positive and a strength of the organizations, this could be equally understood as the basis for personality politics and patronage networks in grant-making—as seen earlier in the chapter, TCF's funding is reliant on personal connections and involvement with local activists, as was the case with Hussein and Kivulini. Thus the diversity of staff backgrounds was used by TCF both to demonstrate their closeness to the grassroots and to justify the relational, personal nature of the way TCF chose the individuals and organizations it funds.

Besides having staff who TCF could claim were themselves 'indigenous' and were integrated into grassroots movements, TCF also built legitimacy and connections through in-person visits to the organizations and communities they fund. In my interviews with TCF staff, these visits became emblematic of TCF philosophy and self-perception. TCF aimed to neither micro-manage its grantees nor be too distant—they were 'not a subcontractor but also not totally removed'. As such, TCF tried to visit their grantee projects in each region about once a year. These visits include trips to the festivals that TCF funds. Ken was accompanied by the programme officer for the region and often a handful of other staff members. The way these visits were described was telling—Yeshi told me that the visits were central, as this was an opportunity to shape views and continue dialogue and exchange with the grassroots. However, Wolde told me that TCF staff members speak publicly only at international festivals; when visiting communities, they only listen and offer their thanks. This contradiction echoes the organization's insistence that they do not impose but rather only empower the local, while admitting that they are deeply involved with the ideas and actions that emerge out of the projects they fund (and, through intermediaries, the shape of the projects themselves). In short, TCF hovers between the desire to forge involvement with communities and projects that shape and change local ideas, knowledge, and actions, and at the same time the desire to gain legitimacy by allowing autonomy, flexibility, and openness in the ways such relationships are formed.

b. Aga Khan Foundation

i. Legitimacy and the Local

When I tried to tease out the role of the head office of AKF with its staff members in Geneva, both Mark and David's response was to stress the agency of the country offices. Indeed, the autonomy of the country offices seemed a vital part of the participation discourse discussed above, and seemed to be a point of pride for the foundation. Mark insisted that AKF programming was country driven; that 'each country has a different story'. For both Mark and David, 'the field' is where new ideas could be born and tried out, with the Geneva head office acting as a support mechanism and eventually formalizing these new ideas by bringing them for approval to the board. For David, the climate change adaptation project was an example of this autonomy and bottom-up idea generation—David credited Laurie with the impetus for its creation, with David's role in the project being to give input, explain what's fundable, and link the project to other agencies and donors. David referred to this as an example of idea generation 'on the ground', and was quick to add that country branches do not have to rely on him for funding advice; AKF Kg also looks for its own funding. However, Laurie herself was an American consultant working in the Kyrgyz Republic, and the attribution of bottom-up, grassroots knowledge formation to her demonstrates more about the autonomy of other development institutions in this network than the uptake of local ideas. Thus David's narrative positions the head offices of AKF as an epistemic filter, bringing ideas from the country office to the board (which includes the Aga Khan himself) and news of funding opportunities and broad currents of thought in the funding communities to the AKF country branches.

This vision of country office autonomy ties into the participation narrative discussed above, and like it, gives legitimacy to AKF's claims to bottom-up development, to carrying out the Aga Khan's mandate of focusing on local concerns and interests. Indeed, AKF was able to achieve this even further by setting up in-country NGOs to implement their programming. These are their Support Programmes, including the Mountain Society Development Support Programme Kyrgyzstan (MSDSP Kg). These are the organizations AKF 'operates through' (Aga Khan Foundation2006a: 20), which means that they could both function as independent NGOs and must align to AKF's oversight. This convenient duality can be seen in the 2006 Annual Report, which claimed that:

> Most Foundation grants are made to local field-based organizations. When an appropriate partner for a programme does not exist, the Foundation will create one—such as its rural development programmes. (Aga Khan Foundation 2006a: 8)

In reality, the majority of the programming was done through the Support Programmes that AKF set up, but since they carry the status of local non-profits, the foundation was able to derive legitimacy from working with 'local' and 'field-based' organizations. When asked about the relative autonomy of these operating NGOs, Mark stated that this varied greatly by country. Sometimes, such as in India, they become independent local organizations with their own local boards, while others (including MSDSP Kg) are much more closely tied to AKF. He insisted that MSDSP and its equivalent had 'lots of freedom . . . to manoeuvre', while the Geneva head office 'raises the profiles' of these organizations—while, admittedly, providing oversight of their activities. But he added that there must be room for local innovations and freedom, and that the Geneva office tries to not be heavy-handed but rather to nurture and support the imagination of local branches and implementing organizations. This narrative leaves a lot of room for knowledge and ideas to travel *up* in the network, to emerge from intermediary organizations rather than to be insisted on by the global node that controls much of the network's access to resources.

Yet the autonomy of country branches and Rural Development Support Programmes had limits. During correspondence David insisted that the AKF Kg office was simply an extension of the AKF as a whole. Mark pointed out that the strategy of the global foundation as a whole is set by the Aga Khan and the board, and that there were common threads connecting all of the country branches, which do run the same broad programmes and themes everywhere. The Geneva office had a concrete epistemic role—according to Mark, besides gathering fundraising from donor boards at the AKF offices in USA, UK and Canada, it gave technical support to the country branches (meaning that it both suggests ideas and sharpens existing ones), provided measurement systems for country programmes, and provided governance and HR for the country offices. All three of these functions guided the country branches' ideas and their implementation. While the country offices could propose new programmes and ideas, the board could also push initiatives and sector and country expansions. This epistemic closeness was maintained by country visits every few months by the staff of the Geneva office. The Geneva staff members were often on the road or involved in trainings of country office staff in the Geneva office. This vision of centralized control spoke to unity rather than autonomy, to a contrasting vision of much stronger epistemic hold over the country offices. It points to gaps between aspirations and actual processes, and ties back to the tension experienced by both AFK and TCF between the epistemic control needed to promote a particular vision of development, and the legitimacy garnered by ceding control to more locally connected organizations, as well as allowing some agenda setting by the local itself.

ii. Creating Knowledge Flows

This contrasting vision between central control and local (or at least regional) autonomy in the Aga Khan Foundation network also manifested itself in the Geneva office's own vision of AKF's role in creating and spreading knowledge. The Geneva office seemed caught between two visions of its epistemic approach. One vision was of implementing and building on local knowledge, which was both in line with AKF's rhetoric of participation and community needs and built the foundation's legitimacy to represent and aid communities in the global South. At the same time, the staff at AKF acknowledged that an essential part of the foundation's work was spreading knowledge and ideas and bringing global, often Western expertise to these communities. Thus Mark admitted that while the Aga Khan wanted AKF to build on local knowledge, this could also be too narrow a perspective for its work. He asserted that the foundation was not 'slavish' to community knowledge, that it aimed to bring to communities 'outside expertise' and 'independent channels of information', and to *develop* knowledge and reduce ignorance. Both Mark and David highlighted the process of spreading knowledge while implementing the ideals of bottom-up development as a challenge that AKF was actively struggling with. In David's words, using bottom-up planning was a hope for AKF, but the foundation relies heavily on Western knowledge. Mark told me that AKF was 'looking for new ways that knowledge and ideas are shared', and that this is a continuing struggle for AKF. He argued that filling broad knowledge gaps is a rocky and slow process with 'high costs of information transfers'. Mark argued that the foundation was doing this by involving local institutions (linking back to its participatory rhetoric), as well as by providing overhead for 'information transfer processes' which the foundation co-ordinates and facilitates. Thus the global foundation openly acknowledges its role in creation and spread of information to the local.

The climate change adaptation programme was a particularly clear example of this tension. Despite David's protestations that climate change adaptation was done for the sake of donor money, he later told me that AKF must give urgency to the conceptual aspects of climate change, and that communities were sceptical of its importance and AKF was trying to change this. David linked this epistemic goal to the broader issue of long-term planning in development, arguing this it was difficult to integrate environmental issues in development projects as most development thinking is short term. Thus for David the climate change adaptation programme had a crucial epistemic aim, and was in fact trying to challenge aspects of the underlying temporal framework of development. Mark echoed the vital role of knowledge flows in the climate change adaptation programme, telling me that it was particularly good at passing along concepts and information, and that this was working well in the Kyrgyz Republic. Indeed, Mark framed epistemic transfers as an issue of responsibility—he told me that AKF does recognize 'the responsibility to raise the [climate change] issue with the community'. Thus, for AKF, spreading knowledge and ideas, particularly around climate change, becomes an essential responsibility as well as an opportunity to challenge development conventions.

III. AKF, TCF, and the State

As we saw in the previous two chapters, knowledge of and about the state is an important facet of civil society knowledge networks in both case studies. However, the importance of this knowledge largely emerges at the intermediary and local nodes of the networks. Neither TCF nor AKF had too much to say about their relationship with or views towards the governments of the countries where they ran their programmes. What they did say broadly supported the arguments developed in more detail earlier in this work—that civil society and the state are not in stark opposition, nor is civil society taking over the functions of the state, or entirely depoliticizing people's engagement with it. When pressed, both AKF and TCF acknowledged that the state is important and that their institutions try to engage with it without alienating it. On several occasions Mark spoke of AKF's interest in working with the state and of using government institutions within AKF's development projects, in particular in bringing 'national and international organizations and national government together'. Yet he also spoke of the problems with government institutions—they 'struggle with bad management and habits' and 'lack community engagement'. At the same time, he did not want to circumvent the state entirely. When it came to the climate change adaptation project, both Mark and David stressed that the government must be brought in 'as a stakeholder'. Mark acknowledged that the state has scope that local communities do not—in his words, 'too many mini-projects [in the climate change adaptation project] do not work', and instead climate change adaptation should be 'integrated into government projects'. As such, it was the project's role to 'link local government and community to implement projects together, to build trust'. Mark admitted that building this trust is difficult. He told me that even AKF's local staff 'are cynical about government programmes' and complained about the government's 'tick-box approach'. In Mark's view, some of this cynicism was justified, as the state is often 'too poor' to build 'productive infrastructure', and it can be difficult for governments in the countries where AKF works to deliver on its promises, which means that communities have to fulfil some of its functions themselves. Thus Mark saw AKF's role as building bridges between communities and government by building trust and knowledge on both sides. Yet this relationship was decidedly ambivalent—he stressed both the limits of the state and its importance. In a parallel fashion, he explained that AKF had 'veered away from becoming a political organization' after Faisal Devji's criticism described earlier, but at the same time noted that AKDN and the Aga Khan himself had the power to 'bring international pressure to national levels', both through the organization and through personal connections in the diplomatic community.

Ken echoed Mark's sentiment towards building trust between the state and local communities. For him, this trust had to largely be built within the state—in his words, TCF 'encouraged [governments] to be less frightened of people gaining rights and autonomy'. To do this, TCF has to engage the state, but 'carefully', with an 'informed relationship' that does not become oppositional to the state. TCF's strategy to achieve this was to build the legitimacy of their grantees in the state's eyes. This could be done by 'transforming social capital'. For instance, Ken told me that many minority-ethnic groups in northern Kenya that were historically not recognized by local and national governments now are as a result of TCF and TCF's grantees' efforts 'on the ground', which enabled local organizations and empowered communities. Thus Ken saw TCF's work as potentially transforming the state both by engaging with it and by supporting grassroots empowerment (as long as it is not too confrontational). This echoes Ken's vision of the power of festivals to change the perspective of local governments. Indeed, for Ken, the long-term goal of TCF was to enable their grantees to have a leading role in their nations and communities, to 'change the mentality' of local institutions towards biological and cultural diversity, including the mentality of the state. Yet the state was worth directly aiding as well. Ken pointed out that 'governments are transforming' due to the 'penetration of socio-economic forces' such as massive energy development. TCF did not aim to stop these processes but rather to help local communities and national governments engage with these 'global processes . . . on their own terms'. Both AKF and TCF thus saw their role as *educators* of the state, as passing the knowledge necessary to guide it towards greater engagement with both local communities and broader development processes without alienating it. They acknowledged that they could operate without state acquiescence, which makes them shy away from contentious politics. Yet they did not shun the political entirely, as both want to have some engagement with the power of the state. This echoes the complicated and at times ambivalent knowledge relationships between NGOs, communities, and governments that are depicted in the preceding chapters.

V. In Conclusion: From Power to Legitimacy

A weakness of the term 'network' is that it can imply flatness and power parity between different nodes. This is very much not the case in this book, yet epistemic power is wielded in covert and over ways by all of the actors in the two case-study networks. In many ways, the global node has the most overt claims to power. Both the Aga Khan Foundation and The Christensen Fund had the advantage of leveraging almost all the financial resources in the networks, as well as having claims to expertise and authority, relationships with, and knowledge of other transnational institutions, and political power. Yet despite their position as gatekeepers or as resourceful 'norm entrepreneurs' on the global realm, and their ability to set the discursive and ideational content of each case-study network, it was not this exercise of power that seemed to interest or concern staff members at the two foundations. Instead, what was emphasized repeatedly was a search less for authority, and more for legitimacy and authenticity via the transfer of power to the local—a need to demonstrate that the foundations were responding to the real needs and desires of real people. Hence Wolde's example of the Borana community who wanted to visit southern Ethiopia (and thus demonstrate the post-material, cultural needs of such communities unaddressed by mainstream development), as well as Mark's insistence that above all the Aga Khan Foundation was responding to community interests. This search for legitimacy and authenticity goes beyond material interests in appealing to other funders and institutions—it points also to the ways that these global organizations and the actors within them are structurally bound within a set of ideas and moral motivations that they themselves help create and promulgate, be they specifically the values and key assumptions of biocultural diversity or the broader participatory development paradigm. To demonstrate this legitimacy and implement these ideas, organizations such as TCF and AKF need information and knowledge of and from the grassroots. They are thus dependent on the buy-in and ideas generated by the local they claim to be responding to—and as an access point and a stand-in for this, both organizations turn to civil society intermediaries.

6
In Conclusion
Civil Society as Knowledge Networks

This book began with a visualization of the two case-study networks. These networks of organizations, individuals, and communities link together high-rise offices in San Francisco and Geneva with villages on the northern Kenyan grasslands and the mountain valleys of the southern Kyrgyz Republic. The interconnections between them rely on interwoven institutions that affect a range of geographies, from the village scale to the transnational, pulling them into global flows and exchanges of information, knowledge, and values that encourage negotiations and hybridity (Fernando 2003). This project conceptualizes civil society as points of contact in these global flows, pulling in knowledge from above and below, shaping or reformulating its content and discourse, and then dispersing knowledge into both the global and local, and the institutions and people along the way. This shared knowledge is verbalized as discourse and transformed into values, which in turn influence practice. In essence, this project traces a case study of the way globalization is in part 'an artifact manufactured and received in the local' (Burawoy 2001: 148). Communities such as Beliqo or Saro-Kamush may have had limited access to global economic or media networks, yet were in many ways embedded in global currents via the spread of NGOs throughout the global South. This is the 'informational model of development' (Castells 2005: 16)—development as a process occurring via the diffusion of people, ideas and epistemic links.

The core inquiry of this work is then the ways in which development institutions can function as networks that create, spread, and modify ideas. This book makes the case that networks of development institutions create connections that can be as profoundly transformative as technology, media, the state, economic transformation, and the like. Resources flow through such networks, but so do ideas, knowledge, and values—and it is these epistemic flows that enable transformation. One of the reasons for their transformative potential is a matter of conscious intention: development institutions engage in a *deliberate* and systematic way; they explicitly aim to teach and to change.

Civil Society Knowledge Networks. E. Fouksman, Oxford University Press. © Elizaveta Fouksman (2026).
DOI: 10.1093/9780198943723.003.0006

Yet despite the complex dynamics of power within such networks of institutions, as well as the many external factors (such as the state) that play a role in the functioning and the effect of such networks, no one organization or individual is able to control or streamline the various goals and ideas of the agents involved in the network. These networks weave together a variety of knowledges, and are far from dominated by the discourse of their global nodes. They function through implicit categories of knowledge, including normative ideas about the authenticity of local knowledge (which is deeply linked with the rhetoric and practices of participatory development) and the authority of 'expert' knowledge. At the same time, even each node is not fully in control of the knowledge and ideas it transmits to the others. This is reflected both in the relationship of global foundations with NGO intermediaries and of these NGOs with local communities. These organizations not only deliberately strive to transfer information, expertise, values, and knowledge (for instance, by teaching through workshops), but inadvertently spread more than that—for instance, knowledge of accessing state resources, or of the values of global charities and foundations. As a result, these links and networks do not so much spread information about concepts such as climate change or deforestation (though they do also do some of this), as spread ways of understanding environmental values and framings and how they can be used to gain access to resources (be they state or non-profit resources).

I. Creating Knowledge Networks

a. Diversity and Alignment

The past three chapters have detailed the ways in which knowledge creation and influence occurred at all points along the two case-study networks. Every organization in the networks was involved in knowledge diffusion and formation, including funding organizations with global reach, national-scale NGOs, grassroots-orientated CBOs, and the local communities where the NGOs' projects take place. While all these actors shape and are shaped by knowledge flows, intermediary NGOs play a uniquely active role in facilitating these flows as their reach spans both the local and the global scale. They can move resources and discourse from the global to the local and information and ideas from the local to the global. Yet they are more than just mediators. They themselves pursue their own goals and ideas, and as such influence not only the grassroots but also the global. This was demonstrated most clearly by Waso Trustland, which, despite pressure and financial incentives, continued to be a land-rights advocacy NGO. Even when taking on projects that Kivulini and The Christensen Fund understood to be related to ecology and cultural diversity, Waso Trustland insistently placed these same projects in a framework of rights, access, and ownership. While Waso Trustland wrote about preserving cultural heritage in its grant application to The Christensen Fund, and even internalized such ideas (as evidenced by Hassan's discussions of the importance of indigenous knowledge and cultural diversity and his attendance and experience at indigenous peoples' conferences), WTL's work in Beliqo remained focused on ecological rights and ownership. WTL was able to do so by contending that ecology and culture too are resources, and are simply extensions of land rights. WTL demonstrated the way civil society knowledge networks are held together by not only shared discourse and language but also the malleability and reinterpretability of concepts, including the willingness of the organizations and actors involved in the networks to allow such malleability. After all, Hussein of Kivulini spent almost as much time speaking about land rights and trustlands as about biocultural diversity, giving the impression that he had been as influenced by WTL's Hassan as Hassan had been by him.

This book has shown that it is the use of a common discourse—in the Kenyan case, the discourse of biocultural diversity and indigenous knowledge—that allows the networks to function at least temporarily as wholes, sharing not only resources but also knowledge (including ecological knowledge) that affects values and action. This shared discourse is constructed out of already held knowledge, goals, and values at every node, enabling a hybrid of ecological understandings and attitudes to emerge out of the network as a whole. Yet each node remains in many ways independent, holding on to its individual goals and perspective. In Kenya, this included Kivulini's interest in ecology as a key aspect of cultural richness and diversity, Waso Trustland's focus on claiming ownership of ecological resources, and CFA and Beliqo residents' views of ecology as central to ensuring livelihoods.

The Kyrgyz case study also demonstrates a similar ability of the network to align behind key ideas while having individual nodes reinterpret and imbibe these ideas with diverse meanings. Such individual agency is all the more striking in the Kyrgyz case, as this network was far more hierarchical, structurally integrated, and disciplined than in the Kenyan case. After all, AKF created AKF Kg and MSDSP Kg rather than connecting largely independent organizations as in Kenya. Nevertheless, both AKF Kg and MSDSP had distinct roles and epistemic contributions to make to the network. They pursued a mix of idealistic and pragmatic interests, and as such their understanding of the climate change adaptation project ranged from resource mobilization to education and local involvement to infrastructure building. While a large swathe of the discourse and ideas of these organizations were, as argued by David Mosse (2005, 2006), representational and focused on building relationships, others reflected the inner values, interests, and knowledge of the institutions and actors involved. Indeed, it was not only organizations but also actors and individual personalities that played a large role in both networks. Hassan and Hussein, Laurie and Talant were not just institutional pawns. While they were institutionally constrained and influenced, they were actors in their own right, pursuing a mix of pragmatic and idealistic goals, influenced by their personal understandings, ideas, and aims. The civil society knowledge networks they found themselves in gave them large scope to do so, while also influencing the values and norms they chose to adopt and pursue.

b. Sites of Connection-Building

The civil society knowledge networks in our case studies functioned in large part through the personal and institutional relationships between such agents. It is these relationships—often formed and nurtured in person—that set and spread the discursive content of the network, which in turn facilitated the creation and sharing of knowledge. While every node was able, within constraints, to pursue its own aims and generate its own ideas, there were points of connection and alignment in the networks that forged epistemic cohesion. These were conferences, universities, workshops, and meetings. It is at these points of connection and knowledge transfer that many of the power dynamics within the case-study network emerged.

Spaces of academic and professional interaction play an integral role in creating connections between geographically dispersed civil society agents, as well as in creating and disseminating the knowledge and discourse within the case-study networks. These spaces function as knowledge commons where knowledge is pooled and shared (Joranson 2008). They connect nodes—particularly global nodes such as The Christensen Fund or AKF with NGO intermediaries—while also privileging and spreading particular types of knowledge. Alongside the exchange of ideas, knowledge, and values, these spaces enabled the creation of personal relationships and interpersonal trust between the key figures at each of the nodes of the network, which are vital to the way that institutional relationships unfold. In other words, formalized spaces of knowledge exchange not only enabled knowledge sharing between many of the organizations in the network but also served as sites for personal interface, which in turn led to continued interaction and knowledge sharing beyond the formalized spaces of the knowledge commons.

As the global node, TCF wielded power in the network by controlling not only the resources that enable the network to function but also access to formalized knowledge commons such as global North universities and 'international' conferences hosted by Northern institutions. By granting local agents access to these spaces, TCF acted as gatekeeper over privileged issues and discourse, as demonstrated by Hassan's experience of realizing the value of traditional culture at a conference in Europe, the same conference where he forged a personal connection with TCF. In a similar fashion, the Aga Khan Foundation in Geneva ran workshops for Kyrgyz staff, at times flying them to Geneva. These workshops forged cohesion and transferred knowledge within the network, while creating relationships of patronage and compliance.

c. Agency and Epistemic Power at the Local

Conceptualizing geographies of knowledge as networks risks having a flattening effect: it may appear as though it fails to take into account the power disparities and structural inequalities that affect both the creation and transmission of knowledge in the network. Our case-study networks are no exception: they too contain disparities of power. Yet I would argue that the network model can itself be a guide to power dynamics. Each node in the network must be understood to possess varying degrees of power relative to its neighbours. Indeed, in Foucault's words,

> Power must by analysed as something which circulates, or rather as something which only functions in the form of a *chain*. It is never localised here or there ... Power is employed and exercised through a *net-like organisation*. And not only do individuals circulate between its threads; they are always in the position of *simultaneously undergoing and exercising this power*. They are not only its inert or consenting target; they are always also the elements of its articulation. (1980: 98, my emphasis)

The chain, net, or network model demonstrates the way power resides not only in resource-rich and Northern-based 'global' nodes. Power also lies in the middlemen and local nodes too, as they are essential for constituting, participating in, and legitimizing such a network.

Despite power dynamics and resource and knowledge imbalances, each node is an agent, not subject. This includes the local nodes. While acknowledging the complexities and power inequalities within such networks, I have argued that the local communities in these networks were not simply passive recipients of global knowledge flows but themselves challenged, ignored, or shaped these flows. It is the local that legitimizes the very existence of the network as a whole, by providing essential 'authentic' knowledge about both the interests and needs and the transformations occurring in local communities (Ebrahim 2003). The knowledge and ideas created and transferred by the networks were reinterpreted by the local to fit into local needs and desires, but also into the secular and religious cosmology of these communities. Both the climate change adaptation project in Saro-Kamush and the forest conservation project in Beliqo fit into a local social logic about the relationship between nature, society, and individuals.

While the individuals and organizations in these case studies were constrained by the economic power of the global, they were free to pursue their own goals within the discursive frameworks set by the network. The local was transformed by development interventions and institutions, but often in unplanned and unexpected ways. The knowledge that remained might not be the knowledge the institutions involved set out to teach. Ideas were not simply adopted by the local—they were ignored, adapted, or transformed to suit local interests and needs, be they livelihood concerns, resource rights, or infrastructure building and upkeep. Thus while local ideas might not in fact have been transforming the global, or even reaching it, they were transforming what happened to global ideas at the local node. This is a demonstration of Ferguson's (2006) critique of the assumptions of power and hierarchy between the local and global, a critique in which he points to the global savvy and connections exhibited by grassroots organizations—much like the connections and the savvy to use them exhibited by CFA and to a lesser extent by the climate change working group and Nurmat. In both the case studies, what the local gains is less the substantive knowledge about the ecological and development issues, but more knowledge of resources that they might access from both the state and development organizations by using the discourse promulgated by the network. In Saro-Kamush, the mini-project was able to borrow equipment from local government structures, and Nurmat began to dream of applying to funds from Norwegian Aid. In Beliqo, the Community Forest Association not only got protective rights over the local forest, but also small grants from government departments. Other grassroots groups in Beliqo had little efficacy without being embedded in global networks, and seemed to be waiting for such opportunities. In both cases, these communities learned that becoming involved in civil society networks enables them to forge ties to and access resources from both Northern institutions and the state.

d. Outside the Network: Connections with the State

Indeed, creating knowledge of and connections to the state emerges as a key theme in both case studies. This was not what I had expected to find—the state does not fit neatly into civil society knowledge networks or a model of the way knowledge is created and spread through development institutions, and complicates the many critiques of the depoliticizing nature of development. It sits outside the networks, but emerged again and again as a key concern for both the intermediary and the local nodes. The contradictory nature—sometimes hostile, sometimes demanding, and sometimes reliant—of the relationship between actors within this network and the state is a theme that recured throughout the analysis of these three chapters. The state plays the role of a key paranodal agent in these networks. It rarely directly interferes or involves itself in the projects examined here, yet its laws, bureaucracy, and resources play a key role in the way the networks function. For instance, legal recognition of civil society groups give such groups legitimacy and the ability to accept funds. Without such mechanisms of state recognition, Pirjan would not have pinned his hopes on Nurmat and Zhalgiz-Alma to lead the climate change working group. Legislation about access and resource rights, such as the Kenya Forests Act, gave the Community Forest Association of Beliqo the necessary legal power to claim control over the nearby forest. And local government officials provided resources such as the excavator to the climate change adaptation working group for canal-building: a minor contribution, but a symbolic one to a community feeling sidelined and ignored by government institutions.

Much of the knowledge and ideas shared by the case study networks concerned how legal frameworks and resources of the state could be used and accessed by the local nodes. Even Waso Trustland—which, unlike MSDSP and AKF Kg, was deeply hostile to and distrustful of the state—took on this role. However, while the networks did create knowledge and relationships with the state, they were able to do so in part by insisting on a less contentious political stance. Kivulini and The Christensen Fund turned Waso Trustland away—at least in part—from campaigning for land rights towards the far less contentious issue of community forestry, even if they were themselves slightly influenced by Waso Trustland's political stance. The climate change adaptation programme was explicitly apolitical, ignoring the politically contentious concerns of local communities such as the impact of the Kumtor mine—or even the strain of overgrazing. Such politically contentious ideas countered AKF's, AKF Kg's, and MSDSP's goals of working with the state and of integrating government bodies in their projects.

At the same time, the state itself is not a passive agent in this process. In both cases state organizations and agencies seemed to welcome the opportunity to reassign some of the responsibilities to local populations and various civil society organizations. Kenya did this by creating the 2005 Kenya Forests Act, transferring primary responsibility for forests from the Kenya Forest Service to local communities. The Act included possibilities for communities to gain access to state resources while doing so, but these opportunities were not common knowledge—and it is organizations such as Waso Trustland and MSDSP that were able to bring knowledge and expertise about how to make use of these resources.

In sum, the organizations that comprise these networks not only made use of the state for resources in exchange for services rendered but also wielded considerable bargaining power through their privileged access to and knowledge of the local. Indeed, John Meyer argues for a similar understanding of the role of civil society as institutions that maintain systems of actors (for him, this is particularly the state, but here can be understood as village residents as well), and that create and stabilize these systems by embedding them through cultural content and normative material (Meyer 1999, 2010). Meyer argues that civil society serves the role of advisors to actors such as states, spreading the norms, knowledge, and expectations that influence the way that states take action, simultaneously constraining and empowering them. The civil society institutions in these two case studies certainly did so; indeed, they wielded power through the very fact that the state turned to them rather than to individual citizens to engage with issues and problems at the grassroots. Yet these institutions were themselves also actors, with their own agency and purpose. They did not simply advise, normalize, or goad the state into action but enacted their own agenda, made use of state resources in the process, and passed knowledge and information between themselves, the state, and the grassroots. Thus the interaction between development and the state results in neither simply an anti-politics machine (Ferguson 1994) or a network state (Chandhoke 2003). While the civil society knowledge networks did at times take on the role of the state and at other times promoted a depoliticizing agenda, they also created links to and knowledge about the resources and workings of the state. The relationships between local communities, NGOs, and the state thus became pluralized and heterogeneous.

e. From Global Civil Society and Transnational Advocacy Networks to Civil Society Knowledge Networks

The diversity and heterogeneity within civil society knowledge networks is precisely what is flattened by alternative conceptualizations of civil society's operations on a global scale, such as the concept of 'global civil society'. If global civil society consists of 'the mechanisms through which individuals negotiate and renegotiate social contracts or political bargains on a global level' (Kaldor 2003: 78), then this is very much what civil society knowledge networks can do as a whole. However, what is missing in the idea of a global civil society is the level of complexity and diversity that civil society knowledge networks embody, as well as the way this diversity is organized via the internal structures and dynamics of the networks. Many of the organizations in the case studies are not global themselves—it is by being connected into transnational civic networks that the Community Forest Association in Beliqo and the working group in Saro-Kamush or Waso Trustland in Isiolo and MSDSP in Osh connect to the global. In this sense, the case-study networks function in many ways like a transnational advocacy network, as 'actors working internationally on an issue . . . bound together by shared values, a common discourse and dense exchanges of information and services' (Keck & Sikkink 1999: 89). Yet as demonstrated by the case studies, the actors in civil society knowledge networks are not all working internationally, or even working on the same issue and sharing the same values (though they do learn a common discourse). Instead, it is only the network as a whole which has both international and local reach. Linking to other civil society organizations, who in turn link to other organizations with global reach, allows local concerns to receive global attention and support, and global knowledge and campaigns to influence what happens at the village level. What these case studies demonstrate is that these inter-spatial networks need not only serve to connect individuals to political bargaining on the global level—indeed, they can connect local actors to the state, or regional actors with the global (exemplified by Hassan and Hussein travelling to, learning, and speaking at international conferences). By proposing both an institutional and a network framework, this book has reworked the global civil society concept into inter-spatial civil society networks, networks that connect not only the local to the global but also the global to the local—and all the meso geographies in between.

II. Creating Knowledge Typologies

a. Expert and Local Knowledge: The Search for Authority and Authenticity

Heterogeneity is a key characteristic of civil society knowledge networks—not only heterogeneity of the organizations involved but also heterogeneity of different types of knowledge, and the way that such knowledge is perceived and utilized by the nodes of the network. The last three chapters have illustrated the way both global nodes and NGO intermediaries create typologies of knowledge in their search for legitimacy, authority, and authenticity. In particular, they have designated certain ways of knowing as either 'expert' knowledge or privileged, authentic 'local' knowledge. This distinction echoes the contrast James C. Scott (1998: 312) paints between 'techne', formal 'epistemic knowledge', and 'metis', practical knowledge that arises from the 'vernacular and local'.

In the case-study networks, expert knowledge is global in scope and typically Western in origin. It is rooted in a common language (not only English, but also the particular discourse of transnational movements) and its practitioners bear insignia of authority such as Western degrees and international experience. For instance, Laurie acted as a source of such knowledge—and of authority and legitimacy—for MSDSP and the climate change adaptation project. Project staff repeatedly referred to her authority, and emphasized her position as an 'international consultant'. The individuals and organizations that are the source of such expert knowledge constitute epistemic communities 'with recognized expertise and competence in a particular domain and an authoritative claim to policy-relevant knowledge' (Haas 1992: 3). Yet these experts do not only attempt to influence states, as is commonly asserted in the epistemic community literature, but rather act as mechanisms for translating knowledge into action, and thus influencing both collective and individual action on the transnational and local scales. Epistemic communities such as the networks described in this work thus 'create reality, but not as they wish' (Adler and Hass 1992: 381) by influencing not only states but also communities and individuals, and themselves taking on projects and actions. Expert knowledge is used to give legitimacy and authority to already existing development practice as much as to develop new knowledge and new ideas. It reproduces the epistemic and discursive consensus of transnational movements, and often incorporates academic knowledge. It has its own spaces of consensus building, such as the conferences, workshops, and trainings discussed earlier—indeed, both knowledge building and knowledge transfer are important goals of such 'experts'.

The two case-study networks also prize another form of knowledge: 'local' (also 'citizen', 'grassroots', 'indigenous', or 'traditional') knowledge. This knowledge emerges out of the incorporation of local leaders, participatory rural appraisals, and partnerships with grassroots organizations and activists. The development actors that cherish such knowledge understand it to be locally tied and spatially bound (Fernando 2003), and 'time, place and culture specific' (Ifejika Speranza et al. 2010: 296). The Christensen Fund valued people like Hassan as repositories of this 'privileged' knowledge, knowledge that is difficult for Western-based organizations to access. The people and institutions such as Hassan and WTL that provide such knowledge are as much 'advisors' and harbingers of legitimacy to development institutions as the 'experts', but rather than being part of global epistemic communities and movements, they symbolize the authentic needs and perspectives of the individuals and communities with whom organizations such as TCF and AKF hoped to engage. The case-study networks' focus on such 'knowledge from below' reflects the central role of participatory approaches to development (Chambers 1986; Chambers 2004; Hickey & Mohan 2004); yet the largely discursive nature of this focus in the case studies demonstrates a key critique of participation as being performative rather than transformative of power relations (Cooke & Kothari 2001). Beyond granting legitimacy (as does expert knowledge) to development practice, I have argued that local knowledge also grants the perception of *authenticity* to global development-focused civil society by seeming to move it out of Western-centred transnational movements and approaches to the perspectives and desires of development 'recipients'.

b. Blurring the Categories

The global and intermediary nodes of the two networks simultaneously privileged and prized both expert and local knowledge typologies, and struggled to reconcile the two. This reflects the contradictions between the privileging of local knowledge and the power of global or Northern knowledge (Beinart 2000; Beinart et al. 2009). Staff at both the Aga Khan Foundation in Geneva and The Christensen Fund reluctantly agreed to this point in the midst of their enthusiasm for bottom-up, local knowledge. Mark and David at the Aga Khan Foundation admitted that some knowledge, such as that of climate change, must be explained or transferred to the local, and even Ken acknowledged a tension in expecting local communities to know everything. At the same time, the way that these two categories of knowledge were delineated by different actors in the case studies points to their fluidity. Different organizations at different points in the network categorized the source of 'local' knowledge in divergent ways. The Christensen Fund wanted WTL staff to speak as indigenous voices at international conferences, while WTL staff members saw themselves as experts who went out into the villages of the district to support what they deem to be 'real' grassroots activism. AKF in Geneva might have referred to MSDSP Kg as their local partner NGO, with 'local' staff members, but MSDSP hired staff for their experience and authority with a variety of international development organizations and projects.

The logic behind these shifting categories emerges out of the interactions and relationships within the framework of a civil society knowledge network. Such malleability extends and reframes concept of epistemic communities. As typically conceived, the epistemic community model leaves no room for people or institutions to fill both expert and local roles, nor does it explain *why* the same person is an expert in one context, but a source of local knowledge in another. Indeed, the concept fails to interrogate why certain agents can claim authoritative expertise, as well as the value ascribed to participatory or local knowledge. Civil society knowledge networks not only make sense of these dynamics via the context and relationships of the network, but also broaden the idea of an epistemic community into 'communities of knowledge.' Such communities of knoweldge encompass a variety of geographies and agents that all take part in the creation, transmission and adaptation of shared ideas and discourse.

An essential aspect of this work has been to challenge the very spatial categories that it utilizes, to question the line between local and global; universalist and indigenous. Geertz (1992) argues against the dichotomy of local and universal, pointing out that not only is local a highly relative term, but while little is purely local, even less is entirely universal. One of the overarching themes of this work has been to examine within the case studies how the two interpenetrate, and the role that networks of civil society organizations play in helping to blur the boundaries between the two. The way these networks create typologies of knowledge is a case in point. Expert knowledge both gains legitimacy from local knowledge and local knowledge itself can be constituted by global movements, such as those which privilege traditional culture or indigenous rights. At the same time, the case studies partially vindicate the utility of the two categories. A variety of patterns emerge out of the relationships, power dynamics, and knowledge transfers between these spatial categories. These consistent relational patterns lend meaning to the terms global and local that extends beyond spatiality, that references the characteristics and abilities of institutions and individuals.

While the development project creates, relies on, and privileges both expert and local knowledge, power and knowledge remain intertwined—not only does knowledge grant power but power enables the shaping of knowledge. Western institutions are able to exercise power over Southern ones in part due to a distribution of resources and historical power, but in part because they justify and explain this very distribution by laying claim to global or universalizing discourse. Thus expert knowledge becomes global knowledge, and this global claim is bolstered and authenticated by the rhetoric of local participation and citizen knowledge. This brings us back to the Enlightenment paradigm of universal, scientific knowledge—now represented as 'expert' knowledge, which continues to play a key role in the development project, despite the apologetics of the particularism and relativism of the local. Of course, as Beinart, Brown, and Gilfoyle (2009) point out, there is utility in both, and to divorce the two would be simplistic. Perhaps one of the staff members at MSDSP Kg highlights the point—the organization had its own in-house civil engineer to plan and help build its infrastructure projects. This was a Kyrgyz man who had never left the country, was educated locally, and spoke no English. He had nothing to do with international organizations (other than getting his salary ultimately from one) and did not have to speak the language of grant-writing. His did not fit the typology of 'expert' knowledge, yet his knowledge of civil engineering was still global: there is broad transnational consensus on how to build an irrigation canal or lay a pipe.

c. Nodes in the Network Society

Networks of development-focused civil society organizations are thus a major harbinger of ideas, not just from above but also, within constraints, from below. These networks can penetrate deeper, further, and in very different ways from the technological networks described by Castells (1997, 2005). I have argued that Castells is limited in considering a global network society from a largely technological perspective. Communication and information technology certainly play a crucial role in enabling this network to function, but even more essential are networks of civil society organizations themselves that reach into the gaps ignored by Castells' technologically based networks. As Lewis and Mosse (2006) have argued, development shapes people's lives not through repression, Western hegemony (Escobar 1995), or bureaucratic or military control (Scott 1998). Instead, it does so via far subtler methods, through norms, values, and ideas within which 'people constitute their aspirations and interests' (Lewis and Mosse 2006: 3). This project has traced the ways these ideas are in themselves created and contested, both from above and from below.

The two networks in our tale spanned wide gaps of distance, culture, resources, scale, and goals. Yet they could build bridges that connected San Francisco, Nairobi, Isiolo, and Beliqo; as well as Geneva, Bishkek, Osh, and Saro-Kamush. These were bridges not simply of resources or even aims or norms: they were bridges of knowledge and ideas, of epistemic connections and intellectual influence. They create what Appadurai (1990, 1996) calls 'ideoscapes': the epistemic landscape which emerges out of flows and interconnections of ideas, terms, and concepts. These connections form in personal and institutional relationships, at spaces that serve as knowledge commons and through chains of circumstances, personal histories, and connections. The spread of knowledge through civil society networks is an uneven and complex process, exemplifying not only disparities of power and access, but also the different typologies of knowledge that are privileged or ignored depending upon the circumstance. Often the knowledge that is spread and created is not what one would expect from the stated aims of the development interventions in question, reflecting instead the interests of the actors and communities involved. Civil society knowledge networks spatially and conceptually extend Castell's network society, reaching via civil society organizations into parts of the world like Beliqo where information technology was still uncommon. Such networks also nuance the concept of global civil society, demonstrating the way organizations which are not at all global in scope can become part of institutional networks with global reach. They expand on the epistemic community literature, demonstrating the fluidity of the label of 'expert' and what can constitute such a community. In short, this book demonstrates and unravels the complex and multiple ways in which civil society organizations can create their own geography of knowledge, building bridges between local and global through the creation, contestation, and spread of ideas.

References

Abrahamsen, R., 2000. *Disciplining Democracy: Development Discourse and Good Governance in Africa*. London: Zed Books.

Adas, M., 1989. *Machines as the Measure of Men: Science, Technology and Ideologies of Western Dominance*. Ithaca, NY: Cornell University Press.

Adler, E. & Haas, P.M., 1992. Conclusion: Epistemic Communities, World Order, and the Creation of a Reflective Research Program. *International Organization*, 46(1), pp. 367–390.

Aga Khan Foundation, 2006a. *Aga Khan Foundation Annual Report 2006*.Aga Khan Foundation, 2006b. *Environment and Development*.

Aga Khan Foundation, 2011. *AKF and AKDN: A Continuum of Development*.

Agrawal, A., 1995. Dismantling the Divide between Indigenous and Scientific Knowledge. *Development and Change*, 26(3), pp. 413–439.

Agrawal, A., 2002. Indigenous Knowledge and the Politics of Classification. *International Social Science Journal*, 54(173), pp. 287–297.

Agrawal, A., 2005a. The Politics of Indigenous Knowledge. *Australian Academic & Research Libraries*, 36(2), pp. 71–81.

Agrawal, A., 2005b. *Environmentality: Technologies of Government and the Making of Subjects*. Durham, NC: Duke University Press.

Agrawal, A., Kononen, M., & Perrin, N., 2009. *The Role of Local Institutions in Adaptation to Climate Change*. Washington, DC: The World Bank.

AKF Kg, 2010. Climate Change Adaptation and Risk Reduction Project Proposal for ActAlliance and the ICCO. Unpublished document. Bishkek: AKF Kg.

Anderson, B., 2005. Globalization and Its Discontents. *Field Day Review*, 1, pp. 177–188.

Anderson, K. & Rieff, D., 2005. 'Global Civil Society': A Sceptical View. In M. Kaldor, ed. *Global Civil Society*. London: SAGE Publications, pp. 26–39.

Appadurai, A., 1990. Disjuncture and Difference in the Global Cultural Economy. *Theory, Culture & Society*, 7(2), pp. 295–310.

Appadurai, A., 1996. *Modernity at Large: Cultural Dimensions of Globalization*. Minneapolis, MN: University of Minnesota Press.

Arero, H.W., 2007. Coming to Kenya: Imagining and Perceiving a Nation among the Borana of Kenya. *Journal of Eastern African Studies*, 1(2), pp. 292–304.

Argote, L. & Miron-Spektor, E., 2011. Organizational Learning: From Experience to Knowledge. *Organization Science*, 22(5), pp. 1123–1137.

Bano, M., 2008. Dangerous Correlations: Aid's Impact on NGOs' Performance and Ability to Mobilize Members in Pakistan. *World Development*, 36(11), pp. 2297–2313.

Beinart, W., 2000. African History and Environmental History. *African Affairs*, 1492, pp. 269–302.

Beinart, W., 2003. *The Rise of Conservation in South Africa: Settlers, Livestock, and the Environment 1770–1950*. Oxford: Oxford University Press.

Beinart, W. & Brown, K., 2013. *African Local Knowledge and Livestock Health: Diseases and Treatments in South Africa*. Oxford: James Currey.

Beinart, W., Brown, K., & Gilfoyle, D., 2009. Experts and Expertise in Colonial Africa Reconsidered: Science and the Interpenetration of Knowledge. *African Affairs*, 108(432), pp. 413–433.

Berkes, F., 1999. *Sacred Ecology: Traditional Ecological Knowledge and Management Systems.* Philadelphia, PA: Taylor & Francis.

Berkes, F., 2004. Rethinking Community-Based Conservation. *Conservation Biology*, 18(3), pp. 621–630.

Berkes, F., 2007. Community-Based Conservation in a Globalized World. *Proceedings of the National Academy of Sciences of the United States of America*, 104(39), pp. 15188–15193.

Berkes, F., Colding, J., & Folke, C., 2000. Rediscovery of Traditional Ecological Knowledge as Adaptive Management. *Ecological Applications*, 10(5), pp. 1251–1262.

Blackden, C.M. & Wodon, Q., 2006. *Gender, Time Use, and Poverty in Sub-Saharan Africa.* Washington, DC: The World Bank.

Boli, J. & Thomas, G.M., 1999. INGOs and the Organization of World Culture. In J. Boli & G. M. Thomas, eds. *Constructing World Culture: International Nongovernmental Organizations since 1875.* Stanford, CA: Stanford University Press, pp. 13–49.

Bordo, M.D., Taylor, A.M., & Williamson, J.G., eds., 2003. *Globalization in Historical Perspective.* Chicago, IL: University of Chicago Press.

Boyle, J., 2003. The Second Enclosure Movement and the Construction of the Public Domain. *Law and Contemporary Problems*, 66(33), pp. 33–74.

Briggs, J., 2005. The Use of Indigenous Knowledge in Development: Problems and Challenges. *Progress in Development Studies*, 5(2), pp. 99–114.

Brown, J.S. & Duguid, P., 1991. Organizational Learning and Communities-of-Practice: Toward a Unified View of Working, Learning and Innovation. *Organization Science*, 2(1), pp. 40–57.

Brown, S. & Sriram, C. L., 2012. The Big Fish won't Fry Themselves: Criminal Accountability for Post-election Violence in Kenya. *African Affairs*, 111(443), pp. 244–260.

Burawoy, M., 2001. Manufacturing the Global. *Ethnography*, 2(2), pp. 147–159.

Burawoy, M., 2004. Public Sociologies: Contradictions, Dilemmas, and Possibilities. *Social Forces*, 82(4), pp. 1603–1618.

Buttigieg, J.A., 1995. Gramsci on Civil Society. *Boundary*, 22(3), pp. 1–32.

Buxton, C., 2011. *The Struggle for Civil Society in Central Asia: Crisis and Transformation.* Sterling, VA: Kumarian Press.

Carpenter, R.C., 2007a. Setting the Advocacy Agenda: Theorizing Issue Emergence and Nonemergence in Transnational Advocacy Networks. *International Studies Quarterly*, 51(1), pp. 99–120.

Carpenter, R.C., 2007b. Studying Issue (Non-)Adoption in Transnational Advocacy Networks. *International Organization*, 61(3), pp. 643–667.

Carpenter, R.C., 2010. Governing the Global Agenda: 'Gatekeepers' and 'Issue Adoption' in Transnational Advocacy Networks. In D. Avant, M. Finnemore, & S. K. Sell, eds. *Who Governs the Globe?* Cambridge: Cambridge University Press, pp. 202–237.

Castells, M., 1997. An Introduction to the Information Age. In G. Bridge & S. Watson, eds. *Blackwell City Reader.* Oxford: Blackwell Publishing, pp. 40–48.

Castells, M., 2005. The Network Society: From Knowledge to Policy. In M. Castells & G. Cardoso, eds. *The Network Society: From Knowledge to Policy.* Washington, DC: John Hopkins Center for Transatlantic Relations, pp. 3–21.

Castells, M. 2023. The Network Society Revisited. *American Behavioral Scientist*, 67(7), pp. 940–946.

Chambers, R., 1983. *Rural Development: Putting the Last First.* London: Longman.

Chambers, R., 1986. Putting the Last First. In P. Ekins, ed. *The Living Economy: A New Economics in the Making.* London: Routledge, pp. 305–322.

Chambers, R., 2004. *Ideas for Development: Reflecting Forwards.* IDS Working Paper 238. Brighton: Institute of Development Studies.

Chambers, R., 2005. Critical Reflections of a Development Nomad. In U. Kothari, ed. *A Radical History of Development Studies: Individuals, Institutions and Ideologies*. London: Zed Books, pp. 67–87.

Chandhoke, N., 2003. Governance and of the Pluralisation of the State: Implications for Democratic Citizenship. *Economic and Political Weekly*, 38(28), pp. 2957–2968.

Choudry, A. & Kapoor, D. 2013. *NGOization: Complicity, Contradictions and Prospects*. London: Bloomsbury Academic.

Cleaver, F., 2001. Institutions, Agency and the Limitations of Participatory Approaches to Development. In B. Cooke & U. Kothari, eds. *Participation: The New Tyranny?* New York: Zed Books, pp. 36–55.

Cocks, M., 2006. Biocultural Diversity: Moving beyond the Realm of 'Indigenous' and 'Local' People. *Human Ecology*, 34(2), pp. 185–200.

Cohn, B.S., 1990. *An Anthropologist among the Historians and Other Essays*. New Delhi: Oxford University Press.

Cohn, B.S., 1996. *Colonialism and Its Forms of Knowledge: The British in India*. Princeton, NJ: Princeton University Press.

Comaroff, J.L. & Comaroff, J., 1999. Introduction. In J. L. Comaroff & J. Comaroff, eds. *Civil Society and the Imagination in Africa: Critical Perspectives*. Chicago, IL: University of Chicago Press, pp. 1–43.

Cooke, B. & Kothari, U., 2001. The Case for Participation as Tyranny. In B. Cooke & U. Kothari, eds. *Participation: The New Tyranny?* London: Zed Books, pp. 1–15.

Cooley, A. & Ron, J., 2002. The NGO Scramble: Organizational Insecurity and the Political Economy of Transnational Action. *International Security*, 53(4), pp. 5–39.

Cowen, M. & Shenton, R., 1995a. Development Doctrine in Africa: The Case of Kenya. In M. Cowen & R. Shenton, eds. *Doctrines of Development*. New York: Routledge, pp. 294–369.

Cowen, M. & Shenton, R., 1995b. The Invention of Development. In J. Crush, ed. *Power of Development*. London: Routledge, pp. 25–41.

Crate, S.A., 2008. Gone the Bull of Winter? Grappling with the Cultural Implications of and Anthropology's Role(s) in Global Climate Change. *Current Anthropology*, 49(4), pp. 569–595.

Dahl, G., 1979. *Suffering Grass: Subsistence and Society of Waso Borana*. Stockholm: Department of Social Anthropology, University of Stockholm.

Devji, F., 2012a. Politics Dies in the Pamirs. *Current Intelligence*, 24 August.

Devji, F., 2012b. The Dictatorship of Civil Society in Tajikistan. *Current Intelligence*, 27 November.

Dicken, P., 2003. *Global Shift: Reshaping the Global Economic Map in the 21st Century*, 4th ed. New Delhi: SAGE Publications.

Dilley, R., 2010. Reflections on Knowledge Practices and the Problem of Ignorance. *Journal of the Royal Anthropological Institute*, 16(N.S.), pp. S176–S192.

Dodgson, M., 1993. Organizational Learning: A Review of Some Literatures. *Organization Studies*, 14(3), pp. 375–394.

Ebrahim, A., 2003. *NGOs and Organizational Change: Discourse, Reporting and Learning*. Cambridge: Cambridge University Press.

Eguavoen, I., 2013. Climate Change and Trajectories of Blame in Northern Ghana. *Anthropological Notebooks*, 19(1), pp. 5–24.

Escobar, A., 1995. *Encountering Development: The Making and Unmaking of the Third World*. Princeton, NJ: Princeton University Press.

Evans, P. & Stephens, J.D., 1988. Studying Development since the Sixties: The Emergence of a New Comparative Political Economy. *Theory and Society*, 17, pp. 713–745.

Evans, Jr., A.E., 2006. Civil Society in the Soviet Union? In A. B. Evans, Jr., L.A. Henry, & L.M. Sundstrom, eds. *Russian Civil Society: A Critical Assessment*. Armonk, NY: M.E. Sharpe, pp. 28–55.

Fechter, A.-M. & Hindman, H., eds., 2011. *Inside the Everyday Lives of Development Workers: The Challenges and Futures of Aidland*. Sterling, VA: Kumarian Press.

Ferguson, J., 1994. *The Anti-Politics Machine: 'Development', Depoliticization, and Bureaucratic Power in Lesotho*. Minneapolis, MN: University of Minnesota Press.

Ferguson, J., 2006. *Global Shadows: Africa in the Neoliberal World Order*. Durham, NC: Duke University Press.

Fernández-Ardèvol, M. & Ribera-Fumaz, R., 2023. The Network Society Today. *American Behavioral Scientist*, 67(7), pp. 839–846.

Fernando, J.L., 2003. NGOs and Production of Indigenous Knowledge under the Condition of Postmodernity. *The Annals of the American Academy of Political and Social Science*, 590(1), pp. 54–72.

Finnemore, M. & Sikkink, K., 1998. International Norm Dynamics and Political Change. *International Organization*, 52(4), pp. 887–917.

Fisher, W.F., 1997. Doing Good? The Politics and Antipolitics of NGO Practices. *Annual Review of Anthropology*, 26(1), pp. 439–464.

Fortin, J., 2013. Ethiopia's 'Festival of a Thousand Stars' Celebrates Diversity in the Cradle of Humanity. *International Business Times*.

Foucault, M., 1980. *Power/Knowledge: Selected Interviews and Other Writings, 1972–1977*. New York: Pantheon Books.

Fraser, N., 2020. From Redistribution to Recognition? Dilemmas of Justice in a 'Postsocialist' Age. In S. Seidman and J. C. Alexander, eds. *The New Social Theory Reader*. London: Routledge, pp. 188–196.

Gaventa, J., 2004. Towards Participatory Governance: Assessing the Transformative Possibilities. In S. Hickey & G. Mohan, eds. *Participation: From Tyranny to Transformation? Exploring New Approaches to Participation in Development*. London: Zed Books, pp. 25–41.

Gasper, D. 1996. Essentialism In and About Development Discourse. In R. Apthorpe & D. Gasper, eds. *Arguing Development Policy: Frames and Discourses*. London: Frank Cass, pp. 149–176.

Geertz, C., 1992. 'Local Knowledge' and Its Limits: Some 'Obiter Dicta'. *Yale Journal of Criticism*, 5(2), pp. 129–135.

Gramsci, A., 1970. *The Modern Prince, and Other Writings*. New York: International Publishers.

Gramsci, A., 1971. *Selections from the Prison Notebooks*. London: Lawrence and Wishart.

Grindle, M. S., 2004. Good Enough Governance: Poverty Reduction and Reform in Developing Countries. *Governance: An International Journal of Policy, Administration, and Institutions*, 17(4), pp. 525–548.

Groenfeldt, D., 2003. The Future of Indigenous Values: Cultural Relativism in the Face of Economic Development. *Futures*, 35(9), pp. 917–929.

Guha, R. & Martínez-Alier, J., 2000. *Varieties of Environmentalism: Essays North and South*. New Delhi: Oxford University Press.

Gupta, A. & Ferguson, J., 1992. Beyond 'Culture': Space, Identity, and the Politics of Difference. *Cultural Anthropology*, 7(1), pp. 6–23.

Haas, P.M., 1990. Obtaining International Environmental Protection through Epistemic Consensus. *Millennium—Journal of International Studies*, 19(3), pp. 347–363.

Haas, P.M., 1992. Introduction: Epistemic Communities and International Policy Coordination. *International Organization*, 46(1), pp. 1–35.

Habermas, J., 1989. *The Structural Transformation of the Public Sphere: An Inquiry into a Category of Bourgeois Society*. Cambridge, MA: MIT Press.

Hailey, J., 2001. Beyond the formulaic: Process and practice in South Asian NGOs. In B. Cooke & U. Kothari, eds. *Participation: The new tyranny?* London: Zed Books, pp. 88–98.

Hall, N., 2016. *Displacement, Development, and Climate Change: International organizations moving beyond their mandates*. London: Routledge.

Hall, N., 2022. *Transnational Advocacy in the Digital Era: Think Global, Act Local*. Oxford: Oxford University Press.

Harbeson, J.W., Rothchild, D., & Chazan, N., eds., 1994. *Civil Society and the State in Africa*. London: Lynne Rienner.

Hardin, G., 1968. The Tragedy of the Commons. *Science*, 162(December), pp. 1243–1248.

Held, D. & McGrew, A., 2003. The Great Globalization Debate. In D. Held & A. McGrew, eds. *The Global Transformations Reader*. Cambridge: Polity Press, pp. 1–50.

Hess, C. & Ostrom, E., 2007. Introduction: An Overview of the Knowledge Commons. In C. Hess & E. Ostrom, eds. *Understanding Knowledge as a Commons: From Theory to Practice*. Cambridge, MA: MIT Press, pp. 3–26.

Hickey, S. & Mohan, G., 2004. Towards Participation as Transformation: Critical Themes and Challenges. In S. Hickey & G. Mohan, eds. *Participation: From Tyranny to Transformation? Exploring New Approaches to Participation in Development*. London: Zed Books, pp. 3–24.

Ifejika Speranza, C., Kiteme, B., Ambenje, P., Wiesmann, U., & Makali, S. 2010. Indigenous knowledge related to climate variability and change: Insights from droughts in semi-arid areas of former Makueni District, Kenya. *Climatic Change*, 100(2), pp. 295–315.

Ikeogu, D.O., Nwokolo, C.K.C., & Chidolue, I.B., 2013. The Impact of Agriculture and Home Economics in National Development. *Journal of Educational and Social Research*, 3(5), pp. 65–72.

Ingham, B., 1993. The Meaning of Development: Interactions between 'New' and 'Old' Ideas. *World Development*, 21(11), pp. 1803–1821.

Inglehart, R., 1971. The Silent Revolution in Europe: Intergenerational Change in Post-Industrial Societies. *The American Political Science Review*, 65(4), pp. 991–1017.

Inglehart, R., 1981. Post-Materialism in an Environment of Insecurity. *The American Political Science Review*, 75(4), pp. 880–900.

Inglehart, R., 1995. Public Support for Environmental Protection: Objective Problems and Subjective Values in 43 Societies. *PS: Political Science and Politics*, 28(1), pp. 57–72.

Isack, H.A., 1986. *People of the North: Boran*. Nairobi: Evan Brothers (Kenya) Limited.

Jayal, N.G., 1997. The Governance Agenda: Making Democratic Development Dispensable. *Economic and Political Weekly*, 32(8), pp. 407–412.

Jeon, H.-K. & Yoon, S.-S., 2006. From International Linkages to Internal Divisions in China: The Political Response to Climate Change Negotiations. *Asian Survey*, 46(6), pp. 846–866.

Joachim, J., 2003. Framing Issues and Seizing Opportunities: The UN, NGOs, and Women's Rights. *International Studies Quarterly*, 47(2), pp. 247–274.

Johnson, J. A. et al., 2023. The Meso Scale as a Frontier in Interdisciplinary Modeling of Sustainability from Local to Global Scales. *Environmental Research Letters*, 18, article number 025007.

Joranson, K., 2008. Indigenous Knowledge and the Knowledge Commons. *The International Information & Library Review*, 40(1), pp. 64–72.

Josephson, P., 2007. Industrial Deserts: Industry, Science and the Destruction of Nature in the Soviet Union. *The Slavonic and East European Review*, 85(2), pp. 294–321.

Josephson, P. et al., 2013. *An Environmental History of Russia*. New York: Cambridge University Press.

Kaldor, M., 2003. *Global Civil Society: An Answer to War*. Cambridge: Polity Press.

Keane, J., 2003. *Global Civil Society?* Cambridge: Cambridge University Press.
Keck, M.E. & Sikkink, K., 1999. Transnational Advocacy Networks in International and Regional Politics. *International Social Science Journal*, 51(159), pp. 89–101.
Kivulini Heritage Trust, 2011. Kivulini Trust: About Us. www.kivulinitrust.org/index.php/who-we-are/about-us.
Klein, R.J.T. et al., 2007. Inter-Relationships between Adaptation and Mitigation. In M.L. Parry et al., eds. *Climate Change 2007: Impacts, Adaptation and Vulnerability. Contribution of Working Group II to the Fourth Assessment Report of the Intergovernmental Panel on Climate Change.* Cambridge: Cambridge University Press, pp. 745–777.
Kollmorgen, J. & Kollmorgen, W., 1973. Landscape Meteorology in the Plains Area. *Annals of the Association of American Geographers*, 63(4), pp. 424–441.
Kothari, U., 2001. Power, Knowledge and Social Control in Participatory Development. In B. Cooke & U. Kothari, eds. *Participation: The New Tyranny?* New York: Zed Books, pp. 139–152.
Kranich, N., 2007. Countering Enclosure: Reclaiming the Knowledge Commons. In C. Hess & E. Ostrom, eds. *Understanding Knowledge as a Commons: From Theory to Practice.* Cambridge, MA: The MIT Press, pp. 139–152.
Kucera, J., 2013. The Aga Khan's Tightrope Walk in Tajikistan. *Al Jazeera.*
Kumar, K., 2000. A Further Note on Civil Society. *European Journal of Sociology*, 41(1), pp. 167–180.
Kutzleb, C.R., 1971. Can Forests Bring Rain to the Plains? *Forest History*, 15(3), pp. 14–21.
Latour, B., 2005. *Reassembling the Social: An Introduction to Actor-Network-Theory.* Oxford: Oxford University Press.
Lauer, M. & Aswani, S., 2010. Indigenous Knowledge and Long-Term Ecological Change: Detection, Interpretation, and Responses to Changing Ecological Conditions in Pacific Island Communities. *Environmental Management*, 45, pp. 985–997.
Lechener, F.L. & Boli, J. eds., 2004. *The Globalization Reader.* Oxford: Blackwell Publishing.
Lessig, L., 1995. The Regulation of Social Meaning. *The University of Chicago Law Review*, 62(3), pp. 943–1045.
Lewis, D., 2002. Civil Society in African Contexts: Reflections on the Usefulness of a Concept. *Development and Change*, 33(4), pp. 569–586.
Lewis, D. & Mosse, D., 2006. Encountering Order and Disjuncture: Contemporary Anthropological Perspectives on the Organization of Development. *Oxford Development Studies*, 34(1), pp. 1–14.
Leys, C. 1996. *The Rise and Fall of Development Theory.* London: James Currey.
Li, T.M., 2007. *The Will to Improve: Governmentality, Development, and the Practice of Politics.* Durham, NC: Duke University Press.
Loh, J. & Harmon, D., 2005. A Global Index of Biocultural Diversity. *Ecological Indicators*, 5(3), pp. 231–241.
Lonsdale, J., 1989. African Pasts in Africa's Future. *Canadian Journal of African Studies*, 23(1), pp. 126–146.
MacDonald, L. 1995. NGOs and the Problematic Discourse of Participation: Cases from Costa Rica. In D.B. Moore and G.J. Schmitz, eds. *Debating Development Discourse: Institutional and Popular Perspectives.* New York: Springer, pp. 201–229.
Maffi, L., 2005. Linguistic, Cultural, and Biological Diversity. *Annual Review of Anthropology*, 34(1), pp. 599–617.
Mahmood, S., 2005. *Politics of Piety: The Islamic Revival and the Feminist Subject.* Princeton, NJ: Princeton University Press.
Manby, B., 2009. *Struggles for Citizenship in Africa.* London: Zed Books.

March, J.G. & Olsen, J.P., 1998. The Institutional Dynamics of International Political Orders. *International Organization*, 52(4), pp. 943–969.

Marchand, T.H.J., 2010a. Making Knowledge: Explorations of the Indissoluble Relation between Minds, Bodies, and Environment. *Journal of the Royal Anthropological Institute*, 16(N.S.), pp. S1–S21.

Marchand, T.H.J., 2010b. Preface. *Journal of the Royal Anthropological Institute*, 16(N.S.), pp. Siii–Sv.

Marcus, G.E., 1995. Ethnography in/of the World System: The Emergence of Multi-Sited Ethnography. *Annual Review of Anthropology*, 24, pp. 95–117.

Martínez-Alier, J., 2002. *The Environmentalism of the Poor: A Study of Ecological Conflicts and Valuation* Cheltenham: Edward Elgar Publishing.

Matanga, F.K., 2010. NGOs and the Politics of Development in Africa. *Development*, 53(1), pp. 114–119.

McIlwaine, C. 2007. From Local to Global to Transnational Civil Society: Re-framing Development Perspectives on the Non-State Sector. *Geography Compass*, 1(6), pp. 1252–1281.

Mejias, U.A., 2009. The Limits of Networks as Models for Organizing the Social. *New Media & Society*, 11(8), pp. 1–18.

Meyer, J.W., 1999. The Changing Cultural Content of the Nation-State: A World Society Perspective. In G. Steinmetz, ed. *State/Culture: State Formation after the Cultural Turn*. Ithaca, NY: Cornell University Press, pp. 123–143.

Meyer, J.W., 2010. World Society, Institutional Theories, and the Actor. *Annual Review of Sociology*, 36(1), pp. 1–20.

Mitchell, T., 2002. *Rule of Experts: Egypt, Techno-Politics, Modernity*. Berkeley, CA: University of California Press.

Mogoi, J., Obonyo, E., Ongugo, P., Oeba, V., & Mwangi, E. 2012. Communities, Property Rights and Forest Decentralisation in Kenya: Early Lessons from Participatory Forestry Management. *Conservation and Society*, 10(2), pp. 182–194.

Molyneux, M., 2001. Ethnography and Global Processes. *Ethnography*, 2(2), pp. 273–282.

Moore, H.L., 2004. Global Anxieties: Concept-Metaphors and Pre-theoretical Commitments in Anthropology. *Anthropological Theory*, 4(1), pp. 71–88.

Mosse, D., 2001. 'People's Knowledge', Participation and Patronage: Operations and Representations in Rural Development. In B. Cooke & U. Kothari, eds. *Participation: The New Tyranny?* New York: Zed Books, pp. 16–35.

Mosse, D., 2003. The Making and Marketing of Participatory Development. In P. Quarles van Ufford & A. K. Giri, eds. *A Moral Critique of Development: In Search of Global Responsibilities*. London: Routledge, pp. 43–75.

Mosse, D., 2005. *Cultivating Development: An Ethnography of Aid Policy and Practice*. London: Pluto Press.

Mosse, D., 2006. Anti-Social Anthropology? Objectivity, Objection, and the Ethnography of Public Policy and Professional Communities. *Journal of the Royal Anthropological Institute*, 12, pp. 935–956.

Mosse, D., 2011. Introduction: The Anthropology of Expertise and Professionals in International Development. In D. Mosse, ed. *Adventures in Aidland: The Anthropology of Professionals in International Development*. Oxford: Berghahn, pp. 1–32.

MSDSP Kg, 2012. *MSDSP Kg Annual Report 2012*. MSDSP KG: Osh.

MSDSP Kg & AKF Kg, 2011. *Aga Khan Foundation, Kyrgyz Republic and MSDSP KG Strategy Update (2012–2014)*.

Munck, R., 1999. Deconstructing development discourses: Of impasses, alternatives and politics. In R. Munck & D. O'Hearn, eds. *Critical Development Theory: Contributions to a New Paradigm*. London & New York: Zed Books, pp. 196–213.

Munck, R., & O'Hearn, D., eds., 1999. *Critical Development Theory: Contributions to a New Paradigm*. London & New York: Zed Books.
Nadelmann, E.A., 1990. Global Prohibition Regimes: The Evolution of Norms in International Society. *International Organization*, 44(4), pp. 479–526.
Nadkarni, M. & Shevchenko, O., 2004. The Politics of Nostalgia: A Case for Comparative Analysis of Post-Socialist Practices. *Ab Imperio*, 2, pp. 487–519.
Narayan, D., Chambers, R., Shah, M.K., & Petesch, P. 2000. *Voices of the Poor: Crying Out for Change*. Washington, DC: World Bank.
Negi, C.S., 2005. Religion and Biodiversity Conservation: Not a Mere Analogy. *The International Journal of Biodiversity Science and Management*, 1(2), pp. 85–96.
Ostrom, E., 1990. *Governing the Commons: The Evolution of Institutions for Collective Action*. Cambridge: Cambridge University Press.
Ostrom, E., 2007. Collective Action and Local Development Processes. *Sociologica*, 3, pp. 1–32.
Ostrom, E. et al., 2002. *The Drama of the Commons*. Washington, DC: National Academy Press.
Pieterse, J. N., 1995. Globalization as Hybridization. In M. Featherstone, S. Lash, & R. Robertson, eds. *Global Modernities*. London: SAGE Publications, pp. 45–68.
Pieterse, J. N., 2009. *Globalization and Culture: Global Mélange* (2nd ed.). Lanham, MD: Rowman & Littlefield.
Pieterse, V. & Black, P.E., 2004. Flow Network. In P. E. Black (ed.) *Dictionary of Algorithms and Data Structures*. National Institute of Standards and Technology. Available at: https://www.nist.gov/dads/HTML/flownetwork.html.
Pilgrim, S. et al., 2009. The Intersections of Biological Diversity and Cultural Diversity: Towards Integration. *Conservation and Society*, 7(2), p. 100.
Posey, D.A., 1996. Protecting Indigenous Peoples' Rights to Biodiversity. *Environment: Science and Policy for Sustainable Development*, 38(8), pp. 6–45.
Price, R., 2003. Transnational Civil Society and Advocacy in World Politics. *World Politics*, 55, pp. 579–606.
Ranger, T., 1992. The Invention of Tradition in Colonial Africa. In E. Hobsbawm & T. Ranger, eds. *The Invention of Tradition*. Cambridge: Cambridge University Press, pp. 211–262.
Rapport, N. & Harris, M., 2007. A Discussion Concerning Ways of Knowing. In M. Harris, ed. *Ways of Knowing: New Approaches in the Anthropology of Experience and Learning*. Oxford: Berghahn, pp. 306–330.
Reimann, K.D., 2005. Up to No Good? Recent Critics and Critiques of NGOs. In O.P. Richmond & H.F. Carey, eds. *Peace: The Challenges of NGO Peacebuilding*. Aldershot: Ashgate, pp. 37–54.
Reimann, K.D., 2006. A View from the Top: International Politics, Norms and the Worldwide Growth of NGOs. *International Studies Quarterly*, 50, pp. 45–67.
Rieff, D., 1999. The False Dawn of Civil Society. *The Nation*.
Robinson, M., 1998. Democracy, Participation, and Public Policy: The Politics of Institutional Design. In M. Robinson & G. White, eds. *The Democratic Developmental State: Politics and Institutional Design*. Oxford: Oxford University Press, pp. 117–150.
Sachs, W., eds., 1992a. *The Development Dictionary: A Guide to Knowledge as Power*. London: Zed Books.
Sachs, W., 1992b. Environment. In W. Sachs, ed., *The Development Dictionary: A Guide to Knowledge as Power*. London: Zed Books. pp. 26–37.
Said, E., 1994 [1978]. *Orientalism*. New York: Vintage Books.
Salick, J. & Ross, N., 2009. Traditional Peoples and Climate Change. *Global Environmental Change*, 19(2), pp. 137–139.

Scott, J.C., 1990. *Domination and the Arts of Resistance: Hidden Transcripts.* New Haven, CT: Yale University Press.

Scott, J.C., 1998. *Seeing Like a State: How Certain Schemes to Improve the Human Condition Have Failed.* New Haven, CT: Yale University Press.

Sillitoe, P., 2010. Trust in Development: Some Implications of Knowing in Indigenous Knowledge. *Journal of the Royal Anthropological Institute,* 16(1), pp. 12–30.

The Christensen Fund, 2009. *TCF Grant Agreement with Waso Trustland Project.* San Francisco, CA: The Christensen Fund.

The Christensen Fund, 2010. *Understanding Christensen's Mission.* San Francisco, CA: The Christensen Fund.

The Christensen Fund, 2014a. African Rift Valley. www.christensenfund.org/programs/african-rift-valley.

The Christensen Fund, 2014b. Global Program. www.christensenfund.org/programs/global-program.

Thornton, T.F. & Manasfi, N., 2010. Adaptation—Genuine and Spurious: Demystifying Adaptation Processes in Relation to Climate Change. *Environment and Society: Advances in Research,* 1, pp. 132–155.

Toke, D., 1999. Epistemic Communities and Environmental Groups. *Politics,* 19(2), pp. 97–102.

Urry, J., 2000. Mobile Sociology. *British Journal of Sociology,* 51(1), pp. 185–203.

Van den Hoonaard, W.C., 2008. Theoretical Sampling. In L. Given, ed. *SAGE Encyclopedia of Qualitative Research Methods.* London: SAGE Publications.

Washbrook, D.A., 1999. Orients and Occidents: Colonial Discourse Theory and the Historiography of the British Empire. In R.W. Winks, ed. *The Oxford History of the British Empire, Vol. V: Historiography.* Oxford: Oxford University Press, pp. 596–611.

Weigle, M.A. & Butterfield, J., 1992. Civil Society in Reforming Communist Regimes: The Logic of Emergence. *Comparative Politics,* 25(1), pp. 1–23.

Whittaker, H. 2012. Forced Villagization during the Shifta Conflict in Kenya, ca. 1963–1968. *The International Journal of African Historical Studies,* 45(3), pp. 343–364.

Whittaker, H. 2015. *Insurgency and Counterinsurgency in Kenya: A Social History of the Shifta Conflict, c. 1963-1968.* Netherlands: Brill.

Wild, R. & McLeod, C., 2008. *Sacred Natural Sites: Guidelines for Protected Area Managers.* Gland, Switzerland: IUCN.

Yin, R.K., 2009. *Case Study Research: Design and Methods,* 4th ed. Los Angeles, CA: SAGE Publications.

Yurchak, A., 2006. *Everything Was Forever, until It Was No More: The Last Soviet Generation.* Princeton, NJ: Princeton University Press.

Ziai, A. 2015. *Development Discourse and Global History: From Colonialism to the Sustainable Development Goals.* London & New York: Routledge.

Index

For the benefit of digital users, indexed terms that span two pages (e.g., 52–53) may, on occasion, appear on only one of those pages.